AFOQT Study Guide 2018-2019:

AFOQT Prep & Study Book for the Air Force Officer Qualifying Test

MOON POINT

TEST PREP

Printed in the United States of America

Contents

FOREWORD

AFOQT BREAKDOWN
THE MOON POINT STUDY GUIDE

1

INSTRUMENT COMPREHENSION 1
VERBAL ANALOGIES 4
TABLE READING 5
AVIATION INFORMATION 6
BLOCK COUNTING 7
SELF-DESCRIPTION INVENTORY 9
SITUATIONAL JUDGMENT 10
ARITHMETIC REASONING 11
MATHEMATICS KNOWLEDGE 31
WORD KNOWLEDGE 51
READING COMPREHENSION 52
PHYSICAL SCIENCE 69

PRACTICE TEST 109

Instrument Comprehension 109
Verbal Analogies 121
Table Reading 128
Aviation Information 129
Block Counting 133
Arithmetic Reasoning 141
Mathematics Knowledge 147
Word Knowledge 151
Reading Comprehension 156
Physical Science 158

PRACTICE TEST ANSWERS 168

Instrument Comprehension 168
Verbal Analogies 168
Table Reading 169
Aviation Information 170
Block Counting 171
Arithmetic Reasoning 172
Mathematics Knowledge 179
Word Knowledge 187
Reading Comprehension 190
Physical Science 191

Foreword

Thank you for purchasing *AFOQT Study Guide 2018-2019* from Moon Point Test Prep!

Your opinion matters!

As a small educational publisher, we depend on you, our customer, to provide feedback. We want to know what we did well and if there is anything we could improve on.

Likewise, your comments can help other shoppers make informed decisions. If you are happy with your purchase, please take a couple minutes to make a review on Amazon!

Feel free to send us an email too at moonpointfeedback@gmail.com and we will respond as quickly as possible to any questions, comments, or concerns.

Thank you for trusting Moon Point for your test prep needs. We are always here for you.

-- Your friends at Moon Point

AFOQT Breakdown

Congratulations! You've decided to become an officer in the United States Air Force! You're in for a long journey ahead, but you've chosen an excellent profession. We wish you the best of luck in your new career.

The first order of business is to successfully pass the Air Force Officer Qualifying Test (AFOQT). The AFOQT is an admissions exam used by the U.S. Air Force to assess potential candidates and their likely future success. Individuals who take the AFOQT must be prepared to complete several subtests on the exam. The table below explains the question breakdown and time limits for the various subtests of the AFOQT.

Subtest	Time	Questions
Instrument Comprehension	5 minutes	25 questions
Verbal Analogies	8 minutes	25 questions
Table Reading	7 minutes	40 questions
Aviation Information	8 minutes	20 questions
Block Counting	5 minutes	30 questions
Arithmetic Reasoning	29 minutes	25 questions
Mathematics Knowledge	22 minutes	25 questions
Word Knowledge	5 minutes	25 questions
Reading Comprehension	38 minutes	25 questions
Physical Science	10 minutes	20 questions
Situational Judgment	35 minutes	50 questions
Self-Description Inventory	45 minutes	240 questions
TOTAL	**~ 3.5 hours**	**550 questions**

The Moon Point AFOQT Study Guide

This AFOQT study guide is designed to be used either as a stand-alone or as a supplemental study aid in preparation for the AFOQT. The lessons and practice questions on the following several pages have been fully updated by our team of AFOQT experts for the latest version of the AFOQT.

For your convenience, this book is broken down into the individual subtests:

- Instrument Comprehension
- Verbal Analogies
- Table Reading
- Aviation Information
- Block Counting
- Self-Description Inventory
- Situational Judgment
- Arithmetic Reasoning
- Mathematics Knowledge
- Word Knowledge
- Reading Comprehension
- Physical Science

So, you know the overall structure of the AFOQT and how to use this study guide to achieve the greatest benefit. Now, it's time to get some practice in.

Good luck, and let's get started.

Instrument Comprehension

The Instrument Comprehension section requires you to determine which image of an aircraft corresponds to a compass heading and artificial horizon. This section is quite easy after you get familiarized with the concept, but you first must know how the artificial horizon works and how the compass corresponds to the images.

The compass is quite simple. If the compass is showing a heading of "East", the correct image of the aircraft will be pointing "left" on the page. If the compass heading is "South", the aircraft image will appear to be heading directly at you. See the below examples:

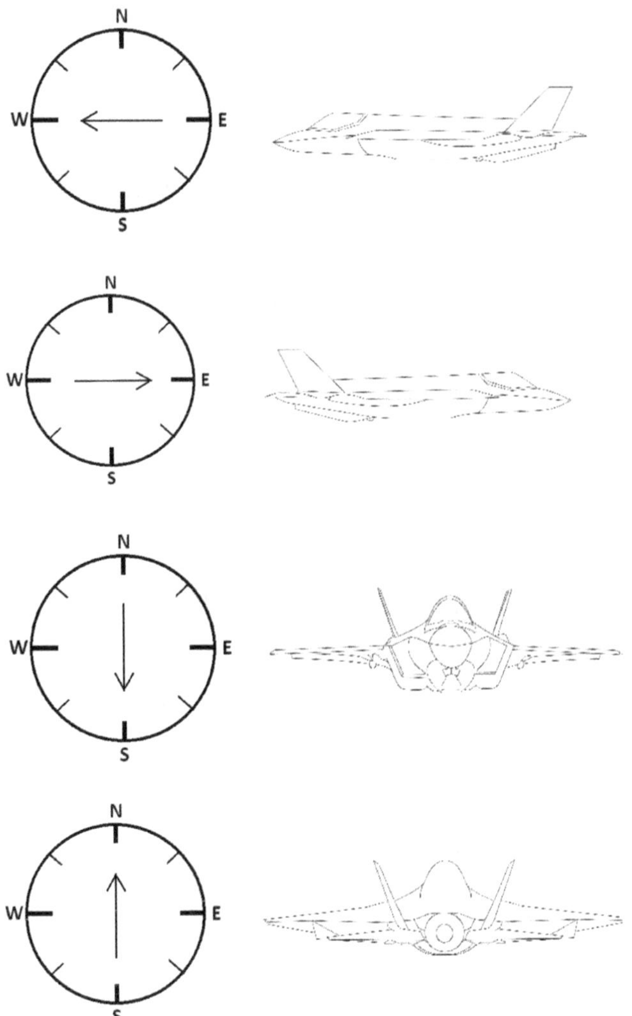

The Artificial Horizon is slightly more difficult to understand for those who haven't seen it before, but only takes a few minutes to grasp the concept. In simple terms, the artificial horizon represents both whether the aircraft is climbing or diving in altitude, as well as if the aircraft is banking.

Below is an artificial horizon showing an aircraft flying level and not banking either direction. This serves as a baseline for your reference. The flat line you see going from left to right that crosses what is called "the carrot" (the plus sign on top of the triangle) is the horizon.

Below is an artificial horizon that represents an aircraft in a dive. As you see, the carrot is now below the horizon.

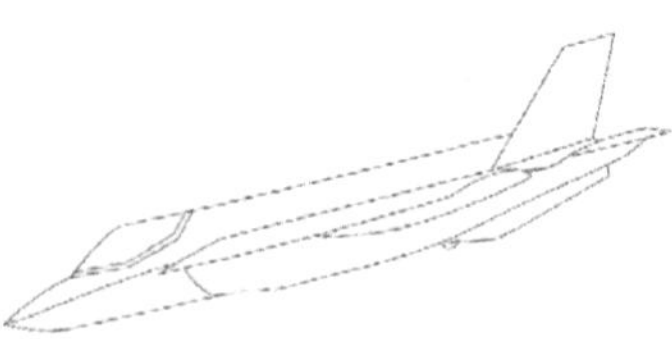

An aircraft banking is the trickier part for many people as it often feels reversed. The tip here is to pretend you are in the aircraft and viewing what the horizon would look like. Below shows an artificial horizon of an aircraft flying level, but banking to the right.

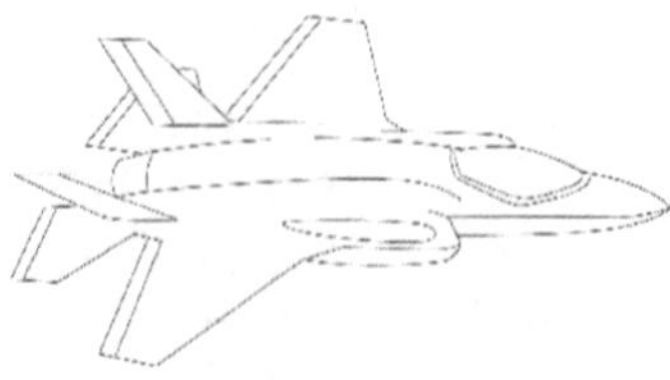

Finally, to put it all together, see the below 3 examples showing the corresponding compass, artificial horizon, and the correct image of the aircraft.

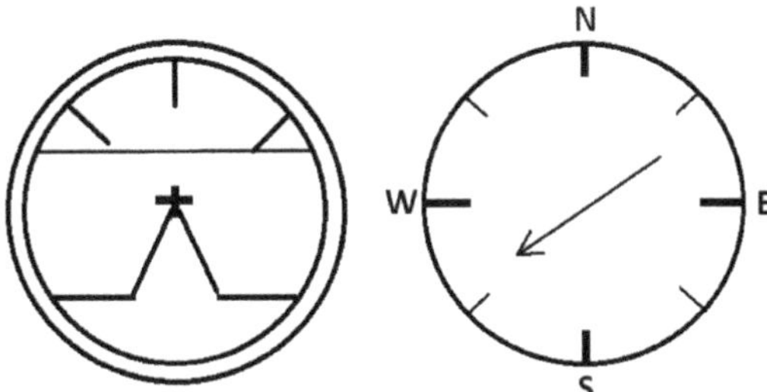

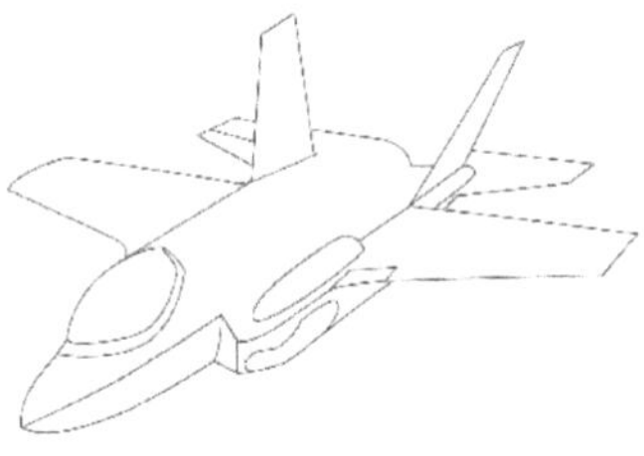

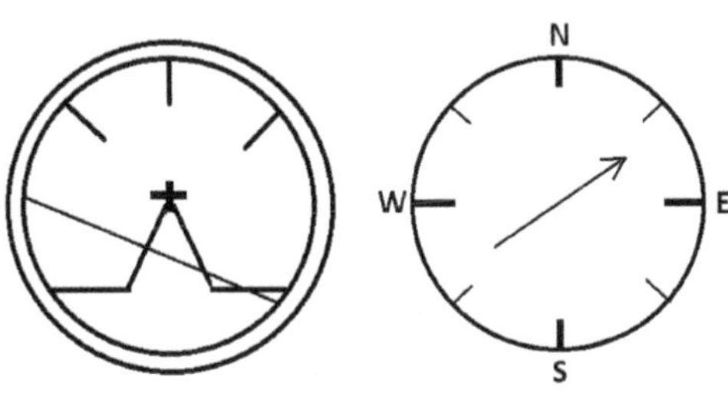

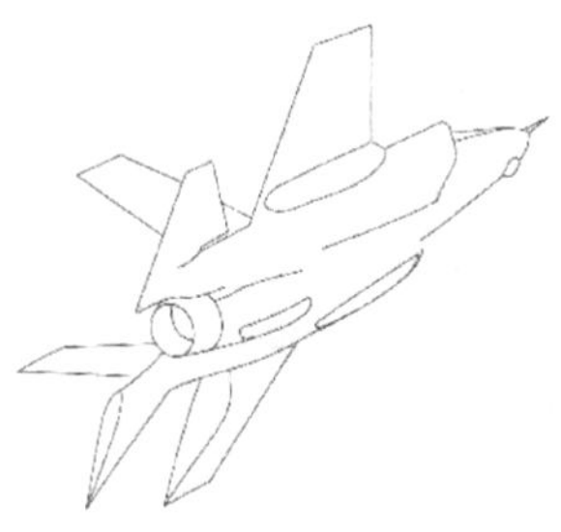

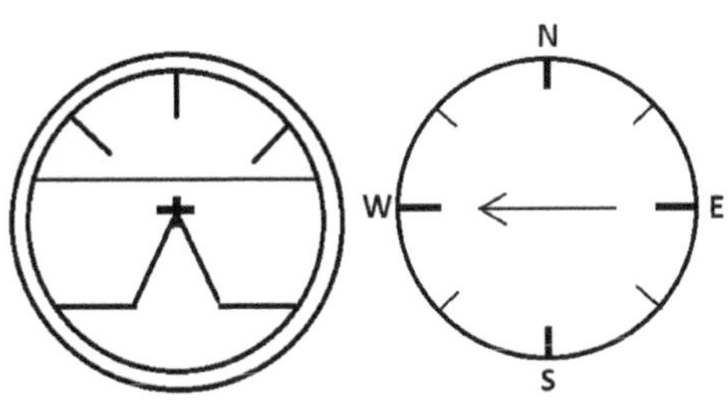

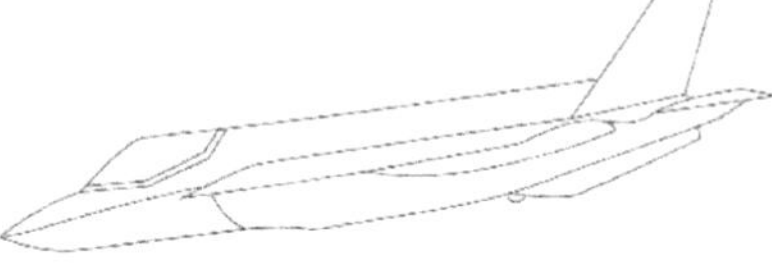

As you know, an analogy is simply a comparison of two similar things, used primarily for the purpose of clarification or description. The verbal analogy section of the AFOQT is the same concept, but you will need to use logic and context to determine the right answer. There are two formats of questions you will encounter. The first looks like this:

Cold is to Hot as Up is to _____:

A) Down
B) Left
C) Colder
D) Hotter
E) Inside out

The second format of question you will encounter will be:

Cold is to Hot as:

A) Up is to Down
B) Parent is to Child
C) Red is to Green
D) Hat is to Sock
E) Fingers are to Toes

Both of the examples here are elementary level used solely to illustrate the format of the questions. The answer to both is of course choice A. However, for the second format, you must remember to keep the order of words the same!

For example, if it says "Parent is to child as ______" and the answer choices were:

A) Puppy is to Dog
B) Cat is to kitten
C) Cake is to bread
D) Cup is to glass
E) Down is to up

Answer choice B is the correct choice. Choice A is incorrect because the order is backwards between the parent/child vs. child/parent.

The questions on the AFOQT will be significantly more difficult and require a solid vocabulary, as well as the ability to use logic, reason, and context clues to determine the correct answer. This list is not exhaustive, but will demonstrate the range of analogies you will encounter:

- Part to Whole: wheel is to car as blade is to fan.
- User to Tool: cook is to chef as operate is to surgeon
- Numerical: 2 is to 6 as 3 is to 9
- Geographic: Austin is to Texas as Denver is to Colorado
- Cause to Effect: push is to move as fire is to burn
- General to Specific: car is to Chevrolet as fast food is to McDonalds
- Object to Function: soccer ball is to kick as baseball bat is to hit

The Table Reading section of the AFOQT consists of 40 multiple choice questions in which the test taker must locate a specific number on large grid using X & Y Coordinates. This seems relatively simple on the surface, but 3 factors make this more challenging:

1) The grid is very large.
2) You may NOT use a straight edge to help you find the coordinates.
3) There is a 7-minute time limit.

As you'll see, your brain can become quickly overwhelmed with the sheer amount of numbers smashed together in fine print. 40 times over, you have to remember the question number you are on, the current XY Coordinates, find the answer, then search for the correct answer number. That is a huge amount of numbers flashing past your eyes. The key to remember is accuracy is more important than speed. Move methodically at an efficient pace, but do NOT rush. Rushing will lead to mistakes and forgetfulness and frustration. It is absolutely better to answer only 20 questions with 100% accuracy than answer all 40 with only 50% accuracy.

You need only practice this section once and get familiar with your pace. There is no tangible benefit to spending any more time on this section after that first round of practice.

Set your timer for 7 minutes, don't cheat, and see how many you can do.

The Aviation Information section tests your knowledge of general flight and airplane mechanics, procedures, and functions. There are only 20 questions with 8 minutes for the section, so plenty of time and no need to rush.

The bad news is that this will be the most time-intensive section for everyone taking the test unless you are already a certified private pilot. There is a vast amount of varying information you'll need to become familiar with; so much so that we do not have a lesson portion for this section. Why? The information is already freely available from the Federal Aviation Administration in the *Pilot's Handbook of Aeronautical Knowledge* found at the below link:

www.faa.gov/regulations_policies/handbooks_manuals/aviation/phak/media/pilot_handbook.pdf

As you'll see, this tome is over 500 pages long. The good news is you don't need to memorize every minor detail. The questions on the AFOQT are more in line with the general concepts of aviation and airplane mechanics. The reality of course is that you are taking this test to join the Air Force, so odds are this will be very basic information compared to what you will need to learn later on. The widely accepted rule of thumb is that the FAA handbook has more information than you need, but it's better to be overprepared than underprepared, and you likewise never know what topics or questions you might see on the exam.

To help familiarize yourself with the types of questions you'll see, try the 20 questions in the practice test developed by a pilot and expert in the field.

The Block Counting section of the AFOQT tests your ability to visualize in three-dimensional space. In simple terms, you are required to count how many other "blocks" are touching a specific one. It is simple on the surface, but a tip is to pause before jumping to an answer and think one moment more before answering. There are 30 questions with a 4.5 minute time limit, so you only have 9 seconds per question to answer. That is not a lot of time, so practice thinking through the questions systematically. Efficiency is the key, not speed.

It is important to remember that ALL the blocks in each arrangement are the same size. There are no "half blocks" or squares or anything else. They all run from end-to-end, just like the parts of the blocks you can see. Likewise, it is important to know that diagonal blocks are NOT considered touching. See below where only TWO blocks are touching block #1.

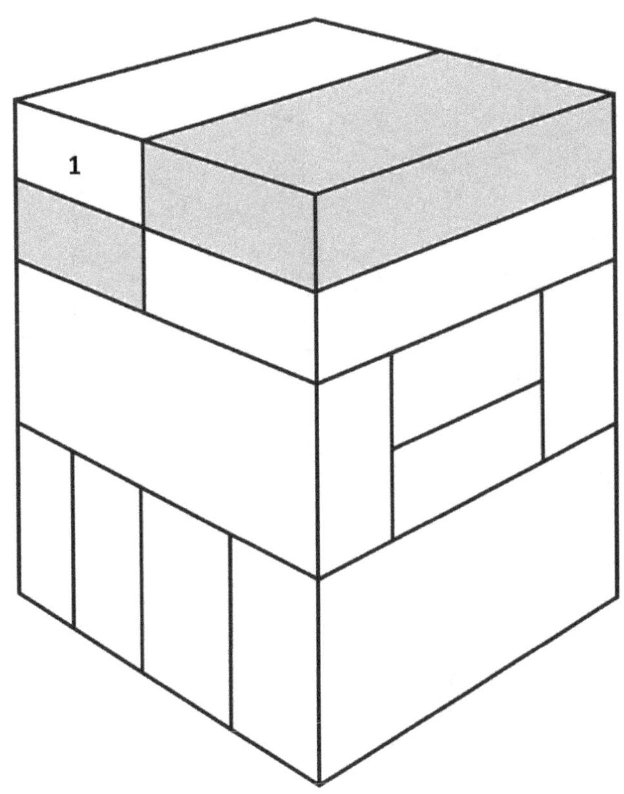

The key to this section is visualizing the parts of the cube that you cannot see. A good method is to start counting the blocks touching the top, then the side, then the bottom, then the last side. Whenever possible, move in the same direction of clockwise or counter-clockwise as you count so that it becomes systematic. A common pitfall is losing track if you already counted a block or not.

To help illustrate this concept, we have highlighted the 8 blocks that are touching block #2 below. Start by counting the 2 blocks touching the top, the two blocks touching the back side, and then you'll count the 4 blocks stacked on the bottom. Obviously, there are no blocks touching the other side of block 2 as it's an outside edge.

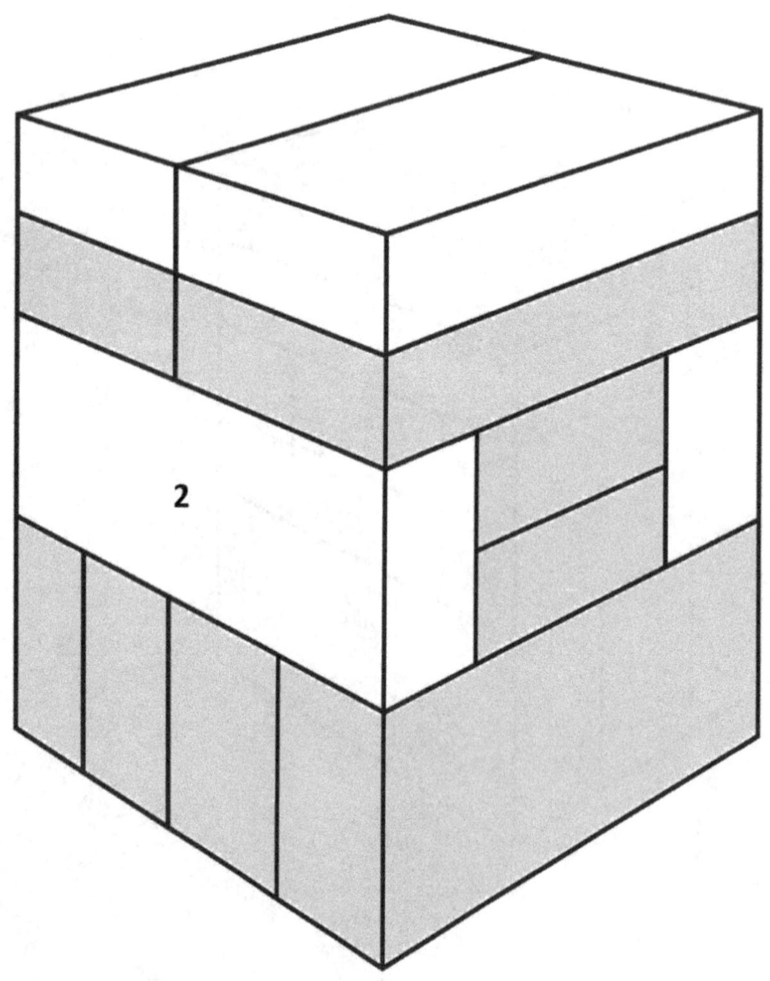

To complete the Self-Description Inventory subtest, you will have 45 minutes to answer 240 questions.

This section is NOT a test, nor is it even scored as part of the AFOQT. It is just a personality gauge. The questions are purely whatever you think most accurately reflects how you perceive yourself. You have about 10 seconds per question, which is just enough time to read it, ponder for a few seconds, then move on. Do not agonize over any one question, nor should you try to answer what you think the test takers want you to answer. Just answer honestly and don't waste time as you go through the questions.

Situational Judgement is a way to measure your baseline ability to effectively lead by asking you to determine what you consider the MOST effective and LEAST effective means to resolve an issue or problem. These problems are intended to be similar to what you might encounter in real life as an officer. You will be presented a short paragraph, typically about interpersonal conflict, and then given 5 possible ways to address that conflict or issue.

A plausible example would be that *"One of your Airman is not performing to standards, but is the favorite person of the group and everyone likes him or her. You've been pressured by your superiors to move that Airmen elsewhere, but that would have a detrimental effect on morale for the Airman remaining in your unit".* Your choices would be some variation or form of:

- Just comply with your superiors, they know what is right and no reason to risk your reputation.
- Ignore your superiors, they are too far removed and don't understand the dynamics.
- Counsel the Airman on how to increase their performance and give them 30 days to improve.
- Do the Airman's work for him or her to cover up the low standards.
- Take a "wait and see" approach, maybe the airman will improve and you can avoid the confrontation.

As you can see, there is no objectively "right" or "wrong" answer here. There is also no way to study for the Situational Judgement portion of the test because all the questions are subjective and you never know what answer choices you will get.

The best tactic for this section is to not approach it as a "test". There is no definitively right or wrong choices. You won't see a question that says "You see an Airman steal weapons ordinance to sell to the enemy. Should you ignore it or stop them?". The issues in the exam are purposefully nuanced and difficult to find the 'best' or 'worst' solution, and there is plenty of room for debate on them. Likewise, there are always more factors to consider in real life than a simple 2 sentence summary like on the exam.

Your answer choices help demonstrate your leadership style, not abilities. Leadership is a paradox, and it is all about balance.

How aggressive are you in making decisions and executing them? Especially in the military, a leader should not 'wait and see' and assertiveness is critical. Decisions must be made, and it's the leaders job to make them. *However*, a leader should also be patient and understand the situation as best as possible and not jump to conclusions.

Are you quick to fire someone, or prefer to counsel them and help improve? Neither is bad, because you must put the mission before an individual. Sometimes you have to get rid of that person for the better of the team and mission success, but that comes at a cost of having to replace that person and potential unforeseen issues. You cannot waste time counseling someone who just cannot improve, but firing people for every little issue doesn't fix the problem either.

Before you begin studying for the arithmetic section of the exam, let's talk basics. Many math exams will test your memory of basic math definitions, vocabulary, and formulas that have become so distant that the questions on this type of exam may feel unfair. You likely don't refer to quotients and integers in your day-to-day life, so testing your recall of high school math class vocabulary and concepts doesn't exactly feel like a valid way to gauge your mathematical reasoning abilities. Well, as the French say, "*C'est la vie!" or* "That's life!" Perhaps the most appropriate English expression would be, "You gotta do what you gotta do."

In this section, it's best for you to begin with a refresher list so that you can master basic math terminology quickly.

Integer: Any whole number, i.e. any number that doesn't include a non-zero fraction or decimal. Negative whole numbers, positive whole numbers, and 0 are all integers. 3.1415 is not an integer. ½ is not an integer. -47, -12, 0, 15, and 1,415,000 are all integers.

Positive and Negative Numbers: A positive number is any number greater than zero. A negative number is any number less than zero. Zero is neither positive nor negative. Adding a negative number is the same as subtracting the positive value of that number. Subtracting a negative number is the same as adding a positive number.

Even and Odd Numbers: An even number is any number that can be evenly divided by 2, with no remainder left over. -4, 2, 6, 24, and 114 are all even numbers. An odd number has a remainder of 1 when it is divided by 2. -19, 1, 3, 5, 17, and 451 are all odd numbers. Another way to think about even/odd is that even numbers are all integers that are multiples of two, and odd numbers are any integers that are *not* multiples of two.

Factors and Multiples: The factors of a number (or a polynomial) are all of the numbers that can be multiplied together to get the first number. For example, the following pairs of numbers can be multiplied to get 16: 1 * 16, 2 * 8 and 4 * 4. Therefore, the factors of 16 are 1, 2, 4, 8, and 16. Note: a polynomial is an expression that can have constants, variables and exponents, and that can be combined using addition, subtraction, multiplication and division.

Prime number: An integer that only has two factors: 1 and itself. There are two things to remember: (1) out of all of the infinite integers in existence, there is only one prime number that is even, and that is the number 2 — that's it, and (2) you can handle almost any prime number question on the test by memorizing all of the primes between 0 and 100. This is not required, but you will save time and mental anguish if you do this. Here they are:

2, 3, 5, 7, 11, 13, 17, 19, 23, 29, 31, 37, 41, 43, 47, 53, 59, 61, 67, 71, 73, 79, 83, 87, 89

Prime Factorization: The prime numbers you have to multiply to get a number. Take the number 24. First, you should find the factors of 24: 1, 2, 3, 4, 6, 8, and 12. Then, you need to pull out all the numbers that are not prime: 1, 4, 6, 8, and 12. What's left? 2 and 3 are the prime factors of 24! Now, that's a simple example, but the concept remains the same, no matter how large the number. When in doubt, start working from the number 2 (the smallest prime), which will be a factor of any number that ends with an even number. Be on the lookout for sneaky questions. For example, if the exam asks you for the prime factors of the number 31, for instance, recall that 31 is a prime number (but 1 is not!) so the only prime factor it can possibly have is itself — 31. The same goes for all prime numbers.

Sum: Add — the number you get when you add one number to another number.

Difference: Subtract — the number you get when you subtract one number from another number.

Product: Multiply — the number you get when you multiply one number by another number.

Quotient: Divide — the number you get when you divide one number by another number.

Expressions

An expression is made up of terms that are numbers, variables, and operators which are added together. If that sounds complicated, expressions are simply made up of the basic symbols used to create everything from first-grade addition problems to formulas and equations used in calculus. The individual terms of the expression are added to each other as individual parts of the expression. Remember that expressions may stand for single numbers, and use basic operators like x and ÷. However, a single expression does not suggest a comparison (or equivalency). But an equation does and can be represented by a simple expression equal to a number. For example, $3 + 2 = 1 + 4$ is an equation, because it uses the equal sign. So, think of $3 + 2$ and $1 + 4$ as building blocks — they are the expressions that, when joined together by an equal sign, make up an equation. Another way to think of an expression is that it is essentially a math metaphor used to represent another number.

Order of Operations

An operation is what a symbol does. The operation of a + sign, for instance, is to add. That's easy enough, but what happens if you run into a problem like this?

$$44 - (3^2 \times 2 + 6) = ?$$

You have to solve this equation by simplifying it, but if you do it in the wrong order, you will get the wrong answer. This is an incredibly important concept. This is where the Order of Operations comes in — here's what you have to remember.

1. Parentheses
2. Exponents
3. Multiplication and division (from left to right)
4. Addition and subtraction (from left to right)

You must do these operations in order, starting with parentheses first and addition/subtraction last, in order to get the correct answer.

$$44 - (3^2 \times 2 + 6) = ?$$

Start by focusing on the expression in parentheses first.

Inside the parentheses, you will find an exponent, so do that first so that you can do the operation within the parentheses:

$$3^2 = 3 \times 3 = 9$$

Then the expression becomes:

$$(9 \times 2 + 6)$$

To complete the operation within the paragraph, you need to remember to do the multiplication operation first:

$$9 \times 2 = 18$$

$$(18 + 6) = 24$$

You don't need the parentheses anymore because there are no operations left to complete inside of them. Now the problem looks like this:

$$44 - 24 = ?$$

$$20 = ?$$

You can use the phrase, **P**lease **E**xcuse **M**y **D**ear **A**unt **S**ally as a useful mnemonic. It has the same first letters as parentheses, exponents, multiplication, division, addition, subtraction.

However, the most common mistake involving the order of operations is the following: doing division after multiplication and subtraction after addition, which results in the wrong answer. You have to do multiplication and division as you encounter it from left to right, and the same goes for addition and subtraction. Remember to do what is inside parentheses first, and that might require you to do exponents, multiplication/division, and addition/subtraction first.

Here's another example of this concept:

$$(4^2 + 5^3 - 120) \times 3 = ?$$

$$4^2 = 4 \times 4 = 16$$

$$5^3 = 5 \times 5 \times 5 = 125$$

$$(16 + 125 - 120) \times 3 = ?$$

$$21 \times 3 = ?$$

$$63 = ?$$

If you didn't understand this example, you should go back and review the Order of Operations again.

Occasionally, you may encounter an equation that uses brackets. You should think of brackets as super parentheses, i.e. it's at the top of the list, and so you do that first, before anything else.

Equations

Equations relate expressions to one another with an equal sign. In algebra, they can get pretty complicated, but in arithmetic, equations often center around finding the equivalent of a single expression. For instance,

$$3 + 2 = 5$$

It may seem pretty simple to say 3 + 2 expresses 5 because they have a clear and simple relationship — they are equal. Other kinds of equations, i.e. relationships, include symbols like $>$ (greater than) and $<$ (lesser than), which can join two expressions together. These are often called inequalities since they are not equal. The greater than or less than relation is a sign of inequality.

Remember that equations can be rearranged by doing the same operations to each side of the equivalency. Here's an example of subtracting 6 from both sides of the equation:

$$34 - 23 = 6 + ?$$

$$34 - 23 - 6 = 6 + ? - 6$$

The number 6 subtracted on both sides of the equation cancel each other out. The equality of the relation remains unaffected.

$$11 - 6 = ?$$

$$5 = ?$$

Greatest Common Factor

Sometimes the term Greatest Common Factor is called the Greatest Common Divisor, but either way, the concept is the same - it's the largest factor that two (or more) numbers share.

To use this concept, you should first work out all of the factors for each number and then find the largest factor they have in common. For example, find the Greatest Common Factor of 18 and 30:

The factors of 18 are: 1, 2, 3, 6, 9 and 18
The factors of 30 are: 1, 2, 3, 5, 6, 10, 15 and 30

The highest number in both sets, i.e. the highest number that are common to both sets, is 6, so that's your Greatest Common Factor.

Least Common Multiple

Sometimes the term Least Common Multiple is called the Lowest Common Multiple or the Smallest Common Multiple or the Lowest Common Denominator when used in a fraction, but in any case, the concept is the same - without knowing this term, you can't compare, add, or subtract fractions, and that's important.

The least common multiple is the smallest number that can be divided by two (or more) given numbers. To get this number, first write out the multiples for each number and then find the smallest multiple that they share.

For example, find the Least Common Multiple of 3 and 7:

The multiples of 3 are: 3, 6, 9, 12, 15, 18, 21, 24, 27...
The multiples of 7 are: 7, 14, 21, 28, 35, 42, 49, 56...

The lowest number in both sets is 21, so that's your Least Common Multiple. Notice that there are other multiples, but we are interested in the lowest or least of the common multiples.

Exponents and Roots

Exponents

An exponent is an algebraic operation that tells you to multiply a number by itself.

For example, 4^2 is the same as 4 x 4, and 4^3 is the same as 4 x 4 x 4. The exponent tells you how many times to multiply the number by itself.

Exponents have a few special properties (you can think of them as shortcuts or even helpful tricks if you want):

1. If two numbers with exponents share the same base number, you can multiply them by adding the exponents:

$$2^5 \times 2^3 = 2^8$$

2. If two numbers with exponents share the same base number, you can divide them by subtracting the exponents:

$$2^5 \div 2^3 = 2^2$$

3. A number with an exponent raised to a negative power is the same as 1 over or the reciprocal of that number with an exponent raised to the positive power:

$$5^{-2} = 1/5^2$$

$$1/5^2 = 1/25 \text{ or } 1 \div 25 = 0.04$$

4. A number raised to a fraction power is the same as a root, or radical:

$9^{1/2} = 3$ (the square root indicated by the two in one half)

Remember that the root of a number *x* is another number, which when multiplied by itself a given number of times, equals x. For example the second root of 9 is 3, because 3 x 3 = 9. The second root is usually called the square root. The third root is usually called the cube root. Because 2 x 2 x 2 = 8, 2 is the cube root of 8. Two special exponent properties are explained more in the two examples below.

1. 1 raised to any power is 1; for example:

$1^2 = 1$
$1^{-4} = 1$
$1^{912} = 1$

2. Any number raised to the power of 0 equals 1 — sounds crazy, but it's true! Here's an example:

$253^0 = 1$

If you can remember these six properties, you'll be able to simplify almost any problem with exponents.

Roots and Radicals

Roots and radicals are sometimes held up as cliché symbols for difficult math problems, but in the real world, they're easy to understand and use to solve equations.

A radical is an expression that has a square root, cube root, etc; the symbol is a √. The number under that radical sign is called a radicand.

A square is an expression (not an equation!) in which a number is multiplied by itself. It is often said that the given number is raised to the power of 2. Here's an example: 4^2 is a square. 4 x 4 is the same square, expressed differently.

The square root of a number is a second number that, when multiplied by itself, will equal the first number. Therefore, it's the same as squaring a number, but in the opposite direction. For example, if you want to find the square root of 25, we have to figure out what number, when squared, equals 25. With enough experience, you will automatically know many of the common square roots. For example, it is commonly known that 5 is the square root of 25. Square and square root are operations that are often used to undo or cancel out each other in problem-solving situations.

A mental image, kind of like a numerical mnemonic, that helps some people is to think of the given number and the square root (in the above case, 25 and 5) as the tree and its much smaller roots in the ground.

The previous example uses the number 25, which is an example of a perfect square. Only some numbers are perfect squares – those that are equal to the product of two integers. Here's a table of the first 10 perfect squares.

Factors	Perfect Square
1 x 1	1
2 x 2	4
3 x 3	9
4 x 4	16
5 x 5	25
6 x 6	36
7 x 7	49
8 x 8	64
9 x 9	81
10 x 10	100

It is helpful to remember that if you find that the square root of any radicand is a whole number (not a fraction or a decimal), that means the given number is a perfect square.

To deal with radicals that are not perfect, you need to rewrite them as radical factors and simplify until you get one factor that's a perfect square. This process is sometimes called extracting or taking out the square root. This process would be used for the following number:

$$\sqrt{18}$$

First, it's necessary to notice that 18 has within it the perfect square 9.

$$18 = 9 \times 2 = 3^2 \times 2$$

Therefore, $\sqrt{18}$ is not in its simplest form. Now, you need to extract the square root of 9

$$\sqrt{18} = \sqrt{9} \times 2 = 3\sqrt{2}$$

Now the radicand no longer has any perfect square factors.

$\sqrt{2}$ is an irrational number that is equal to approximately 1.414. Therefore, the approximate answer is the following:

$$\sqrt{18} = 3 * 1.414 = \text{approximately } 4.242$$

Note that the answer can only be an approximate one since $\sqrt{2}$ is an irrational number, which is any real number that cannot be expressed as a ratio of integers. Irrational numbers cannot be represented as terminating or repeating decimals.

Factorials

If you have ever seen a number followed by an exclamation point, it's not yelling at you – it's called a factorial. Simply put, a factorial is the product of a number and all of the positive integers below it, stopping at 1. For example, if you see 5!, its value is determined by doing the following example:

$$5! = 5 \times 4 \times 3 \times 2 \times 1 = 120$$

Factorials are typically used in relation to the fundamental principle of counting or for the combinations or permutations of sets.

Addition, Subtraction, Multiplication, Division Operations with Decimals

The sign conventions for positive and negative decimal arithmetic operations are the same as those for whole number operations. But, there are special details to recall when performing arithmetic operations with decimal values to ensure correct answers.

When adding and subtracting decimal values, it is important to make sure that the decimal points are aligned vertically. This is the simplest method to ensure a reliable result. For example, adding 0.522 and 0.035 should be performed as follows:

$$\begin{array}{r} 0.522 \\ +0.035 \\ \hline 0.557 \end{array}$$

Subtraction operations should be aligned similarly.

$$\begin{array}{r} 0.522 \\ -0.035 \\ \hline 0.487 \end{array}$$

It is important to note that multiplication requires a different convention to be followed. When multiplying decimals, the operations are NOT aligned necessarily the same way as addition and subtraction. For example, multiplying 0.7 and 2.15 is performed as follows:

$$\begin{array}{r} 2.15 \\ \times\ 0.7 \\ \hline 1.505 \end{array}$$

When multiplying decimal values, the decimal point placement in the answer is determined by counting the total number of digits to the right of the decimal point in the multiplied numbers. This detail is often overlooked in testing choices where the same numbers may appear in several multiple-choice answers, but with different decimal point placements.

Division of decimal values is simplified by first visualizing fractions that are equivalent. The mathematics terminology is that a dividend / divisor = quotient. For example:

7.35 / 1.05 is the same as 73.5 / 10.5, which is the same operation as 735 / 105.

The last fraction, in the example above, means that to solve 7.35 / 1.05 we can divide 735 / 105 and find the correct whole number answer. This method just requires that when dividing by a decimal number, the divisor must be corrected to be a whole number. This requirement is achieved by moving the decimal points in **both the dividend and divisor** the same number of decimal places. If the dividend still contains a decimal point, the place is maintained in the long division operation, and the correct quotient is still achieved. The quotient remains in the form of a decimal number.

Addition, Subtraction, Multiplication, Division Operations with Fractions

The sign conventions for positive and negative fractional arithmetic operations are the same as those for whole number operations. However, there are special details to recall when performing arithmetic operations with fractional values to ensure correct answers.

Remember that fractions are made up of a numerator and a denominator. The top number of the fraction, called the numerator, tells how many of the fractional parts are being represented. The bottom number, called the denominator, tells how many equal parts the whole is divided into. For this reason, fractions with different denominators cannot be added together because different denominators are as different as "apples and oranges." So, when adding or subtracting fractions with different denominators, a common denominator must be found. In this case, simple geometric models will be used to explain the common denominator principle. Usually, this principle is illustrated with circles divided into "pie slices." A simpler and more effective example involves the use of squares or rectangles divided into fractional parts.

Representing fraction parts, $^1/_3$ and $^1/_4$ will be demonstrated with the following square diagrams. In this case a whole square is the number "1" and the fractional parts will be the slices of the square as follows:

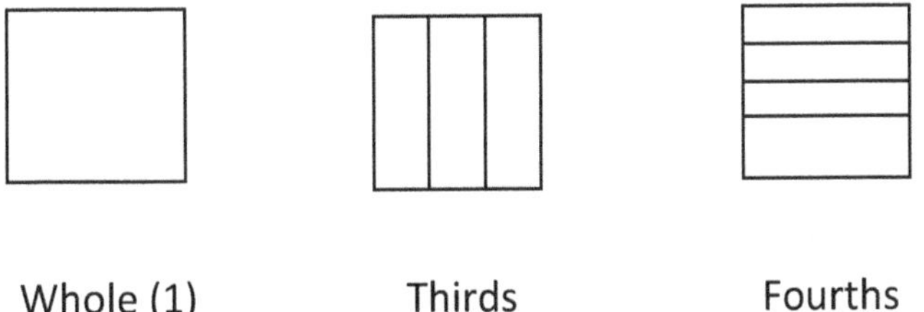

Whole (1) Thirds Fourths

If we superimpose the four horizontal slices over the three vertical slices, there are twelve separate parts of the whole as follows:

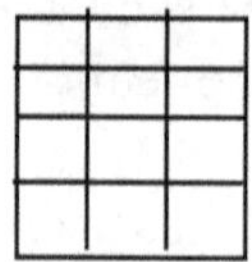

In the last diagram, any column representing a third, has four of the twelve small rectangles from the diagram, or $^4/_{12}$ as the equivalent fraction.

Similarly, any row of the last diagram, representing a fourth, has three of the twelve small rectangles from the diagram, or $^3/_{12}$ as the equivalent fraction. With this modification of the two fractions, both are now in the form of a common denominator, and the addition of the two fractions can be completed:

$$^1/_3 + ^1/_4 = ^3/_{12} + ^4/_{12} = ^7/_{12}$$

Notice that this result is exactly analogous to the simple diagram above. Common denominator fractions need not be simplified with this type of diagram, but it is a valuable example to explain the principle. The common denominator is required whenever adding or subtracting fractions with different denominators. If the denominators are the same, then the addition or subtraction of numerators is all that is required. Remember that the individual fractions will retain the same value only if the numerator and denominator are multiplied by the same value.

Multiplication of fractions is a simple operation because fractions multiply as follows:

$$^7/_8 * ^3/_4 = ^{(7*3)}/_{(8*4)} = ^{21}/_{32}$$

This fraction is in its simplest form because there are no common factors. If common factors exist in the numerator and denominator of a fraction, then that fraction must be simplified.

Division of fractions should never be attempted in the form of a ratio. The method is confusing, elaborate and unreliable in a testing situation. Instead, **every** fraction division problem is a simple operation because the division operation can be rewritten as a multiplication operation. To begin, as stated previously:

dividend / divisor = quotient

This can be rewritten as:

dividend * ($^1/_{\text{divisor}}$) = quotient

This yields exactly the same outcome as division. The quantity ($^1/_{\text{divisor}}$) is called a reciprocal, and for a fraction, it's as simple as flipping the fraction upside down. Therefore:

$$(^5/_8) / (^1/_4) = ^5/_8 * ^4/_1 = ^{20}/_{32} = ^5/_8 \text{ (in simplified form)}$$

Fraction to Decimal Conversions

Every fraction represents a division problem. The decimal value of any fraction is represented by the numerator, (top value), divided by the denominator (bottom value). Certain combinations, such as $^1/_3$, will result in repeating decimals that will always be rounded in a multiple-choice testing situation.

The fraction $^1/_2$ has a decimal value of 0.5, which is the value of 1 divided by 2. The values of improper fractions such as $^3/_2$, $^5/_2$, or $^7/_2$ (larger numerator than denominator) are determined by dividing as previously stated or more easily by multiplying the numerator by 0.5. So the improper fraction of $^7/_2$ is 7 * 0.5, or 3.5. Often, the determination of the unit fraction (1 divided by the denominator) followed by the decimal multiplication is simpler in a testing situation.

The fraction $^3/_5$ has a decimal value of 0.6, which is the value of 3 divided by 5. Alternately, the value of the unit fraction of $^1/_5$ is 0.2, and that unit fraction multiplied by 3 is 0.6. If you know the unit fractions for common fraction values, the answer selection process may be simplified.

When a fraction such as $^5/_7$ is evaluated, the quotient of 5 divided by 7 results in a lengthy decimal value of 0.71428.... That extended value will never appear as a multiple-choice test answer selection. Typically, that value will be rounded to either 0.71 or 0.714. Remember that testing instructions say to choose the **best answer**. Your best choice may be a rounded number.

Decimal to Fraction Conversions

All decimals are also fractions and can be written in that form. The fractions that result all have powers of 10 in the denominator and usually need to be simplified in order to be compared to multiple-choice answers in a testing situation.

For example, simple decimal values, such as 0.25, can be written as the fraction $^{25}/_{100}$. This fraction must be simplified to be correct. $^{25}/_{100}$ can be rewritten as a product:

$$^{(25 * 1)}/_{(25 * 4)}$$

or

$$^{25}/_{25} * {}^{1}/_{4}$$

The fraction can be expressed correctly as $^1/_4$ since the fraction $^{25}/_{25}$ is simplified to 1. Recognizing the common factors in the numerator and denominator is the essential element in making these conversions.

For testing purposes, decimal conversions will often be based on common fraction values. For example, $^1/_{16}$, if divided with long division, is 0.0625. Any integer multiple of this value results in a fraction with 16 in the denominator.

The value 0.0625 is first rewritten as the fraction:

$$^{625}/_{10000}$$

Simplifying with factors of 5 in the numerator and denominator gives the fraction

$$^{125}/_{2000}$$

Simplifying with factors of 25 in the numerator and denominator gives the fraction

$$^{5}/_{80}$$

Simplifying with factors of 5 in the numerator and denominator one more time gives the simplified fraction

$$^{1}/_{16}$$

While either of these methods may require an extra amount of time to complete, usually the answer choices may be logically reduced to two of the four examples. Testing the answer choices is simply a matter of multiplying the decimal value by the denominator to determine if the numerator is correct.

Another solution method, logical deduction, can be used as a simple, reliable and time saving approach to finding the fractional value of 0.435. In this example, the following is a list of possible multiple-choice answers:

A $^{3}/_{16}$
B $^{5}/_{16}$
C $^{7}/_{16}$
D $^{9}/_{16}$

Logically, any fraction greater than $^{1}/_{2}$ is immediately eliminated since:

$$0.435 < 0.5$$

So, first eliminate answer D. Incorrect answer choices will be eliminated with this type of logical deduction.

Second, notice that in the answer choice:

$$^{3}/_{16} < ^{1}/_{4}$$

and in decimal form

$$^{3}/_{16} < 0.25$$

So, choice A can logically be eliminated since our answer comparison is with 0.435.

Third, notice that in the answer choices:

$$^{5}/_{16} > {}^{1}/_{4}$$

and in decimal form

$$^{5}/_{16} > 0.25$$

Since $^{5}/_{16}$ is just slightly more than $^{1}/_{4}$, choice B can be eliminated since our comparison is with 0.435.

Finally, C is chosen as the most likely answer choice. It is the logical choice since:

$$^{7}/_{16} < {}^{1}/_{2}$$

and

$$0.435 < 0.5$$

Percentages

Percentages is a concept you are most likely familiar with from real-world applications, so these are some of the less scary math problems that appear on tests. However, test writers take that confidence into account and can use it against you, so it's important to be careful on problems with percentages. Let's look at an example:

> A sweater went on sale and now costs $25.20. If the original price was $42.00, what is the percent discount?
>
> A 16.8%
>
> B 20.0%
>
> C 25.0%
>
> D 40.0%
>
> E 60.0%

Take a minute to work out the problem for yourself. If you get the wrong answer, it will be helpful to you to see where you went wrong – several of the answer choices are distinct traps that often appear on test questions like this.

Solution:
With percentages, you can always set up a fraction. First, you want to know what percent the sale price is of the original price. The reference point, or original price, will go on the bottom of the fraction. The numerator will be the sale price. The ratio of 25.2 / 42 is equal to 6 / 10.

The sale price, $25.20, is 0.6, or 60%, of the original price. A percentage is just the decimal times 100.

This is answer choice E. However, the question did NOT ask what percent the new price is of the original price. Read carefully: it asks for the percent *discount*. This language is commonly used for questions with prices. Here's what it means, in math terms:

Percentage discount = 100% - Percentage of the Sale Price

The percent discount is the amount less than 100% that the sale price is of the original price. We can use this equation to solve, which yields:

(42 – 25.2) / 42 = 0.40

Remember, a percent is a decimal times 100%. So, we can convert the decimal on the right side to a percentage by multiplying by 100%:

100% * 0.40 = 40%

The sale price is 40% *less than* the original price, which is answer choice D. Another mathematical reasoning approach would be to take the original fraction subtracted from 1:

1 - 25.2 / 42 = 0.4

From here, just recognize that if the sale price *is* 60% of the original price, then it is 40% *less than* the original price.

You can solve for the discounted amount and then find that as a percent of the original amount to solve for the percentage of the discount:

42 - 25.2 = 16.80

16.80 / 42 = 0.4

Those are three different ways to approach one problem, using the same concept of percentage and recognizing that a percent *discount* requires subtraction from the original. Here's another percentage problem, this time with a different trick:

168 is 120% of what number?

Solution:
First, convert 120% to a decimal. Remember, converting a percentage to a decimal is done by dividing by 100%:

$$120 / 100 = 1.2$$

We are told that 168 is this percent *of* some other number. This means that 168 goes in the numerator of our percent fraction equation. Here is the resulting equation:

$$168 / x = 1.2$$

Here, *x* signifies the unknown number in the problem. Writing the percent equation is indispensable to solving this type of problem. Multiply both sides by *x* and then divide both sides by 1.2 to isolate the variable:

$$168(x) / x = 1.2(x)$$

$$168 = 1.2x$$

$$168 / 1.2 = 1.2x / 1.2$$

$$140 = x$$

Therefore, 168 is 120% of 140. We can verify this answer by plugging the numbers back into the original equation:

$$168 / 140 = 1.2$$

This problem is tricky because the percentage is greater than 100%, or greater than 1.0, so it violates our intuition that the bigger number should go on the bottom of the fraction. Usually, percentages are less than 100. However, when percentages are larger than 100, the numerator is bigger than the denominator. The inverse of this question could be the following:

168 is what percent of 140?

Many people, after reading this question, would automatically set up the following fraction equation:

$$140/168 = 0.83$$

83% would likely be an answer choice, but it's the wrong answer. The question is asking for 168 / 140. Read these questions carefully, and don't automatically place the larger number in the denominator.

Let's look at one more example, which combines these concepts, and then do a couple practice problems:

> An ingredient in a recipe is decreased by 20%. By what percentage does the new amount need to be increased to obtain the original amount of the ingredient?

Solution:
Here is a pro's tip for working with percentages:

When a problem is given only in percentages with no given numbers, you can substitute in any value to work with as your original amount. Since you are solving for a percent, you'll get the same answer no matter what numbers are used because percentages are ratios. The easiest number to work with in problems like this is 100, so use that as the original recipe amount. 100 what? Cups of flour? Chicken tenders? Chocolate chips? Doesn't matter. Here's how your equation should look:

$$x / 100 = 0.20$$

Solve for x, which gives the amount the ingredient has been decreased by:

$$x = 100 * 0.20$$

Remember that 20% is a decimal, so 0.20 * 100 = 20. The ingredient has been decreased by 20 units. What is the new amount?

$$100 - 20 = 80$$

What was the question asking for? *By what percent does the new amount need to be increased to obtain the original amount of the ingredient?* Let's parse this mathematical language. We've found the new amount of the ingredient, 80. The original amount, we decided, was 100.

The next step in answering the question is to find the *amount* that we would need to add to get back to the original amount. This part is pretty easy:

$$80 + x = 100$$

$$x = 20$$

It's the same amount that we subtracted from the original amount, 20. But the question asks what percentage of 80 is required to add 20?

Set up the percentage equation. 80 times what percent (x / 100) will give that extra 20 units?

$$80 * x / 100 = 20$$

Solve as normal by dividing both sides by 80 and then multiplying both sides by 100:

$$x / 100 = 0.25$$
$$x = 25$$

The new amount must be increased by 25% to equal the original amount.

Working with Sets

All standardized math exams will touch on the basic statistical descriptions of sets of numbers: mean (the same as an average, for a set), median, mode and range. These are terms to know. Let's look at an example set and examine what each of these terms means:

Set of numbers: 42, 18, 21, 26, 22, 21

Mean/Average

The mean of a set of numbers is the average value of the set. The formula for finding the mean is:

$$\frac{Sum\ of\ the\ numbers\ in\ the\ set}{Quantity\ of\ numbers\ in\ the\ set} = mean$$

Use this formula to find the mean of the example set:

$$\frac{42 + 18 + 21 + 26 + 22 + 21}{6} = \frac{150}{6} = 25$$

You add together all the numbers that appear in the set, and then divide by the quantity of numbers in the set. The mean, or average, value in the set is 25. Notice that the mean is not necessarily a number that appears in the set, although it can be.

Median

The median of a set is the number that appears in the middle **when the set is ordered from least to greatest.** Therefore, the first step in finding the mean is to put the numbers in the correct order, if they are not already. You should always do this physically, on your scratch paper, to make sure that you don't leave any numbers out of the reordering. For the example set, that would be:

18, 21, 21, 22, 26, 42

Make sure you've included all the numbers in the order, even if there are duplicates. If a set with a lot of numbers, it's helpful to cross them off in the original set as you order them on your scratch paper. This helps ensure that you don't leave one out.

If there is an odd quantity of numbers in the set, the median will be the middle number. For example, if a set is comprised of nine numbers, the median will be the fifth number of the ordered set.

However, the example set has six numbers. Since no single number is in the exact middle, we average the two middle numbers to find the median:

$$\frac{21 + 22}{2} = 21.5$$

The median of this set is 21.5.

Mode

The mode of a set of numbers is the number that appears most often. Speakers of French will find this easy to remember: *mode* is the French word for style. The number that appears the most is "in style" for this particular set.

The example set has one number that appears more than once: 21. Therefore, 21 is the mode. Sometimes, it's easiest to see this after the set is ordered, when duplicate numbers appear next to one another.

If a set has two numbers that equally appear most often, such as two 21s and two 22s, then both 21 *and* 22 are the mode. We don't average them together, as we do to find the median. Therefore, the mode is the only descriptor of a set that must always be a number in the set. Since there are two modes, the set would be described as "bimodal."

Range

The range of a set of numbers is the distance between the highest and lowest values. Once you've reordered a set, these values are easy to identify. Simply subtract the two values to get the range:

$$Highest\ value - Lowest\ value = Range$$

For the example set, this would be:

$$42 - 18 = 24$$

The range of the set is 24.

Sets can include negative numbers, decimals, fractions, duplicates, etc. They may also appear in table form. Let's look at another example set to see what kinds of tricky questions you may encounter.

Month	Rainfall (inches)
August	0.8
September	1.3
October	2.1
November	1.3
December	3.7

What is the average rainfall for the months September, October, November and December?

Solution:
Notice the first trick in this question – you are asked for the average of only four months, not all five listed in the table. This introduces two possible sources of error – you could add all five months' rainfall and/or divide by five when calculating the average. To find the average of only the four months stated in the question, the solution is:

$$\frac{1.3 + 2.1 + 1.3 + 3.7}{4} = 2.1\ inches$$

Here's another question for the same data table, but it uses a different approach to averaging:

> The average monthly rainfall from July through December was 1.7 inches. What was the rainfall, in inches, in July?

Solution:
This question gives you the average and asks you to find the missing rainfall value. This is a common way to make a mean/average problem a little tricky for the average (mean) test-taker. You can solve these types of questions by applying the basic equation for finding the mean:

$$\frac{Sum\ of\ the\ numbers\ in\ the\ set}{Quantity\ of\ numbers\ in\ the\ set} = mean$$

Next, fill in all the known values:

$$\frac{July + 0.8 + 1.3 + 2.1 + 1.3 + 3.7}{6} = 1.7$$

Solve algebraically:

$$July + 0.8 + 1.3 + 2.1 + 1.3 + 3.7 = 1.7 * 6$$

$$July = (1.7 * 6) - 0.8 - 1.3 - 2.1 - 1.3 - 3.7$$

$$July = 1\ inch$$

Now, try to solve this question:

> What is the difference between the mode and the median of the rainfalls for August through December?

Solution:
Simply find the mode and median values. Remember, the first step is to order the set:

0.8, 1.3, 1.3, 2.1, 3.7

The mode is 1.3 because that is the only number that appears more than once.

The median is 1.3 because, of the five numbers in the set, 1.3 is the third (middle) number.

Therefore, the difference between the mode and the median is:

$$1.3 - 1.3 = 0$$

Scientific Notation

Scientific notation was originally developed as a simplified way for scientists to express extremely large or small numbers. In mathematics, scientific notation is used to easily compare large and small numbers. Let's take a look at how to translate a real number to its scientific notation equivalent.

Converting standard numbers to scientific notation is performed without calculation, although counting place values is still essential. For example:

> The number 2,345,000 is equal to 2.345 * 1,000,000. By writing the value of 1,000,000 as 10^6 (10 multiplied by itself 6 times), the formulation of the scientific notation equivalent of the original number is completed: 2.345 * 10^6.

Similarly, small decimal numbers can be written using scientific notation as well. For example:

> The number 0.00736 is equal to 7.36 * 0.001. By writing the value of 0.001 as 10^{-3} (1 divided by 10, three times), the formulation of the scientific notation equivalent of the original number is completed: 7.36 * 10^{-3}.

Instead dividing (or multiplying) by 10, the translation to scientific notation can also be simplified by counting the number of places that the decimal point is transferred in the conversion process. In the first example above, when the scientific notation was written, it began with writing 2.345. This number was formulated by moving the decimal point six places to the left in the original number. Therefore, the exponent of 10 was 6 (10^6).

Similarly, in the second example, the decimal part of the scientific notation number, 7.36, was written by moving the decimal point three places to the right. Therefore, the exponent of 10 was -3 (10^{-3}).

Using this method, no calculation is required. The included benefit is that the "significance" of numbers is easily determined. Answering the question of the number of significant figures for the two examples is a simple matter when using scientific notation. The number of digits in the decimal part of the scientific notation is always the number of significant figures. 2,345,000 has four significant figures. 0.00736 has three. The zeros in these numbers are often referred to as "place holders" when converting to scientific notation.

Notice that the exponent is NOT determined by counting zeros, but by counting the number of decimal places that are moved when formulating the scientific notation. The decimal part in scientific notation always has only one digit to the left of the decimal point.

Algebra Concepts

Algebra is a branch of Mathematics with symbols, referred to as variables, and numbers, as well as a system of rules for the manipulation of these. Solving higher-order word problems is a valuable application of the Algebra properties described in this chapter.

Expressions

Algebra uses variables, numbers and operations as the basic parts. Variables are typically represented by letters and may have any number of values in a problem. Usually the variable is the unknown quantity in a problem. All letters can and often are used, but x, y, and z are letters that appear most often in algebra textbooks. In a testing situation, letters other than x, y, and z are often used to mislead test takers. Algebraic expressions are variables and numbers with operations such as addition, subtraction, multiplication and division. The following are all examples of algebraic expressions:

x	y	a	(letters)
7u	$^1/_2\,q$ (or $^q/_2$)	3.9 p	(product of a variable and number)
s + 5	u+v	2.3+r	(sum of a variable and number)
z – 3.5	k-n	t – 1.3	(difference of a variable and number)
m/6	($^z/_2$)	3.9 /p	(quotient of a variable and number)
c^2	$b^{0.5}$	$\sqrt{3}$	(variable or number with an exponent)

Finally, the sum, difference, product or quotient of these items are also expressions.

Equations

Equations are defined as algebraic expressions that are set equal to a number, variable or another expression. The simplest identifier of an equation is the equal sign (=). When an equation is written to express a condition or represent a situation for problem solving, the solution is normally completed by manipulating the equation correctly so that a variable or unknown quantity is on one side of the equal sign and the numerical answer(s) are on the other side of the equal sign. Let's review some problem-solving methods in the following examples.

If the simple equation is written in word form, the first step must be to write the equation that represents that written question. The simple problem of ages of individuals is a common example:

> Example 1: Jane is 8 years older than Nancy. In 5 years, she will be 27 years old. What is Jane's age now?

The variable J will represent Jane's age and the expression J+5 will represent Jane's age in 5 years. In this example, we read that this expression is equal to a number, in this case 27. Our equation becomes:

$$J+5 = 27$$

In the words of the problem, we have the correct expression set equal to a number. Our basic principle is to perform algebraic operations until the "J" is alone on one side of the equation and the numerical answer is on the other side. This type of solution involves the opposite of the addition (+5) so 5 is subtracted from both sides.

$$\begin{array}{r} J+5 = 27 \\ -5 \quad -5 \\ \hline J+0 = 22 \end{array}$$

Therefore, the answer says that the variable J, Jane's age, is now 22 years.

If the simple equation involved multiplication, the steps would involve an opposite operation that in this case would be division.

$$\begin{array}{c} 7J = 84 \\ 7J/7 = 84/7 \\ \hline J = 12 \end{array}$$

These examples are typical of "one-step solutions" since a single operation is involved to solve the problem.

Of course, there are multiple step solutions in more involved problems. But the rules are still the same, i.e.

1. Opposite operations are performed to solve
2. The same operations must be performed on both sides of the equation
3. The solution is complete when a variable is on one side and the answers are on the other side

> Example 2: Jane is 8 years older than Nancy. In 5 years, she will be twice as old as Nancy. What is Jane's age now?

The first step to solving this type of problem is to identify the variable. In this solution, we will select the variable "J" to represent Jane's age and "N" to represent Nancy's age.

The two equations from the word description, become:

$$J - 8 = N$$

and

$$J + 5 = 2(N+5)$$

Dividing both sides of the second equation by 2 means that it becomes

$$(J+5)/2 = N+5$$

Adding 5 to the original equation we have

$$J - 8 + 5 = N + 5$$

In this method, there are two expressions which contain "J" that are both equal to "N + 5" so therefore, they must be equal to each other. So:

$$J - 3 = (J + 5)/2$$

Multiply both sides by 2 (same operation on both sides) and the equation is:

$$2J - 6 = J + 5$$

Subtract J and add 6 to both sides and the answer becomes:

$$\begin{array}{rcl} 2J - 6 & = & J + 5 \\ -J + 6 & & -J + 6 \\ \hline J & = & 11 \end{array}$$

By this solution, the problem is completed and the following statements are clarified:

1. Now, Jane is 11 years old, and Nancy is 3 years old.
2. In 5 years, Jane will be 16 years old, and Nancy will be 8 years old.

We are able to answer the question, "What is Jane's age now?" and all the other ages in the question because of an algebra principle that requires two equations for two unknowns. In the problem, there are two variables (J and N) and two relationships between them (now and 5 years from now). If we are able to formulate two equations with the two unknowns, then algebra principles will allow for the solution of a complex problem.

Quadratic Equations

Quadratic equations are algebraic equations where the largest variable exponent is equal to two. This is often referred to as a "second degree" equation. If there are multiple terms, it can also be referred to as a second degree polynomial, where polynomial indicates that there are multiple terms in the equation. Quadratic equations are valuable in higher-order problem solving situations, with particularly important application in Physics problem solving. Examples are depicted below:

$$7x^2 = 0$$

$$\frac{1}{2}(9.8)\,t^2 = 27$$

$$ax^2 + bx + c = 0 \text{ where a, b and c are real numbers}$$

Note that all quadratic equations can be written in the form of the last example because coefficients can be zero and algebra operations can be performed so that the 0 is on the right side of the equation. This last statement is the standard form and is of great importance. **Every** quadratic equation in this form can be solved with the quadratic formula. It is presented here with a qualifying statement. In a timed testing environment, the use of the following formula is typically used when factoring is not feasible, since it a time consuming option. The quadratic formula for equations in the standard form states:

$$X = -b/\ (2a) +/- \sqrt{(b^2 - 4ac)\ /\ (2a)}$$

Due to the complexity of the quadratic formula, it will normally be used when the term

$$(b^2 - 4ac)\ /\ (2a) = 0$$

$$(b^2 - 4ac)\ /\ (2a) = \text{a perfect square}$$

Since the use of technology is not allowed, any more intricate application of the quadratic formula will be too time consuming to be useful. Note that the operations before the square root sign are both correct. The plus and minus signs indicate that every quadratic equation has the possibility of two answers. It does not say that both answers will be valid to the multiple-choice word problem that is in quadratic form. This is easily explained with a simple statement. Since two negative numbers and two positive numbers multiplied together give a positive answer, any quadratic equation may have two possible correct answers. When answering questions about quadratic equations in multiple-choice problems, that statement should be considered.

FOIL - Polynomial Multiplication

Polynomial multiplication is routinely taught with a method described as FOIL, which stands for First, Outside, Inside and Last. In a binomial multiplication problem, the form will usually look like this, with A, B, C, D whole number coefficients:

$$(Ax + B) * (Cx + D)$$

The "First" means that Ax and Cx are multiplied together to equal ACx^2
The "Outside" means that Ax and D are multiplied together to equal ADx
The "Inside" means that B and Cx are multiplied together to equal BCx
The "Last" means that B and D are multiplied together to equal BD

The polynomial answer becomes: $ACx^2 + (AD + BC)x + BD$

In testing conditions, this method can be cumbersome, confusing and unreliable because mistakes are too common.

A simplified alternative is called the Box Method, and it is simpler for multiple reasons.

1. There is a box that provides the organization for the multiplication.
2. The box also provides organization for the addition of like terms.
3. This method is expandable for use with longer polynomial multiplication.

To use the Box Method for polynomial multiplication, follow these steps:

1. Create a box that has a row and column for each term in the multiplication problem.

2. Perform the multiplication of each pair of terms.
3. Place the answers in the cells of the box.
4. Add the like terms that are aligned diagonally.
5. Write the polynomial.

The following diagram explains the outcome with the previously noted example:

(Ax + B) * (Cx + D) becomes:

	Ax	B
Cx	ACx^2	BCx
D	ADx	BD

The diagonal boxes in the upper right and lower left are always the "like terms" so there are no questions as to which terms must be added. This is true if you have ordered the binomials correctly with the "x term" of the binomials on the left and on top, respectively.

The final outcome is the same as the FOIL answer previously noted:

$$ACx^2 + (AD + BC)x + BD$$

Notice also that the Box Method has the additional benefit of separating the addition and multiplication operations completely.

In a multiple-choice problem such as this, there is a significant benefit in using the box method as a time saving consideration.

Example: (x + 6) (4x + 8) = (choose a correct answer below)

A $4x^2 + 32x + 48$

B $4x^2 + 32x + 32$

C $4x^2 + 32x + 14$

D $4x^2 + 14x + 48$

The lower right box entry means that the last term in the answer must be 6 * 8, or 48. So, both answers B and C can be eliminated because the last term is not 48.

The upper right and lower left box entries are added and the middle term must be 24x + 8x = 32x. So, answer D can be eliminated because the middle term is not 14x.

The correct answer must be A, a choice that can be made logically by looking at the box entries. Eliminating choices is expedited with the Box Method because the box entries can be easily compared to coefficients in the answer choices.

Substitute Variables

Many mathematics applications involve using equations and then substituting variables. This terminology means that the algebra equation will typically have a single variable with all other parameters defined as whole, decimal or fractional numbers. Then to solve a specific problem, the value of the specific variable will be uniquely defined (in some cases, multiple values may be supplied for comparison) and the variables used to determine a problem solution. For example, let's use the equation that was previously discussed, for a car traveling 70 miles per hour:

Distance traveled equals 70 mph multiplied by time in hours

Without the words, in strictly algebraic terms:

$$D = 70t \text{ (t in hours)}$$

To find the amount of distance traveled, solve the equation by substituting the value of time that is appropriate for the problem. If the problem stated that the time traveled was two and one-half hours, then the equation would be solved with the following:

$$D = 70 \text{ x } 2.5$$

After multiplying, the answer for the distance traveled is 175 miles.

In some equations, you may be asked to evaluate an equation that involves a second-degree variable. For example, a word description might read as follows:

Distance traveled is equal to one-half 9.8 m/sec^2 multiplied by the time squared

Again, without words, in strictly algebraic terms the equation would be:

$$D = {}^1/_2 * 9.8 * t^2$$

Evaluating this equation for a time of 2 seconds becomes:

$$D = {}^1/_2 * 9.8 * 2^2 = {}^1/_2 * 9.8 * 4 = 2 * 9.8 = 19.6 \text{ meters}$$

The answers have distance units that are determined by the units of measure that are given in the word problem.

Miles per hour multiplied by hours will provide distances in hours. Meters per second per second will provide distances in meters. The units of time and distance within the problem must be consistent. Substituting variables will be simple if the variables are consistent.

Inequalities - Greater Than and Less Than

Inequalities are an algebra topic that is often misrepresented and taught in a more difficult manner than necessary. When we find solutions to algebra equations there is a single number (or two numbers in the case of a quadratic equation) that represents the set of all numbers that are **equal to** the algebraic expression on the other side of the equal sign.

Inequalities represent the set of all numbers that are either greater than or less than that specific solution. If the number 3 represents the solution of an algebra equation, then the following number line diagram may help visualize what the inequalities may look like:

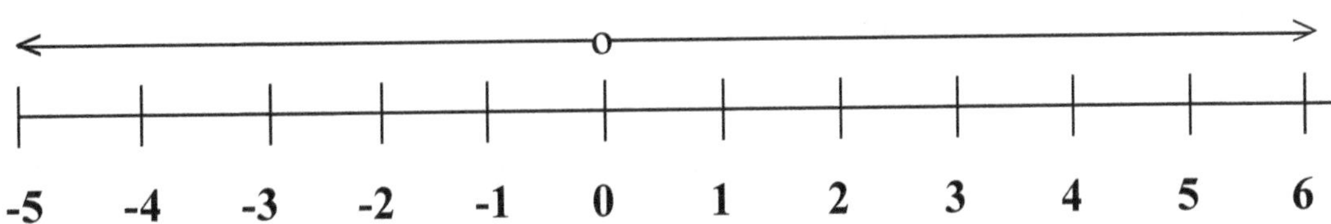

The arrow on the left side of the "o" is the less than inequality, and the arrow on the right side of the "o" is the greater than inequality. Of course, the "o" represents the exact solution of the inequality. This simplicity tells us that the simplest way to solve the inequality is to first solve the equality and then find out which arrow is required. The solution with quadratics will be discussed at the end of this section.

The inequality $7x + 2 > -5$ will be solved by first solving the equality:

$$7x + 2 = -5$$

Following the steps discussed in section 2, the first step is to subtract 2 from both sides and divide both sides by 7. The solution of the equality says:

$$x = -1$$

To see which way the arrow points, we will use the value of $x = 0$ in the inequality to see if it is true. If it is true, then the arrow pointing to the right is correct (>), which is what we would expect. If $x = 0$ is not true then the arrow must point the other direction (<). The test helps by ensuring that the point at $x = 0$ is or is not in the solution set of the inequality, allowing the correct answer to be chosen. Therefore, substituting $x = 0$ means:

$$7(0) + 2 = 2$$

Since 2 is greater than negative 5 the answer looks like the following diagram:

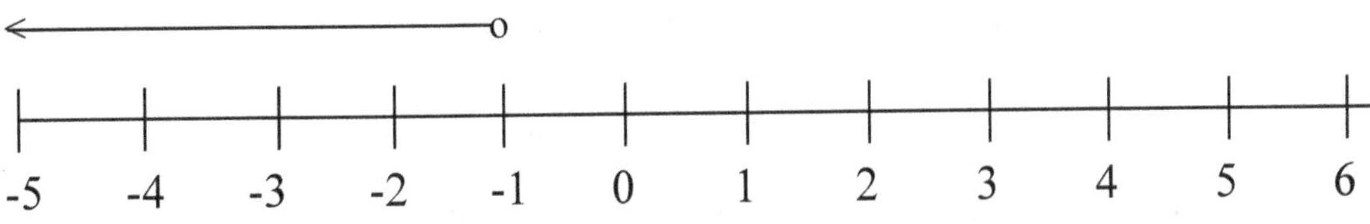

The arrow does not include the point "0" on the number line because the "Zero Test" tells us that that point does not satisfy the inequality. If the "0" is not included then the arrow must point to the left of the point at -1, which was the answer to the equality. If our test showed that the "0" satisfied the equality, then the arrow would have pointed to the right. For this reason, both "Greater Than" and "Less Than" are addressed in this section. They are determined the same way, specifically:

First, find the solution to the **equality**.

Second, test to see if x = 0 is true for the **inequality**.

If the test is true, the solution must include the point x = 0.
If the test is not true, the inequality goes the opposite direction.

There may be the question as to why the value of x = 0 is chosen for the test. Simply, it represents the simplest solution for evaluating algebra equations with variables. Any term which has an "x" (or x^2 or higher order) simply disappears when x = 0, leaving only the constant numerical terms.

If there is a need to solve an inequality where the equality solution is x = 0, then the inequality test can be performed with x = 1. The test is **almost** as simple as the zero test, and it applies if the equality solution is 0. The same logical decision process used for the zero test also applies here.

Rates and Systems of Equations

These are some of the most common questions on standardized math exams and also some of the most criticized. How many pop culture references are there to the nightmare of the "if train A is traveling west of Detroit at 70 miles an hour and train B is traveling north of Denver at 90 miles an hour, what is the weight of the moon" variety? Excluding the nonsensical nature of the joke (would we weigh the moon in terms of its own gravity, or Earth's? Do bodies in orbit actually weigh *anything*?? Wait, wrong subject), this is simply a rate problem! Train A has a speed and a direction, Train B has a speed and a direction, and given those facts, you can answer all kinds of questions easily.

A *rate* is anything that relates two types of measurement: distance and time, dollars and workers, mass and volume, x per y. Exchange rates tell us how much of one currency you can get for a certain amount of another currency. Speedometers tell us how many miles we travel per unit of time. Growth rates tell us how much additional population we get over time. Rates are everywhere in the world, and they are everywhere on standardized math tests. To express a rate mathematically, think of the following:

All rates express one measurement *in terms of* another.

For example, *miles per hour* gives us a measurement of distance (miles) for one unit of time (an hour). "Per" is a term that means divide. It looks like this:

If a car is traveling 70 mph, it goes 70 miles for every one hour of time that passes.

All rates work this way. If you can get €0.81 (Euros) for one American dollar, the exchange rate is:

€0.81 (Euros) / 1 Dollar = 0.81 Euros per Dollar

A rate is written as a fraction. A rate *equation* gives you a value of one of the measurements if you know the rate and the value of the other measurement.

If a car travels 70 mph: Distance = 70 miles/hour * hours

This recipe for the equation always works for a rate problem:

Examine the mph example: when you multiply 70 miles/hour times a number of hours, the hours units cancel out, leaving you with a number of miles. This works for any type of rate. The thing being measured on the *top* (numerator) of the rate measurement is equal to the rate times the unit being measured on the *bottom* of the rate measurement.

To solve a rate problem, follow these steps:

1. Read the question carefully to determine what you will be solving for. Is it an amount of time? A distance? Something else? Make sure you understand this before anything else. It can be helpful to name the variables at this point.

2. Write equations to express all of the information given in the problem. This is just like we've demonstrated for percentage problems, averaging problems, etc. The ability to express information in an equation is one of the main mathematical reasoning abilities that you can demonstrate to succeed on tests like these. Remember the equation:

Distance = Rate * Time

3. Solve!

First, a simple example:

A train is traveling west at 75 mph. How long will it take to travel 60 miles?

Step 1: Identify what the question is asking for: in this instance, it's *how long*, or the time it takes to travel 60 miles.

Step 2: Write an equation: 60 = 75 * time

Step 3: Solve! We know that the rate is 75 miles per hour and that the miles traveled is 60. To solve for time, just plug those values into the equation:

Isolate the "x hours" by dividing both sides by 75 mph:

60 miles / 75 miles per hour = 0.8 hours
0.8 hours * 60 minutes per hour = 48 minutes

Rate problems can also require a system of equations. This just means that you need to write two equations to relate two unknown variables, instead of one equation to solve for one unknown variable, like the problem above. The algebra is not any more difficult for these types of problems. They just require the extra step of writing another equation.

For example: Jessica assembles one model airplane per hour. James assembles one model airplane per 45 minutes. If they work for the same amount of time and assemble twelve planes all together, how many planes did James assemble?

Step 1: Identify what the question is asking for: the number of planes that James assembled.

Step 2: Write equations:

$$x = 1 \text{ Airplanes per hour} * T \text{ hours}$$
$$y = 1/0.75 \text{ Airplanes per hour} * T \text{ hours}$$
$$x + y = 12$$

You convert "45 minutes" to 0.75 hours, since 45/60 = 0.75. If you'd rather not do that, you could leave the rate in minutes, but then change Jessica's rate to 60 minutes instead of one hour. The important thing is to use the same units for time across the whole equation.

Step 3: Solve! Notice that the "T hours" term is the same in both of the rate equations. The problem stated that the two of them worked for the same amount of time. To solve for the number of planes James assembled, first we need to find T hours. The *number of planes Jessica assembles* and the *number of planes James assembles* can be added together since we know that the sum is 12. This is the new equation from adding those together:

$$12 = 1 \text{ Airplanes per hour} * T \text{ hours} + 1/0.75 \text{ Airplanes per hour} * T \text{ hours}$$

The algebra here is a little bit hairy, but we can handle it! To solve for time, isolate T step by step. First, multiply every term in the equation by "1 hour":

Now, the unit "hour" cancels out of both terms on the right side of the equation. Remember, when you multiply *and* divide a term by something, that cancels out:

$$12\, planes * (1\, hour) = \cancel{(1\, hour)} * \frac{1\, plane}{\cancel{1\, hour}} * T\, hours + \cancel{(1\, hour)} * \frac{1\, plane}{0.75\, \cancel{hours}} * T\, hours$$

Now, we have:

$$12 \text{ plane hours} = 1 \text{ plane} * T \text{ hours} + 1/0.75 * T \text{ hours}$$

We need to isolate "T hours." Gather together the "T hours" terms on the right side of the equation. Right now, they are separated into an addition expression. If we add them together, they will be collected into one term. Since 1/0.75 is equal to 4/3, change that term first:

$$12 \text{ plane hours} = 1 \text{ plane} * T \text{ hours} + 4/3 \text{ plane} * T \text{ hours}$$

Now add:

12 plane hours = (1 plane + 4/3 plane) * T hours
12 plane hours = (1 and 4/3 plane) * T hours

You add together 1 and 4/3. This is the same as saying that $1x + 2x = 3x$. We just collected the like terms.

Now, divide both sides by 1 plane to isolate the T hours term. Since mixed fractions are difficult to work with, change this into an improper fraction:

12 plane hours = (7/3 plane) * T hours

The planes unit cancels out on the right side. So we are left with:

12 hours / (7/3) = T hours

One arithmetic trick: dividing by a fraction is the same as multiplying by the inverse of the fraction. If you are comfortable dividing by fractions on your calculator, you can do the rest of the problem that way, or else you can flip the fraction over and simplify the arithmetic:

12 * 3/7 = T hours
36/7 = T hours
5 1/7 = T hours

The answer is x = $5\,^{1}/_{7}$ hours, or approximately 5.14 hours.

That was a long problem! But it included rates, a system of equations, unit conversions (changing minutes into fractions of an hour) and algebra with complex fractions. That is about the most difficult type of rate problem you would ever see on a standardized math exam, so if you were able to follow along with the solution you're in good shape.

Remember, on exams like this, the vast majority of points come from the easier problems. The harder problems (which on most exams tend to be at the end of a section) are always worth giving a shot, but they are not necessary to get a good score. Problems like these are great for practice because they include a lot of different concepts. Don't be discouraged if you don't always get the tougher problems correct on the first try. They are preparing you to do well on a wide range of different problem types!

Probability

Every probability is a ratio as described below.

$$\text{Probability} = \frac{\text{Total number of desired events}}{\text{Total number of possible outcomes}}$$

The simplest example of this type of ratio is found when tossing a coin. There are always two total outcomes, heads and tails, so the probability of either a head or a tail is always 1/2 for that coin.

Similarly, if you tossed that same coin 14 times, you would expect to see it land 7 times with the head showing and 7 times with the tail showing. Because these events are totally random, flipping the coin 14 times will not always provide an equal number of outcomes in a group of trials. So we say that the number of heads in a trial of 14 is the "expected value" of 7. Similarly, 7 would be the "expected value" for tails.

A common misconception is that there "has to be" a certain outcome based on the number of outcomes that have already occurred. In the repeated trial of an event, each outcome is it's own trial and is not influenced by the previous trial or trials.

The other common type of probability problem is with dice, where each of six faces of a cube has its own number from 1 to 6. Each of these numbers has the probability of 1/6 for a single roll of the die.

If we formulate a table of outcomes for two dice, thrown together, the details are slightly different. In this table, the individual numbers are shown across the top and vertically along the side. The entries in the table represent the total of the two dice.

Cube "B" \ Cube "A"	1	2	3	4	5	6
1	2	3	4	5	6	7
2	3	4	5	6	7	8
3	4	5	6	7	8	9
4	5	6	7	8	9	10
5	6	7	8	9	10	11
6	7	8	9	10	11	12

A look at the table shows that there are 36 possible outcomes when two dice are thrown together (6 * 6). The individual probabilities are shown below.

P (1) =	0		(never appears)
P (2) =	$^1/_{36}$ does not simplify		(appears once)
P (3) =	$^2/_{36}$	simplifies to $^1/_{18}$	(appears twice)
P (4) =	$^3/_{36}$	simplifies to $^1/_{12}$	(appears three times)
P (5) =	$^4/_{36}$	simplifies to $^1/_9$	(appears four times)
P (6) =	$^5/_{36}$	does not simplify	(appears five times)
P (7) =	$^6/_{36}$	simplifies to $^1/_6$	(appears six times)
P (8) =	$^5/_{36}$	does not simplify	(appears five times)
P (9) =	$^4/_{36}$	simplifies to $^1/_9$	(appears four times)
P (10) =	$^3/_{36}$	simplifies to $^1/_{12}$	(appears three times)
P (11) =	$^2/_{36}$	simplifies to $^1/_{18}$	(appears twice)
P (12) =	$^1/_{36}$	does not simplify	(appears once)
P (13) =	0		(never occurs)

The symmetry of the table helps us visualize the probability ratios for the individual outcomes. By the definition of probability, any number larger than 13 will never appear in the table so the probability has to be zero. The probability of any impossible outcome always has to be zero. By the same reasoning, any event that must happen will have a probability of one. So, the probability of rolling a number from 2 to 12 is one.

If you are finding the probability of two events happening, the individual probabilities are added. For example, the probability of rolling a ten or eleven is the same as the probability of rolling an eight. The number eight appears in the table the same number of times as the combined total of appearances of ten or eleven.

The formulation of ratios for probabilities is simplest when using fractions. Often, the expression of a probability answer will be in a percent or a decimal. A coin from the first example would have the following probabilities P (heads) = 50% or .5 or 0.5.

Formulating probabilities from a word problem can always be structured around the ratio defined at the beginning of this section. However, the words can mislead or misdirect problem-solving efforts.

For example, a problem that describes a class distribution may often be stated as the number of boys and the number of girls. The probability of selecting a boy in a random sample is defined as the number of boys divided by the TOTAL number of boys AND girls. This is simple to see, but problems can be worded to mislead you into selecting the incorrect answer or to lead to the wrong conclusion when calculating an answer.

Another way that probability problems can be misleading is when multiple choices are used when simplified ratios are required. For example, if a class is made up of 6 girls and 10 boys, the probability of randomly selecting a girl from the classroom is $^6/_{16}$ or $^3/_8$. The misleading multiple choices that may be listed would often include 60%, (6/10) or 50% (since there are two outcomes — boys and girls). Reading a probability problem carefully is extremely important in both formulating the probability ratio and in making sure that the correct ratio is selected in the correct form. If the probability ratio for the example is formulated as $^6/_{16}$, the simplified form of $^3/_8$ is the only correct answer.

Ratios and Proportions

Ratios and fractions are synonymous when discussing numerical values. The ratios or fractions always imply division of the numerator by the denominator. In this section, the discussion is directed toward how words appear in ratio problems and how those words should be interpreted.

A commonly used ratio is contained in the term "miles per hour", usually abbreviated by mph. When the term "miles per hour" is interpreted numerically, it is the ratio of the total number of miles traveled divided by the number of hours traveled. The key word in this commonly used term is "per". It literally means for each hour of travel, a specific number of miles will be traveled. It has the same implication when the term is "gallons per hour" (how fast a tub is filled or a lawn is watered) or "tons per year" (how much ore is mined in one year).

Another way that ratios can appear is when a phrase defines a ratio as one value to another. A commonly used comparison is usually the ratio of "men to women" or "boys to girls". When this terminology is used, the first term is in the numerator, and the second term is in the denominator by convention.

There is an inherent problem when this terminology is used as illustrated by the example below:

> In a classroom setting, the ratio of girls to boys is 3 to 4 (or 3:4 in strictly mathematical terms). How many boys are there in the classroom if the total number of students is 28?

There are two ways that this word problem may be easily solved. If the ratio of $(^{girls}/_{boys})$ is ¾, the actual numbers may be ¾ or $^6/_8$ or $^9/_{12}$ or $^{12}/_{16}$ and so forth. These fractions are all equivalent fractions since they all simplify to the value of ¾. The equivalent fractions are easily determined as the ratios of multiples of the numerator and denominator of the original fraction. There is only one fraction where the numerator and denominator add to 28, and that is the ratio $^{12}/_{16}$. Therefore, the solution is the classroom has 16 boys and 12 girls.

Notice that the words specify which group (boys or girls) is the numerator and denominator in the original problem and in the solution. When choosing multiple-choice answers, make sure that the correct answer is chosen based upon the wording in the original problem. Most often, the correct ratio and its reciprocal are in the answer choices. For example, if the sample problem appeared on the exam, the multiple-choice answers would most likely include 16 boys and 12 girls AND 12 boys and 16 girls. But 16 boys and 12 girls is the correct answer choice.

Geometry

To tackle geometry questions on a mathematical reasoning test, there are a few formulas and rules that you need to know. This section takes you through those basic rules. It covers intersecting lines, triangles, squares and rectangles, and circles.

Basic Vocabulary

Vocabulary that is important to know for geometry questions includes the following:

Line – A line is a set of all points between two endpoints. Lines have no area or width, only length.

Angle – An angle is the corner formed by two intersecting line segments, and it is measured in degrees. Degrees measurements show the magnitude of the "sweep" of the angle. In the figure below, angle x is shown as the measure between the two line segments.

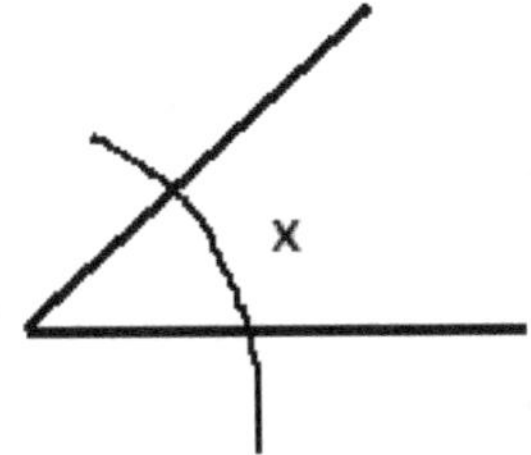

360° describes the angle measurement all the way around a full circle. Half of that, 180°, is the angle measurement across a straight line. Two lines at right angles to each other, called perpendicular lines, have an angle measurement of 90°.

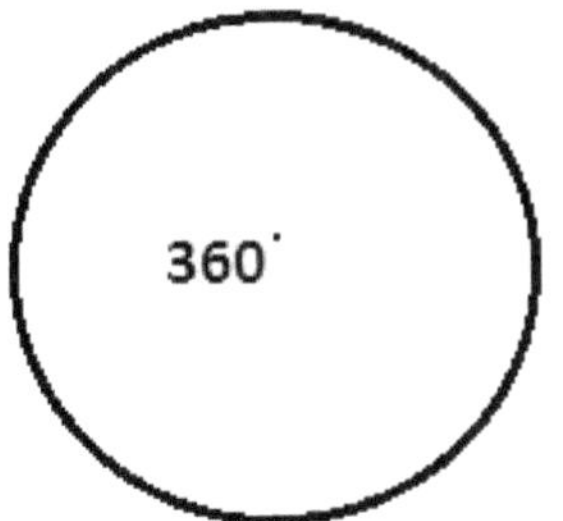

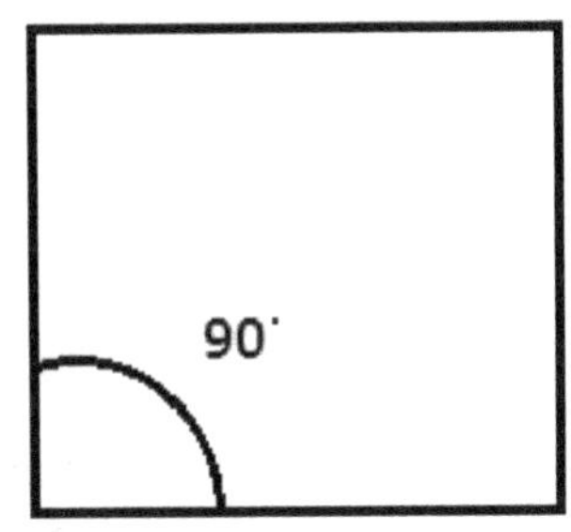

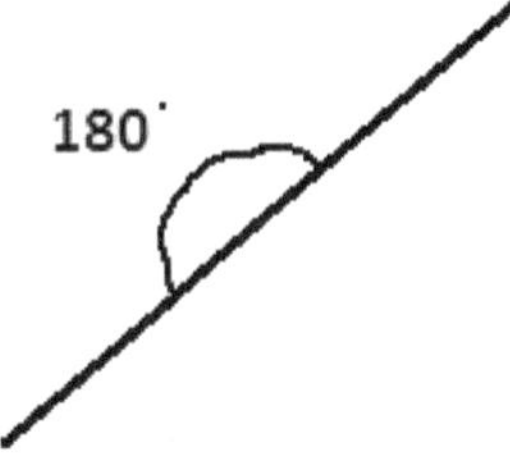

Area – The area is the measure of space inside a two-dimensional figure. It has units of length * length, or length^2. For example, rooms are described as being a number of square feet. Counties are described as being so many square miles. Each basic shape has a special formula for determining area.

Perimeter – The perimeter is the measure of the length around the outside of a figure.

Volume – For three-dimensional figures, the volume is the measure of space inside the figure. Volume has three dimensions: length * width * height. Because of this, it has units of length^3 (cubic length). For example, you may have heard "cubic feet" used to describe the volume of something like a storage unit. This formula applies only to square and rectangular three-dimensional shapes. Other figures have their own formulas for determining volume.

Intersecting Lines

There are two important properties to know about pairs of intersecting lines:

1. They form angles that add up to 180° along the sides of each line.
2. They create two pairs of equal angles.

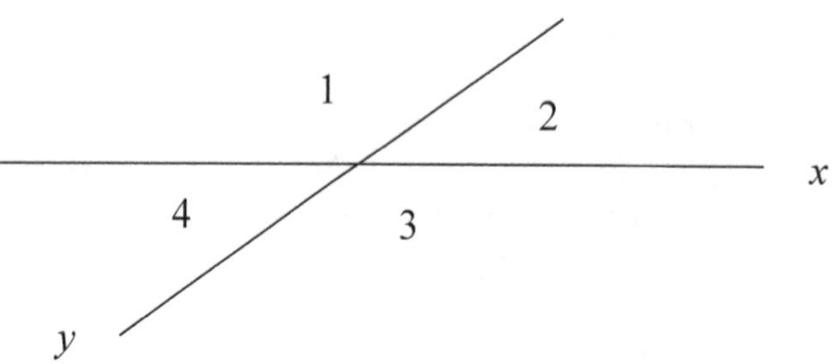

For example, in the diagram above, line x intersects line y, forming the four angles 1, 2, 3 and 4. Any two angles along one side of a line will add up to 180°:

$$Angle\ 1 + Angle\ 2 = 180°$$
$$Angle\ 2 + Angle\ 3 = 180°$$
$$Angle\ 3 + Angle\ 4 = 180°$$
$$Angle\ 4 + Angle\ 1 = 180°$$

All four of the angles added together would equal 360°:

$$Angle\ 1 + Angle\ 2 + Angle\ 3 + Angle\ 4 = 360°$$

The two angles DIAGONAL from each other must be equal. For the figure above, we know that:

$$Angle\ 1 = Angle\ 3$$
$$Angle\ 2 = Angle\ 4$$

This property is very useful: if you are given any one of the angles, you can immediately solve for the other three. If you are told that Angle 1 = 120°, then you know that Angle 2 = 180° - 120° = 60°. Since Angle 3 = Angle 1 and Angle 4 = Angle 2, you now know all four angles.

Parallel/Perpendicular Lines

Parallel lines are lines that lie on the same 2-D plane (i.e., the page) and never intersect each other. The thing to remember about parallel lines is that if a line intersects two parallel lines, it will form a bunch of corresponding angles (like the ones discussed above). Also, you can never assume that two lines are parallel just from a diagram. You need to be told or given enough information that you can deduce it. Parallel lines have the same slope.

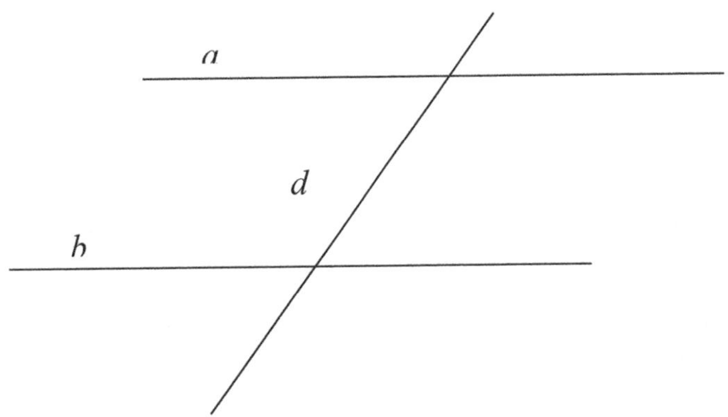

Lines *a* and *b* are parallel and are intersected by line *d*.

In the diagram above, all four of the acute angles (the ones smaller than 90°) are equal to each other. All four of the obtuse angles (the ones greater than 90°) are equal to each other. Why? Because a line intersecting parallel lines forms equivalent angles. This is simply an expanded case of the intersecting lines concept discussed earlier.

Squares and Rectangles

By definition, a square has four sides of equal length and four angles of 90°. A rectangle has two pairs of sides of equal length and four angles of 90°. This means that the sum of all four angles in a square or rectangle is 360°.

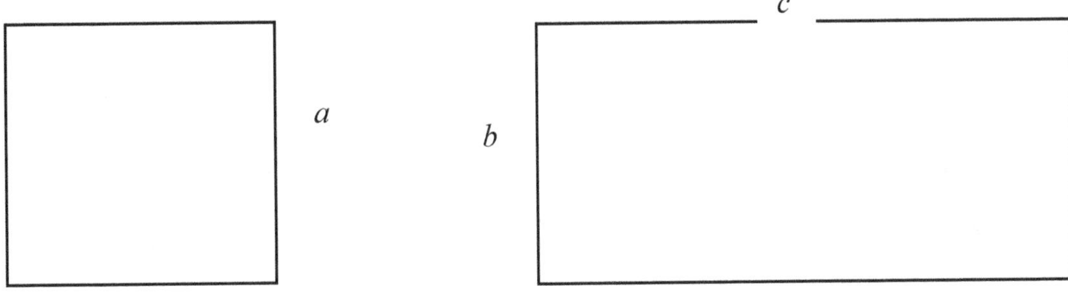

In the diagram above, the shape on the left is a square. So, if you are given the length of side *a*, you automatically know the length of every side. You already know the measure of every angle, because they are all 90° - the measure of right (perpendicular) angles.

The shape on the right is a rectangle. So, if you are given the length of side *b*, you know the length of the opposite side. However, you do not know the length of the longer two sides unless they are given.

The **perimeter** of a square is the sum of all four line segments. Since the line segments are equal, the equation is as follows:

$$Perimeter\ of\ a\ square = 4 * (side\ length)$$

The perimeter of the square above is $4a$.

The perimeter of the rectangle is also the sum of its sides. However, since there are two pairs of equal length sides in a rectangle, the equation is as follows:

$$Perimeter\ of\ a\ rectangle = 2 * (long\ side\ length) + 2 * (short\ side\ length)$$

The perimeter of the rectangle above is $2b + 2c$.

The **area** of a square is its length times its width. Since length and width are the same for a square, the area is the length of one of its sides squared (that's where the term "squared" comes from) and the equation is as follows:

$$\text{Area} = a^2$$

For a rectangle, length times width is not equal to one side squared (it's not a square, so the sides are not all the same length). The equation for the area of a rectangle is as follows:

$$\text{Area} = b * c$$

Triangles

A triangle is a polygon (closed shape) made of three line segments. While the four angles in a square and rectangle always add up to 360°, the three angles in a triangle always add up to 180°. However, these angles are not always the same measure, as they are for squares and rectangles.

Below are the different types of triangles:

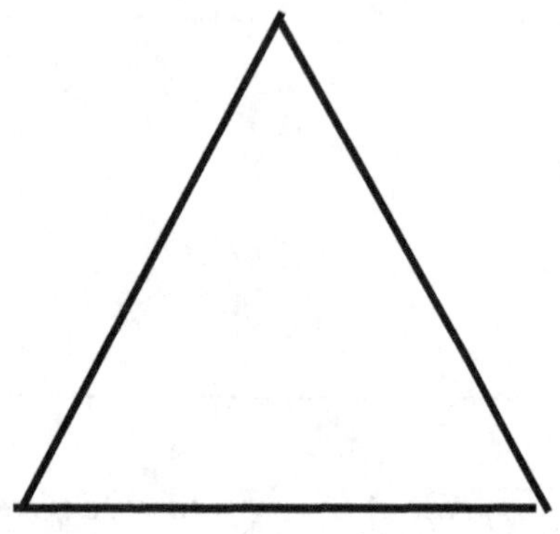

Equilateral
sides of same length
angles of 60°

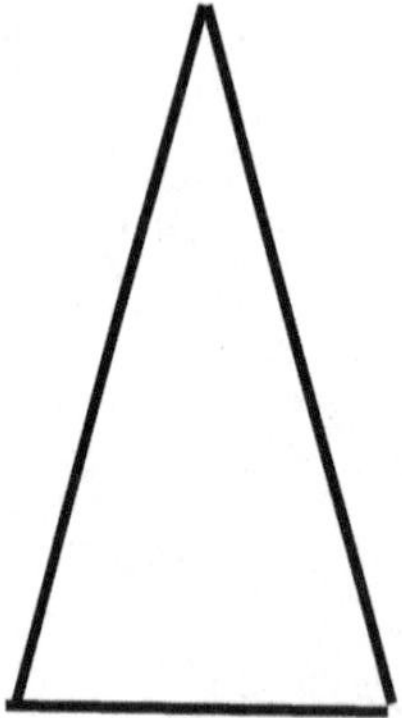

Isosceles
two sides of same length
two angles of same measure

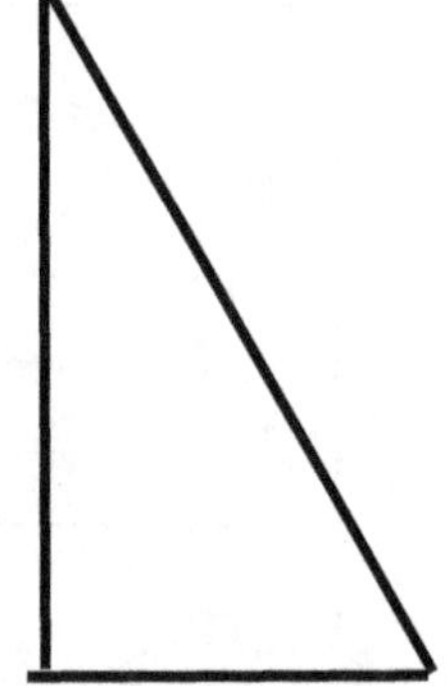

Right
one angle of 90°

The area of a triangle will always equal one half of the product of its base and its height. You can choose any side to be the base (the one at the bottom of the triangle is probably best), and the height of a triangle is the perpendicular line from the base to the opposite angle. The height is NOT the length of a side, unless the triangle is a right triangle.

For example:

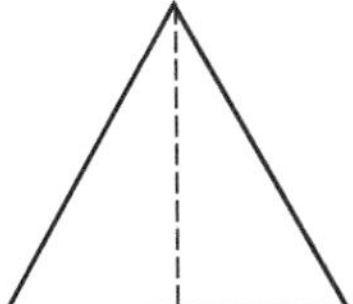

In this triangle, the bottom leg is the base, and the dotted line is the height.

$$A = \frac{1}{2}\,(\boldsymbol{base} * \boldsymbol{height})$$

Another important formula to know when working with triangles is the Pythagorean Theorem. This tells you how to relate the lengths of the sides of right triangles – the ones that include 90° angles.

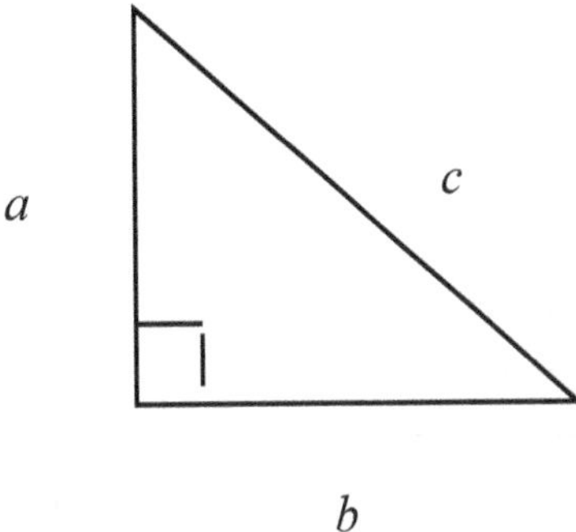

In the diagram above, you have right triangle ABC. You know it's a right triangle because it has a 90° angle – not because it *looks* like one. Never assume the measure of an angle without being given that information. Side *c* is called the hypotenuse, which is the longest side of a right triangle. Sides *a*, *b* and *c* are related to each other according to the Pythagorean Theorem:

$$c^2 = a^2 + b^2$$

Regardless of how the sides of the right triangle are labeled, the length of the longest side squared is equal to the sum of the lengths of the two shorter sides, each squared. There will likely be a few problems that will require you to use this relationship to solve.

Here are some important details to remember about triangles:

- A triangle has three sides and three angles.
- The angles of a triangle will always add up to 180°.
- A triangle is a "right triangle" if one of the angles is 90°.
- If a triangle is equilateral, all angles are 60°, and all sides are the same length.
- The area of a triangle is one half times the base times the height.
- For right triangles, you can relate the lengths of the sides using the Pythagorean Theorem.

Circles

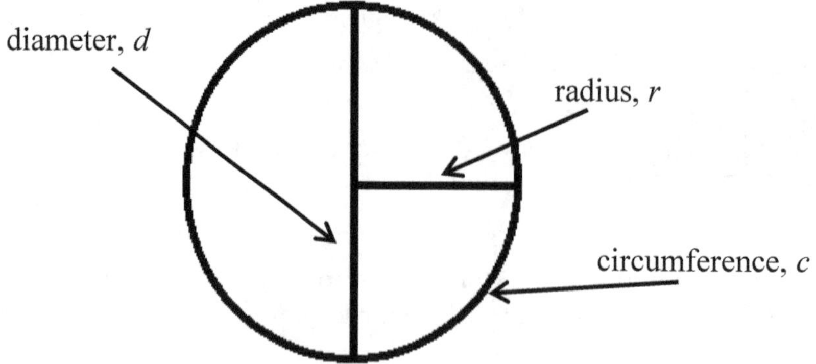

A circle is a figure without sides. Instead, it has a circumference with a set of points equidistant from the center of the circle.

Here are some important details to remember about circles:

- The measurement around the outside of a circle is called the **circumference**.
- The line segment going from the center of the circle to the circumference is called the **radius**.
- The line segment that goes across the entire circle, passing through the center, is the **diameter**.
- The number of degrees in the central angle of a circle is 360°.

The circumference of a circle can be found using the following formula:

$$C = 2\pi r$$

In this formula, r is the radius (or the distance from the center of the circle to an outside point on the circle). If you are given the diameter, then you can find the circumference using this formula:

$$\boldsymbol{C = \pi d}$$

The radius is twice the length of the diameter:

$$\boldsymbol{D = 2r}$$

The area of a circle can be found using this formula:

$$\boldsymbol{A = \pi r^2}$$

So, the area is equal to the radius squared times the constant π (pronounced pi). Sometimes, answer choices are given with π as a part of the value, 2π, for example. When you see this, work out the problem without substituting the value of π (approximately 3.14). You can, in fact, estimate that π is 3.14 or 22/7 in your calculations, but you'll end up with a decimal or fraction for your answer.

True to its name, the Word Knowledge section tests your knowledge and understanding of the meaning of words. In simple terms, the goal is to choose a synonym for the given word.

The section has 25 questions with a 5-minute time limit, giving you an average of 20 seconds per question. This is ample time if you move smoothly and with a plan. It is impractical to memorize tens of thousands of words for a 5-minute exam section; rather, your time studying should be focused on learning or refreshing yourself on the base roots, prefixes, and suffixes of words. After that, use practice time to streamline your process of elimination so that worst case, if you are unsure, you can greatly increase the probability of an educated guess (not lucky guess!).

As with most sections of the AFOQT, the concept of the test is straightforward with Reading Comprehension. As an AFOQT test-taker, you undoubtedly have encountered this type of section before on the SAT or ACT. The difference here is the level of difficulty of the questions themselves is a bit higher, but not by much.

The main challenge to keep in mind is that you only have 38 minutes to answer 25 questions. This gives you approximately 1.5 minutes per question, which might seem ample, but there is a lot of reading to be done. Science tell us that the "average reader" can read 200 words per minute with 60% or better comprehension. Generally speaking, between the passage itself and the answer choices, you'll have about 150-250 words total to read, and the test of course measures your comprehension of what you read.

So, while the questions themselves may not be terribly difficult, your ability to read AND comprehend, both quickly AND accurately is what is being measured.

Finding the Main Idea

Many of the reading comprehension questions you will encounter on the exam are structured around finding the main idea of a paragraph. The last section on root words was all about finding the main idea of a word – notice a theme developing here?

In this section, you will need to find the main idea of a paragraph. Luckily, that's nice and simple once you know what to look for.

First of all, we're going to re-define a few terms you might think you already know, so don't rush through this part:

Paragraph

A paragraph is a tool for organizing information. It's simply a container for sentences in the same way that a sentence is a container for words. Okay, maybe you knew that already, but you'd be surprised how many professional writers get their minds blown when they realize that almost all books are structured in the same way:

Books are made of *chapters*, which are made of *sections*, which are made of *paragraphs*, which are made of *sentences*, which are made of *words*.

It's a simple hierarchy, and smack in the center is the humble paragraph. For the purposes of the test, you need to be able to comb through given paragraphs to find two kinds of sentences: topic and detail.

Topic Sentence

A well-written paragraph, which is to say all of the paragraphs that you'll find on the test, contains just one topic. You'll find this in the topic sentence, which is the backbone of the paragraph. The topic sentence tells you what the paragraph is about. All of the other sentences exist solely to support this topic sentence which, more often than not, is the first or last sentence in the paragraph. However, that's not always the case, so use this foolproof method: Ask yourself, "Who or what is this paragraph about?" Then find the sentence that answers your question.

Detail Sentence

Detail sentences exist to support the topic sentence. They do so with all kinds of additional information, such as descriptions, arguments and nuances. An author includes detail sentences to explain why they're writing about the topic in the first place. That is, the detail sentences contain the author's point, which you'll need in order to find the main idea. To easily spot the author's point, just ask yourself, "Why is the author writing about this topic?" Then pay close attention to the detail sentences to pry out their motivations.

Got it? Good. Now, let's do some really easy math: **The topic + the author's point = the main idea**.

Now, let's put that in English: **What + Why = Main Idea**.

In the Real World

All right, you've got the abstract concepts nailed down. Now, let's get concrete. Imagine a scenario where a friend is explaining the movie Toy Story to you. Also, imagine that she has already picked her jaw up off the floor, because seriously, how have you not seen Toy Story? You should fix that.

She tells you what the movie is about: There are these toys that get lost, and they have a bunch of adventures trying to get back to their owner. Then she tells you why you should see it: It's cute and funny, and it's a classic.

Two sentences: The topic (what the movie is about) and the author's point (why she's telling you about it.) And now you have the main idea: Your friend thinks you should see the movie Toy Story because it's a cute, funny classic about toys having adventures.

Illustrating the Main Idea

Here is a paragraph similar to one you might encounter on the test, followed by the types of questions that you will need to answer:

EXAMPLE 1 – from The Art of Conversation by Catherine Blyth:

"Silence is meaningful. You may imagine that silence says nothing. In fact, in any spoken communication, it plays a repertoire of roles. Just as, mathematically speaking, Earth should be called Sea, since most of the planet is covered in it, so conversation might be renamed silence, as it comprises 40 to 50 percent of an average utterance, excluding pauses for others to talk and the enveloping silence of those paying attention (or not, as the case may be.)"

This one is relatively easy, but let's break it down:

Who/What is the paragraph about? Silence.

Why is the author writing about this topic? It is often overlooked, but it's an important part of conversation.

What is the main idea? Silence is an important part of conversation. Or, put it another way: "Silence is meaningful" - it's the first sentence!

Okay, you've seen the technique in action, so now it's your turn. Read the following paragraphs and determine the topic sentence, the author's main point, and the main idea.

To find the main idea of any piece of writing, remember: The topic + the author's point = the main idea or What + Why = Main Idea

Let's see what you have learned about finding the main idea and focal points of a passage. Read the following passages below. Search for topic and main idea, and try to determine the focus of each one. Then answer the questions presented after each passage.

Good Luck!

Passage 1

Regardless of your reasons and motivations, if you choose to homeschool your child, there are many factors that must be considered. One of the most hotly debated is that of providing a means of socialization for students. The fear some people have is that students taught at home rather than a traditional school setting do not get the social interaction with peers that regular students do. There are many ways children can socialize and interact with others their age:

Group field trips- there are groups and certain organizations that help host group fields trips. Homeschooled students can also get together with other homeschool students or their friends and peers who are in public or private schools and attend field trips together. These trips also can serve as credit for the homeschooled student's class work- historical monuments can count as history credit and a report written about what was seen can count as an English assignment; they also get the benefit of having time with their friends and peers.

Community service- there is always an opportunity to get involved in the community and these are perfect opportunities to interact with others. Students can get together to work on a project or can work on their own and work alongside others who are volunteering at the same location. It helps get your child interacting with others and can also help to instill valuable life lessons at the same time.

Scouts, clubs, and programs- there are many organizations that offer the opportunity for students to work, learn, and grow alongside each other. Boy Scouts and Girl Scouts offer a chance for students to interact with their peers while developing their own life skills. The 4-H Program also offers a unique opportunity for homeschooled students to get life experiences and interaction; some 4-H clubs are set up especially for homeschooled students.

Co-op Groups- these exist to help families organize group events with fellow homeschool students. Group projects and study sessions are just some of the options that are available. Group study sessions can also be prepared to practice for things such as SAT testing, Finally, homeschooled families can take advantage of co-op groups to help set up study sessions and events for students.

These are just a handful of simple ways home school families can answer society's question about how students can be socially active and interact with students their own age. Following the simple tips and taking a stab at any others that may be out there is a great way to meet your child's socialization needs while providing them with peace and protection and the education you want them to receive.

1. Which sentence best states the main idea of this passage?
   A) Homeschool children lack any good socialization and peer interaction.
   B) There are many ways children can socialize and interact with others their age.
   C) Children who are homeschooled lack major social skills.
   D) None of the above.

Answer: B.
Throughout the piece, the author talks about how homeschooled children can still find ways to socialize and interact with their peers.

2. Which of the following is not a way homeschooled students can interact with their peers that was discussed in this passage?
   A) Join a club or social group
   B) Volunteer in the local community
   C) Go on field trips
   D) They all are ways homeschooled students can meet peers

Answer: D.
All three of those methods of socialization were talked about in detail within the passage. Every one of them had several examples and explanations given as to why they were effective means of getting homeschooled students around their peer group.

Passage 2

The world around us is filled with the weird and usual. When we think of freaks of nature we usually bring to mind images of massive rabbits, six legged cows, and two headed dogs. However, the usual species and 'freaks of nature' also spill over into the plant world. Usual plants offer a unique look at plant biology gone haywire. From excessive size to usual smell, these freaky plants are real and can be found today -if you know where to look.

Although more than 90% of plant types have leaves, used for photosynthesis, there are some scenes and varieties of plants that do not. The most common of these are members of the mushroom family that are parasitic in nature. They feed off the decaying material of plants or suck nutrients from healthy living plants. One such parasitic plant truly earns the title of usual. It is the Rafflesia arnoldii. This plant bears a bloom that can grow more than three feet in diameter. The flower smells like rotting flesh and has a hole in the center big and deep enough to hold up to six quarts of water. To top off the list of usual traits, this plant has no stems, roots, or leaves, a true freak of nature.

Flowers can range in size from a fraction of the size of the plant, to more than 80% of the plant itself. Flowers serve as the reproductive part of the plant and is responsible for producing seeds to further the next batch of plants to be grown according to that plant's individual biology. One of the plants that show this wide range in plant size is the group of plants known as Amorphophallus. Closely related to the peace lily, these plants have a similar flower. Found in the subtropics, more than 200 different species and varieties have been identified. One of these species, Amorphophallus titanum, has a bloom that is several times larger than the plant itself; the blooms can get so large on some plants that they can exceed the height and width of a grown adult. Truly amazing what plant biology is capable of.

Main species of trees and flowering plants are quite old. The methuselah trees of the desert and the great redwood giants of the forests are just two well-known examples of ancient species still living. But perhaps the most ancient of all is a plant that was believed to have been long extinct. Until 1944, the plant known as Wollemia nobilis was known only by the fossil remains. Then living plants of this type were discovered in remote tropical areas. The bark is unique as it is a deep chocolate color and looks like it is comprised of many tiny bubbles. This is not tiny plant either as some specimens have been records at heights of over 120 feet. It is believed that there are maybe only 100 of these plants left in the wild.

Plant biology is an interesting branch of science. A great deal can be learned about nature and the world around us by studying plants. This field of study gets even more interesting when the unusual plant species that populate the world are taken into consideration. Every corner of the world hold surprises. Who knows, there may still be colossal giants hidden away in remote rainforests and miniscule plants hiding in the crevasse of a mountain side just waiting to be discovered.

1. Which point do the details in this passage support?
   A) Plants have many different features
   B) All plants are basically the same in their biologic makeup
   C) Plants must share similar characteristics in order to be plants
   D) None of the above

Answer: A.
All the details in this passage talk about how plants are different from each other yet still are considered to be plants- some have leaves whole others do not and some are big while others are little. Plants can look vastly different from each other and still belong to the plant family.

2. What did the author want the reader to get out of reading this passage?
   A) That plants are amazing and very diverse in the way they look
   B) Not all plants look like the flowers and trees we are familiar with
   C) Some plants are very old and some are still waiting to be discovered
   D) All of the above

Answer: D.
All of these points are correct because they are all mentioned within the passage and discussed and described in detail.

How did you do? If you still need some help figuring out the main idea and topics of passages like these, keep practicing!

Detail Questions

Reading passages and identifying important details is an important part of the critical reading process. Detail questions ask the reader to recall specific information about the main idea. These details are often found in the examples given in the passage and can contain anecdotes, data or descriptions, among other details.

For example, if you are reading a passage about certain types of dogs, you may be asked to remember details about breeds, sizes and coat color and patterns.

As you read through the following passages, make sure you take note of numbers, figures and the details given about the topic. Chances are you will need to remember some of these.

There is a wealth of information, facts, pieces of data and several details that can be presented within any passage you read. The key to uncovering the main idea and understanding the details presented is to take your time and read through everything contained in the passage. Consider each example and figure presented. Think about how they relate to the main idea, how they support the focus, and how those details add to the information and value of the passage.

Strategies for Answering Specific Detail Questions

• Identify the key words in the question that help you find details and examples that will help answer the question.

• Make mental notes as you read the passage about how words are used and the phrases that are repeated. Also look for the overall meaning of each paragraph and passage.

• Some questions will pull words or phrases from the passage and use them in the question. In this case, look through the passage and find those words or phrases and make sure they are being used the same way in both the passage and the question. Many questions will change the meaning of these to make the question wrong or confuse the reader.

• Some questions will ask you to determine if a particular statement about the passage or topic of the passage is true. In this case, look over the paragraphs and find the overall theme or idea of the passage. Compare your theme or idea to the statement in the question.

Read the following news article and answer the following questions.

Passage 1

Police of Chicago are searching for two men who under investigation for charges of impersonating cops. The men stopped a person on the city's Northwest Side. In a bit of an ironic twist, the two fake cops ended up pulling over an actual Chicago cop.

Officials say the officer who is in his 40's was finishing his shift and on his way home when he was pulled over. It was in Chicago's Avondale neighborhood just after midnight when the officer had a white SUV pull up behind him and flash its lights. The officer saw the signaling, said the SUV looked like a police issued undercover vehicle, and pulled over. According to reports, one of the two men exited of the unmarked car, wearing normal civilian clothes. The man approached the cop, who was still wearing his bullet proof vest, and said he was with the Chicago police.

The officer said that the civilian clothes and lack of standard police issued items alerted him that something was wrong and he challenged them on that statement. The two men ran back to the unmarked car and sped off and disappeared into the dark streets. The Chicago police describe the suspects as two Hispanic men in their early to mid 20s who are both around 6 feet tall and around 150 pounds. Anyone with tips should call the Chicago Police Department.

1. What is the passage above mostly about?
   A) Problems with the Chicago Police Department
   B) A news report about people pretending to be police officers
   C) How the Chicago Police are cracking down on crime
   D) None of the above

Answer: B.
There is a sentence that specifically states that the report is about two men who were pretending to be Chicago Police officers.

2. According to the passage, what details were given about the incident?
   A) Civilian clothes and lack of standard police issued items made the cop suspicious
   B) The event occurred in Chicago's Avondale neighborhood just after midnight
   C) The two men who posed as Chicago Police officers were of Hispanic decent
   D) The police officer was in his 40's and the two fake cops were in their 20's
   E) All of the above

Answer: E.
All of these details were mentioned throughout the news report.

3. All of the following are things we know about the real officer in this story except:
   A) His Age
   B) His duty status at the time
   C) How long he's been with the Chicago Police
   D) We know all these things

Answer: C.
Nowhere in the article is it mentioned how long the real officer has been serving with the Chicago Police Department.

Remember:
There is a wealth of information, many facts, countless pieces of data, and a lot of details that can be presented within any passage that you read. The key to uncovering the main idea and understanding all the details that are presented is to take your time and read through everything contained in the passage. Read everything and take the time to consider every example and every figure presented and see how it relates to the main idea and how to supports the focus and how those details add to the information and value of the passage you are reading.

Reading passages and picking out these important details is a big part of being an effective reader. Practice makes perfect and the more you read the more you analyze and the more you work on it the better you will get and the more you will be able to pull from any article, blog, story, or report you read!

Understanding Question Stems

In addition to careful reading of the passages (including marking up the text for topic and concluding sentences, transitional words and key terms), you must also be able to identify what is being asked of you in each of the questions. Recognition of the task in each question can be easily accomplished if you are familiar with the question stems, or the most commonly phrased wording that will be associated with each type of question on the test.

Keep reading for an explanation of each question type, along with sample stems, and suggested approaches for tackling them.

Supporting Details
Supporting details are those that back up the main ideas presented in the passage. These can include examples, clarifying explanations, or elaborations of basic ideas presented earlier in the reading. Supporting details are directly stated in the passage, so you must rely on your careful reading to guide you to the correct answer. Answers may not be stated in the original language of the passage, but the basic ideas will be the same

Here are some common ways this type of question is asked:
- The passage states...
- The author says...
- According to what you read...

Main Idea
Questions asking you to identify the main idea expect that you will be able to determine the overall point of the passage (often called the *thesis*), NOT secondary details or supporting points. Attempting to put the main idea into your own words after reading WITHOUT looking at the text again is a very helpful strategy in answering this type of question. If you can sum up the author's main point in your own words, then you will find it very easy to find the right "match" amongst the answers provided for you. Alternately, the main idea may often be found in the opening or concluding paragraphs, two common places where an author may introduce a topic and his perspective about said topic, or he summarize the main points.

Here are some common ways this type of question is asked:
- The main idea for this paragraph...
- The central point of the passage...
- A possible title for the passage...
- The author's primary point...

Inference
Inferences are those ideas which can be gleaned from the suggestions that may be implied in other statements made by the author. They are never explicitly stated, but we understand that they are true from "reading between the lines". The answers to inferences questions, therefore, are assumptions, and cannot be found from direct statements in the text. You will have to rely on your ability to

logically deduce conclusions from your careful reading. More than one answer may sound correct, but only one is. Make sure that, whichever answer you choose, you can find statements in the text which would support that idea. If you cannot do that, then that choice is likely not the right answer. Here are some common ways this type of question is asked:
• The passage implies...
• The author suggests...
• The reader could logically conclude that...
• The reader would be correct in assuming that...

Tone/Attitude
Some questions will ask you about the author's tone or attitude. A good place to start with this type of question is to consider whether the passage is positive, negative or neutral. Does the author seem **angry**? Maybe **sad**? Or **torn** between two points of view? The language that an author uses can be very telling about his tone and attitude. Is the author **critical**? **Praiseworthy**? **Disappointed**? Even if you find some finer details of passage difficult to understand, the tone and attitude are often fairly easy to identify. Look for adjectives and statements that reveal the author's opinion, rather than facts, and this will help you know his tone or attitude.

Here are some common ways this type of question is asked:
• The tone of the passage is...
• The attitude of the author is...
• The writer's overall feeling...

Style
Style refers to a writer's "way with words". Most seasoned writers have a well-developed and easily recognizable style, but often the topic of a written work can dictate style. If the topic is serious the language will likely be more formal. Works for academic settings may be heavy with the jargon of that discipline. Personal reflections can be rife with imagery, while instructional manuals will use simple and straightforward language. Identifying style is not difficult; simply pay attention to the words used (simple or fancy?), the sentence structure (simple or compound-complex?), as well as the overall structure of the piece (stream of consciousness or 5-paragraph essay?). You must answer these questions in order to determine the style of the passage.

Here are some common ways this type of question is asked:
• The overall writing style used in the passage…
• The author's style is…
• The organizational style of the passage is…

Pattern of Organization
Pattern of organization questions want you to consider how the writing of a piece was developed. What features did the writer utilize to make his point? Did he include personal anecdotes? Data or statistics? Quotes from authorities on the topic? These are all modes of organizing a passage that help the writer support his claims and provide a logical focus for the work.

Here are some common ways this type of question is asked:
• The author proves a point through...
• In the passage, the author uses...
• Throughout the passage, the author seems to rely on...

Purpose and Attitude

Questions asking about purpose and attitude require you to consider why the author took the time to write. The authors motivations are directly behind the purpose of the piece. What question did he wish to answer? What cause did he want to show support for? What action did he wish to persuade you to take? Identifying these reasons for writing will reveal the purpose and attitude of the passage.

Here are some common ways this type of question is asked:
• The purpose of the passage is...
• The author's intent for writing the passage is...
• The attitude the author displays is...

Fact/Opinion

There will be some questions on the test that will ask you whether a statement is a fact or an opinion. Without being able to fact-check, how will you do this? A rule of thumb would be that opinions reflect only the thoughts, feelings or ideas of the writer, whereas facts are verifiable as true or false, regardless of one's feelings. if a writer cites a statistic about the environmental effects of oil drilling on migratory mammals in the Pacific Northwest, then that is verifiable and can be considered factual. If, however, the writer claims that oil drilling in the Pacific Northwest United States is bad and should be stopped, then that is his opinion. He may at some point provide examples of why this is so, but that viewpoint is based on his thoughts and feelings about oil drilling, and can only be considered opinion.

Here are some common ways this type of question is asked:
• Which statement is a fact rather than an opinion?
• This statement is meant to be...
• An example of fact is when the author says...
• An example of opinion is when the author states that...

Now you know the basics of Question Stems and how to determine the answers you need to be searching for. Use these question stem tips with every passage you read!

Eliminating Wrong Answers

An author often writes with an intended purpose in mind, and they will support their main idea with examples, facts, data and stories that help the overall meaning of their written text to be clear. You may be asked a question regarding one of these details or examples, or you may be asked something about the overall theme or main idea of the passage. These types of questions require you to read the passage carefully for meaning and to look at all the supporting details used. However, it's also important to learn how to identify incorrect answer choices and eliminate them right away. This will help you narrow down the answer choices that are likely to be correct.

Now it is your turn to try it out and see how you do.

Read the following passages and answer the questions, making sure you eliminate the wrong answers as you look for the right one.

There will be three passages for you to read and several questions about each one- there will be one right answer and at least three wrong answers you will need to eliminate as you read.

Good luck!

Passage 1

Online game play has become standard for many video games. While it allows your kids the opportunity to play with other fans of their favorite games, it also brings with it new risks and dangers. By being proactive and staying active with their children, parents can ensure video games remain safe and fun for their kids.

Parents need to stay current on several things- video game ratings, content clues, and their kid's use and involvement. The ratings on video games can help parents know what is and is not acceptable content for their kids.

Parents also need to keep an eye on the content of the games once the game play starts- peek in now and then to make sure there is nothing surprising lurking in a game you thought was fine. Also, parents need to monitor how often their kids are playing the games, the time spent playing, and how much time is spent thinking about the game. Balance is critical to make sure video game use remains fun and safe.

Make sure you keep communication lines open with your kids. They need to know that they can come to you with questions, concerns, or problems. They need to feel safe talking to you and not be fearful that you will be made or angry with them. When your child comes to you with a problem do not brush it off- be sure to give it the attention it deserves and make sure they know you are glad they are coming to you.

Parents who are involved and who talk to their kids and take an interest in what they are doing often times have kids who stay safe and smart when playing online games and video games.

1. Parents can ensure video games remain safe and fun for their kids by doing what?
   A) Be proactive with your decisions
   B) Be active and involved with your kids
   C) Be willing to let your kids do what they want
   D) A and B
   E) B and C

Answer: D.
Both A and B are correct since they were mentioned in one of the first sentences in the opening paragraph of the passage

2. What do parents need to do to keep their kids safe while playing video games?
   A) Stay current on trends and news
   B) Monitor kid's game activities
   C) Communicate with kids often
   D) All of the above
   E) None of the above

Answer: D.
All of these are things mentioned in the passage when it talks about the things people can do to keep their kids safe while playing games and playing online.

Remember reading all the paragraphs is a great way to get the overall idea of the passage. Also every paragraph of a passage should be discussing a different example or point that ties back to the main idea of the passage and helps further demonstrate the main idea.

Passage 2

Kids of all ages have long loved drawing and many kids will draw on anything and everything they can get their hands on. Thy will draw on paper, the floor, their clothes, themselves, and of course the walls! Many parents turn to the tried and true chalkboards for their kids' play room, or play area.

However, chalk can be messy, is harder to clean up, and some kids just don't like the light powdery look of their chalk artwork. If this is the situation you are in, you will want to consider dry-erase paint as the most practical solution to your dilemma. Years ago when dry erase was something you saw only in school or in office buildings, it was hard to come by if you wanted that option at home.

Dry erase easels and boards were cumbersome, bulky, heavy, and expensive. However, now you can actually get specially formulated dry erase paint that you can use on your walls to turn them into massive dry erase boards! Dry-erase has low odor, low-chemical content, and is suitable for a range of surfaces such as wood, brick, concrete, and many others.

Why stifle their creativity when you can unleash it and let them create, design, and explore the wonders of their own imagination? Many companies carry dry erase paint so you can transform your child's bedroom or play room into the best place in the world. Whether you want to give them a section of the wall, one entire wall, or all the wall space they can reach, this one little addition can help make it easy for you to give them ample room to be creative.

Image the smile on your child's face to see a daily message written to them on the wall when they wake up or when they come home from school. Send gentle reminders about chores and homework or use the dry erase space for a fun approach to the nightly homework sessions. Be creative and you will never run out of uses for the Create Pain dry erase paint.

1. What are some reasons mentioned in the passage for why dry erase walls are a good choice for a kid's room?

A) Easy to clean and helps kids be creative
B) Safe and less chemicals
C) Are able to be used for every day needs
D) All of the above

Answer: D.
All of the answers are correct and are mentioned in the passage- they are not all mentioned in one paragraph but they are mentioned throughout the passage and all tie back to the idea of dry erase being a good option for your kid's room.

2. True or False?

Only a few companies carry dry erase paint to be used on walls, which makes it hard to find and use for kid's room designs.

Answer: False.
In the passage it does mention getting dry erase paint from companies but says that many companies carry it. So this means it is fairly easy to find and use and is a good choice for kid's rooms.

Passage 3

We hear a lot of talk about recycling nowadays. We recycle glass, plastic, newspaper, and there are countless ways to reuse everyday items to keep them out of the landfill for a little longer. An equally important, but not as discussed method of recycling is scrap metal recycling. You may be wondering why it is such a big deal and what good metal recycling can make- well, let's take a look.

One of the biggest impacts this form of recycling has is it conserves raw resources and eliminated the carbon footprint for many metal production facilities. The Institute of Scrap Recycling Industries (ISRI) states that in 2010, more than $64billion was added to the United States economy; all of it came from the recycling, reuse, and production of new products from recycled metals. All of this metal scrap would otherwise end up in the landfills or in the environment and that much more raw material would have to be mined and refined and produced from scratch to make new tools, machines, and products. Scrap metal recycling is a very important aspect of conservation and pollution reduction.

In addition to the economic impact from profits of reusing scrap metal, the act of metal recycling also generates jobs. The ISRI estimated that in 2008, over 85,000 jobs were supported and made possible in some way thanks to scrap metal recycling. It also helps in trade sand exports, as it was estimated that over $28 billion and roughly 44 million metric tons of metal was shipped and sold overseas.

Scrap metal recycling comes in many forms. Sometimes it is a junk yard or scrap yard that buys scrap metal and then sells it to manufacturers who can melt it down, refine it, and use it to make new products and materials. Or it could be the neighborhood scrap collector who visits yard sales and stops by your trash pile to pick up that old dishwasher or microwave you threw out. There are also community sponsored recycling programs where cans are collected and turned in for cash, or programs such as the electronics recycling and business incentives for recycling scrap metal left over from production or building projects.

It is easy to see the benefits and importance of scrap metal recycling. Whether it is some materials left over after a home renovation project, tin cans your kids have collected, or the last remaining pieces to that old junk car you scraped, recycling the scrap metal can do a world of good and have a lasting impact on the environment, economy, and your local community. So do your part and be on the lookout for scrap metal to add to your recycling piles.

1. True or False?

The ISRI is a company that oversees scrap metal and recycling practices.

Answer: True.

The ISRI is the Institute of Scrap Recycling Industries and in the passage we see that they offer reports about money earned from scrap metal recycling and also talks about the job market associated with scrap metal recycling.

2. True or False?

Recycling scrap metal helps the environment by keeping that junk out of landfills.

Answer: True.
The passage talks about recycling and how it is a very important aspect of conservation and pollution reduction.

Good job- remember to read every passage you are given carefully and don't be afraid to go back and read something again or scan the passage for key words and phrases that show up in the questions.

Inferences and How to Make Them and Use Them

*Inference is a mental process by which you reach a conclusion based on specific evidence. Inferences are the stock and trade of detectives examining clues, of doctors diagnosing diseases, and of car mechanics repairing engines. We infer motives, purpose and intentions.

You use inference every day. You interpret actions to be examples of behavioral characteristics, intents or expressions of particular feelings. You infer it is raining when you see someone with an open umbrella. You infer that people are thirsty if they ask for a glass of water. You infer that evidence in a text is authoritative when it is attributed to a scholar in that particular field.

You want to find significance. You listen to remarks and want to make sense of them. What might the speaker mean? Why is he or she saying that? You must go beyond specific remarks to determine underlying significance or broader meaning. When you read that someone cheated on his or her income taxes, you might take that as an example of financial ingenuity, daring or stupidity. You seek purposes and reasons.

Inferences are not random. While they may come about mysteriously with sudden recognition, you usually make inferences very orderly. Inferences may be guesses, but they are educated guesses based on supporting evidence. The evidence requires that you reach a specific conclusion.

Inferences are not achieved with mathematical rigor, and they do not have the certainty obtained with deductive reasoning. Inferences tend to reflect prior knowledge and experience as well as personal beliefs and assumptions. Thus, inferences tend to reflect your stake in a situation or your interests in the outcome. People may reason differently or bring different assumptions or premises to bear. This is why bias is addressed so carefully in our criminal justice system, so defendants are given a fair trial.

Given evidence that polychlorinated biphenyls (PCB) cause cancer in people and that PCB's are in a particular water system, all reasonable people would reach the conclusion that the water system is dangerous to people. But, given evidence that there is an increase in skin cancer among people who sun bathe, not all people would conclude that sunbathing causes skin cancer. Sun bathing, they might argue, may be coincidental with exposure to other cancer-causing factors.

[*Daniel J. Kurland (www.criticalreading.com/inference_process.htm)]

Inference Questions

Inference questions ask about ideas that are not directly stated, but rather are implied by the passage. They ask you to draw conclusions based on the information in the passage. Inference questions usually include words like "imply," "infer" or "conclude," or they may ask you what the author "would probably" think or do in a given situation based on what was stated in the passage.

With inference questions, it is important not to go *too far* beyond the scope of the passage. You are not expected to make any guesses. There is a single correct answer that is a logical, next-step conclusion from what is presented in the passage.
Let's take a look at some sample inference questions. Read through the following passages and use your inference skills to answer the questions. Remember that the inferences you make are not always obvious or directly stated in the passage.

Passage 1

Despite the fact that the practice is illegal in many states, some people set off their own fireworks at home each summer, especially on Independence Day. Most cities have public fireworks displays run by experienced professionals in a controlled environment, but many people still enjoy the thrill of setting off their own fireworks. However, this practice can be dangerous, and many people are injured each year from fireworks-related accidents. Having Independence Day fireworks in your own backyard is not worth the safety risk, especially when public fireworks display are available in most areas.

1. The author of this passage would most likely support:
   A) The complete legalization of fireworks nationwide
   B) The reduction of public fireworks displays
   C) More rigorous enforcement of restrictions on home fireworks
   D) Promoting home fireworks use

Answer: C.
In the passage, the author takes a negative tone toward home fireworks use, citing the fact that the practice is dangerous, illegal in some areas and unnecessary since many areas have safe public fireworks displays on holidays. Someone who is critical of home fireworks use would support strong enforcement of restrictions on their use.

Passage 2

A man took his car to the mechanic because the engine was overheating. The mechanic opened the hood to inspect the situation. He removed the radiator cap and could see that there was a sufficient amount of coolant in the radiator. He took the car for a drive and also noticed that the engine would overheat at a stoplight, but not on the highway.

1. According to the passage, what can you infer about the engine?
   A) The engine needs to be replaced
   B) The radiator is leaking
   C) The engine is operating normally
   D) The radiator fan is broken

Answer: D.
Although an overheating engine does indicate an abnormal condition, it does not necessarily indicate a catastrophic failure. Thus, the engine can be repaired instead of replaced. The radiator was full of coolant, so that eliminates the possibility of a leak. When a vehicle is moving, the airflow across the radiator cools the coolant. However, when a vehicle is stationary, the fan is responsible for cooling the coolant. If the fan is not working correctly, this would explain the overheating at a stoplight, but not on the highway.

Passage 3

One man in St. Paul Minnesota is making a difference for people in the community, and his impact was felt stronger than ever this Thanksgiving Holiday. Jeff Ansorge once was in charge of almost 20 staff members and earned $80,000 a year as the head executive chef at a classy downtown Minneapolis restaurant. Only for the very well-off, the restaurant featured items such as a 24-ounce dry aged Porterhouse steak that went for almost $50. However, Jeff gave it all up to and has taken on the job of head cook of a Salvation Army soup kitchen. Where meals would cost $40-$60, now his meals are free.

As head cook he is making salmon, ribs, and stews for those who come to The Salvation Army Eastside Corps Community Center in St. Paul. For the Thanksgiving meal that's Jeff had the traditional meal of turkey with stuffing, along with mashed potatoes and gravy, and even the extras like cranberry sauce and rolls. Even the ambiance was completed with dinner being served on tables covered with white tablecloths and simple decorations. Jeff Ansorge, who is 40, says that it was a spiritual awakening that prompted him make the move to the soup kitchen in October 2012, where he is now making just one-third of his previous salary.

Not only did Jeff bring his culinary skills but his eye for bargain shopping and his ability to make food stretch has allowed the Salvation Army to serve great food and actually save some money in the process. The Salvation Army works along with Second Harvest Heartland food bank and with Jeff's help, they can now get 40-pound cases of mixed poultry for as little as five bucks. Jeff Ansorge also does his best to bring nutritional value to every meal that he serves. He knows that for many who come to the soup kitchen, it may be the only meal they get for the day. He's eliminated desserts and is also working to cut back on the fat and sugars in meals, giving more room for fresh fruits and vegetables and healthy meats.

1. True or False?

    Jeff is a caring and compassionate individual who has a deep sense of right and wrong and is likely governed by deeply held beliefs and ideas of mortality and civil duty.

Answer: True.
Several things mentioned in this passage can lead you to infer this about Jeff- he was raised in the Catholic faith, he works in a soup kitchen, volunteers, gave up a good job to help others, and genuinely seems to care about those who are less fortunate than himself.

2. True or False?

    All people who are well off and making good money dislike people like Jeff who make them look bad.

Answer: False.
Nowhere in the passage is this hinted to or implied at all.

Remember inferences can be tricky things to master. Practice makes perfect so keep at it!

The Physical Science section covers a broad spectrum of middle to high school level science concepts. These include Chemistry, Mechanics, Electronics, and Earth Science.

The time limit is 10 minutes for 20 questions. 30 seconds per question may not seem like much time, but the questions will be straight forward and will not require calculation. In most cases, you either know the answer or you don't, but often times some basic process of elimination can help if you need to guess (there are no lost points for guessing).

Geology

The Earth's Structure

Geology is the study of the Earth, including its history and physical properties. Much of this history is learned through studying rocks at various layers.

The structure of the Earth can be described as similar to an onion – it has a series of spherical layers that are differentiated by chemical formation, type of rock, and whether the material is solid or liquid (molten).

Earth's Layers

In school, most of us learned the chemical layers of the Earth, but you may encounter questions on the test about the mechanical layers of the Earth.

Starting at the top, is the crust, which includes continental crust and oceanic crust.
The lithosphere is solid and includes the crust and the most outer part of the mantle.
Next is the asthenosphere. This is technically solid, but it has some fluid properties, due to heat.
The mesosphere (not to be confused with the mesosphere of the atmosphere) is solid due to pressure.
Finally, at the innermost center of the Earth is the core. The core is comprised of two parts:

The outer core is mostly made of molten liquid iron and nickel. This layer is liquid due to extremely high temperatures.
The inner core is mostly made of iron and shaped like a ball. The inner core is hotter than the outer core, but it's actually solid. This is due to extremely high pressures that prevent the iron from melting.

Magnetic Poles

As it turns out, that giant chunk of iron at the inner core means our planet is also a humongous magnet. That means Earth has a magnetic field encircling it, which protects it from all kinds of nasty particle radiation blasting through the solar system that would otherwise destroy, damage or alter life as we know it. There are just two weak spots in our planet's cosmic suit of armor, which are coincidentally at the opposite sides of its magnetic field: the north and south poles. If you're near either and it's a clear night, you can sometimes witness that radiation funneling down through the night sky. In the northern hemisphere, it's called the aurora borealis, and in the southern hemisphere, it's called the aurora australis.

Types of Rocks

Depending on how, when, and from what materials they were formed, rocks are categorized into three groups:

Sedimentary Rocks

Formed of pebbles, sand, shells and other sediment (hence the name), these rocks form by accumulating layers that form and fuse together over very long periods of time. Sedimentary rock is soft by comparison to other rocks, and can break apart relatively easily. Limestone, shale, coal, and sandstone are examples of sedimentary rock.

Metamorphic Rocks

These rocks are formed below the Earth's surface, and are created by intense heat and pressure. These very hard rocks often have ribbons of color from the different layers of various materials and minerals. Slate and marble are examples of metamorphic rock.

Igneous Rocks

These rocks are formed by the hardening of molten magma from deep within the Earth as it cools. Lava that erupts from volcanos is igneous rock. Depending on how quickly it cools, the rock can be shiny and smooth, or it can be bumpy and rough from gas bubbles erupting as it cooled more slowly. Granite, pumice, basalt, and obsidian are examples of igneous rocks.

The uppermost layer of the earth, the crust, is comprised of approximately 7 or 8 major plates, but as many as 30 plates all together. These plates shift and move over time. The movement of these plates over very long periods of time is what causes mountain formations, earthquakes, ocean trenches, and volcanic activity.

When these plates move, one of three types of plate boundaries occurs: transform, divergent, or convergent. Transform boundaries occur when two plates slide past each other, which neither creates nor destroys plate material. Divergent boundaries occur when two plates move away from each other, which creates new plate material. Convergent boundaries occur when two plates move toward each other, which destroys existing plate material.

Earthquakes occur along fault lines (also called fault zones), which are mostly found at transform plate boundaries. Earthquakes are measured using the Richter Scale, which starts at 1 and increases by a power of 10 to each subsequent number. For example, a score of 2 is 10 times more powerful than a score of 1. And a score of 3 is 10 times more powerful than a score of 2 and 100 times more powerful than a score of 1.

Geologic Time Scale

The geologic time scale is used by scientists to better study and understand the history of the Earth and events of life and organisms that took place at certain times. This is done by studying different strata of the Earth's crust for fossils, types of rocks, and other indicators of events in Earth's history. There is a lot of history too…the Earth is approximately 4.5 billion years old and life on Earth first appeared 3.5 billion years ago!

Precambrian Time

The Precambrian's beginning age cannot be defined for certain, but ended approximately 542 million years ago. About 90% of the Earth's history occurred in the Precambrian time.

Paleozoic Era

This era began 542 million years ago and lasted about 291 million years. Sea-life and other reptile life started during this period.

Mesozoic Era

This era began 251 million years ago and lasted about 186 million years. This was the age of reptiles, when dinosaurs lived.

Cenozoic Era

This era began 66 million years ago and includes the geological present time. This is the age of mammals, including homo sapiens (or humans).

Meteorology

The Atmosphere

The atmosphere of the earth is the layer of gas that surrounds the earth and is kept in place by gravity. The atmosphere is what allows life on earth to exist, providing the air we need to breath, but also protecting us from the sun's radiation. Dry air is made up of approximately 78% nitrogen, 21% oxygen, with the remaining 1% or so including argon, carbon dioxide, and a few other gases. There are 5 main layers of the atmosphere:

Exosphere

700 to 10,000 km (440 to 6,200 miles) – The uppermost layer of the atmosphere, it merges with empty space where there is no atmosphere whatsoever. Molecules of gas are so far apart that they may be miles away from each other.

Thermosphere

80 to 700 km (50 to 440 miles) – This layer is still very far out. In fact, the space station is in this layer. Temperatures are extreme here, getting as hot as 1,500°C (2,700°F), however, the molecules of gas are so far apart (miles away from each other), that the temperature would feel cold.

Mesosphere

50 to 80 km (31 to 50 miles) – This is the layer where most meteors burn up, making them visible to the naked eye. Clouds can form here, but they are very difficult to see and requires the sun to be at just the right angle, typically around sunrise or sunset. Temperatures get as cold as -85°C (-120°F).

Stratosphere

12 to 50 km (7 to 31 miles) – Due to the lack of weather patterns, few clouds form here. This is the highest altitude in which jet airplanes can fly. Temperatures can range from 0°C to -60°C (32°F to -76°F)

Troposphere

0 to 12 km (0 to 7 miles) – The lowest layer, extending from the surface of earth upwards to about 7 miles. This is where clouds and other weather patterns form, and temperatures are generally stable.

Clouds

There are three main types of clouds you need to be familiar with:

Stratus

Stratus clouds are the lowest to the ground (and can actually be at ground level; what we call fog). These clouds are broad and generally flat, covering large areas. When you see dark stratus clouds, you can expect rain.

Cumulus

Cumulus clouds are the big puffy clouds higher up than stratus clouds. They are generally pretty flat on the bottom, but look like big puffs of cotton on top. These clouds also turn dark when rain is coming.

Cirrus

Cirrus clouds are at very high altitudes, approximately 20,000 feet or more. They are wispy and thin.

Weather Fronts

The two main types of fronts are warm fronts and cold fronts and are exactly what they sound like. When a warm front moves through, it rides up and over the top of the colder air and clouds. The end result is often precipitation in the form of rain, sleet, snow, or hail.

Cold fronts are the opposite. Cold air moves in and overtakes the warm air. Though there might be some precipitation right before the front moves through, there is usually no rain accompanying a cold front. You know when one comes through because of the sudden drop in temperature.

The Hydrologic Cycle

The Hydrologic Cycle is simply the movement of water on Earth. This cycle includes all forms of water (solid, liquid and vapor or gas) and has 4 main stages:

Precipitation

When the air maximizes the amount of condensed water it can hold, it rains. Snow, hail and sleet are also forms of precipitation.

Run-off and Collection

Once the water falls back to Earth, it has to go somewhere. Some of it starts to evaporate soon after it rains, but most of it will run downhill to streams and lakes. Some rain water will end up in underground aquifers through a process called infiltration.

Evaporation

This is when water vaporizes, such as from the street after it rains. It also includes transpiration, which is when water vaporizes directly from plant life, such as leaves.

Condensation

This is when the vaporized water goes up and forms clouds.

Astronomy

The Solar System
You'll need to be familiar with our solar system and the relationships between the different planets and bodies in our system. The main bodies of importance in our solar system are the sun and 8 planets, of which Earth is one.

The Sun
Our sun is actually a star and is referred to as a yellow dwarf. Despite its enormous size compared to Earth (the sun's diameter is 100X that of Earth), it is actually small in comparison to other stars. The surface of the sun is approximately 6,000°C (11,000°F). The core of the sun is assumed to be as hot as 15,000,000°C! The sun is extremely dense, comprised of a plasma that produces energy from atomic reactions in the core. The sun is so dense, in fact, that it accounts for 99.9% of the mass of our entire solar system.

The Planets
There are a total of 8 planets in our solar system, although kids from the 90's will remember there being 9. Recently, however, scientists determined that the furthest planet, Pluto, does not actually meet the qualifications of a planet and was removed.

The easiest way to remember the order of the planets is this mnemonic: My Very Educated Mother Just Served Us Nachos. There are others, but this is the one suggested by the International Astronomical Union.

The four planets closest to the sun, including Earth, are called terrestrial planets. These planets have similar compositions, although only Mars and Earth have moons. The Earth is the biggest of these 4 planets. The 4 planets beyond Mars are called outer planets. These planets are very large and all have rings (made up mostly of ice crystals). The most well-known rings belong to Saturn. These planets are also known as Gas Giants since their mass is made up mostly of gas with rocks and mineral material at their core.

Our Planet Earth
The Earth revolves around the sun in 365 days, which is where we get our calendar year. This rotation is also responsible for our seasons of spring, summer, fall and winter. The Earth is on an axis, so as we go around the sun, different parts of the Earth are slightly closer or further, making the temperature slightly warmer or colder.

Vital to life on Earth, our moon revolves around the Earth in approximately 29 days. The moon is vital to Earth because it provides a gravitational pull that causes high and low tides, which move water on our planet. This occurs twice per day when the moon is closer or further away from a specific area of Earth as our planet rotates.

Solar and Lunar Eclipses
A solar eclipse occurs when the moon revolves directly in front of the sun during the day. This phenomenon occurs only 2 to 5 times per year because the moon's orbit is not tilted slightly, so it does not always align directly with the sun. A solar eclipse can only occur during a new moon, which we will cover next.

A lunar eclipse is when the Earth's shadow covers the moon. This obviously happens at night and requires a full moon.

Phases of the Moon

Some people confuse a "lunar eclipse" for a new Some people confuse a lunar eclipse for a new moon, meaning when the moon isn't visible in the sky. Actually, when you cannot see the moon at night, it is because it is currently on the other side of the Earth where it is daylight, not because it is being eclipsed (remember, the moon revolves around the Earth). As the moon comes back around, you can see the sunlight reflecting partially (or completely) off the moon. To better visualize this process, look at the diagram below.

A complete lunar cycle isn't a month as most people believe, but actually 29.5 days. This means that there are 13 lunar cycles during a year. Let's review a few details of each moon phase:

New Moon

This first phase of the moon occurs when the Earth, moon and sun have the same elliptical longitude. The moon is not visible except when seen as a silhouette during a solar eclipse. The new moon seems to last up to 3 days since the amount of illumination changes relatively slowly.

Waxing Crescent

This second phase of the moon is where the illumination of the disk seen from Earth starts increasing.

First Quarter

The third phase lasts a short period of time, just a single rising and setting. Exactly one-half of the moon appears illuminated by direct sunlight.

Waxing Gibbous

The fourth phase lasts a similar amount of time as the crescent phase, about 6 days as the illumination continues to increase.

Full Moon

The fifth phase occurs when the Earth, moon and sun all return to the same elliptical longitude as they had during the new moon. However, the moon is now on the outside of the alignment, allowing the sunlight to illuminate the complete disk of the moon visible from Earth. This phase lasts about 2 days.

Waning Gibbous

The sixth phase begins the decreasing of illumination against the disk of the moon as seen from Earth. This phase also lasts about 6 days.

Last Quarter

The seventh phase is similar to the first quarter where only 50% of the surface of the moon is visible. This phase also lasts only a single rising and setting.

Waning Crescent

The eighth and final phase is directly opposite of the waxing crescent. This phase also lasts about 6 days until another new moon occurs to start the cycle all over again.

Comets and Asteroids

In addition to our sun, the planets, and moons, there are thousands of bodies in our solar system known as comets, asteroids, and meteoroids. While comets and asteroids have many things in common, the difference between the two is that comets are comprised mostly of ice, dust, and organic material whereas asteroids are comprised of rock and metal. As they pass by the sun in their orbit, comets lose some material since the ice will burn off. However, asteroids typically remain mostly intact. In either case, both comets and asteroids are made up of "left-overs" from the formation of the universe billions of years ago. Comets, such as the well-known Haley's Comet leave long tails as they orbit near the sun and can be visible to the naked eye (these tails are sometimes millions of miles long!). It will be a while before Haley's Comet orbits again… approximately July of 2061.

Whereas most comets are found far away in what is called the Kuiper Belt, most asteroids orbit between Mars and Jupiter in an asteroid belt.

Fragments of asteroids and comets are known as meteoroids. Meteors are fragments of meteoroids that have broken off and fallen through the Earth's atmosphere. If the meteor doesn't burn up completely in the atmosphere, the material that lands on Earth is called a meteorite.

Mechanical Foundations

Mass & Weight

Mass is defined as the amount of matter that exists in an object. Matter possesses inertia, and mass is a measure of an object's resistance to movement. On the other hand, weight is defined as the product of mass and the gravitational acceleration being applied to that mass, or w = m*a. For example, if you have a mass of 50kg, and the gravitational acceleration is 9.8 m/s^2, then your weight is 50 kg x 9.8 m/s^2, or 490 Newtons. The terms mass and weight are often used interchangeably. However, in physics, they mean something quite different, and they each have different associated units. As a result, make sure you know whether the problem is about mass or weight.

Force

Force is an interaction that changes the acceleration of an object. If an unbalanced force acts on a mass, then the mass will begin to move. This is also known as Newton's Second Law, and it is expressed in equation form as F = M*A. Although forces are almost always present on a given object, only unbalanced forces will result in movement.

Velocity

Velocity is defined as displacement over time, or V = D/T. Common measures of velocity are feet per second (ft/s), meters per second (m/s), or miles per hour (mph). Velocity is different from speed in that velocity has a defined or given direction, whereas speed is simply displacement over time.

Acceleration

Acceleration is defined as the change in velocity over time. In other words, $A = \Delta V/\Delta T$. For example, at time = 0, a car was moving at 5 m/s. 5 seconds later, the car is moving at 10 m/s, so the difference in velocity of the car (5 m/s) divided by the time (5 s), equals the acceleration, 1 m/s^2.

Distance

Distance is also known as displacement, and it is measured in units such as feet, meters, miles, or kilometers. For example, the distance from your home to work might be 5 miles. Since 1 mile = 5280 feet, we could also say that the same distance is equal to 26,400 ft. To solve problems faster, you should learn a few of the common distance conversion factors, such as 1 meter = 3.2808399 feet, typically approximated as 1 meter = 3.3 feet. Memorizing some of the most common measurement conversions will be extremely helpful.

Momentum

Momentum is an object's tendency to keep moving. The momentum of an object is equal to its mass multiplied by its velocity, or M = M*V, and the units of momentum are measured in kg*m/s (mass x velocity). For example, a car traveling at 15 m/s with a mass of 500 kg would have a momentum of 500 kg * 15 m/s = 7500 kg*m/s.

Energy

Energy is the ability to do or perform an action. It is a fundamental property of objects and can take many forms. These forms of energy include heat energy, kinetic energy, potential energy, chemical energy, and electrical energy (these are outlined below).

1. Heat – Heat energy is the temperature of an object. The hotter an object is, the more heat energy it contains.
2. Kinetic – Kinetic energy is found in an object that is actively moving. The faster the object is moving, the more kinetic energy it possesses.
3. Potential – Potential energy is found in an object that is some distance from the force being applied to it. Potential energy is not actively being used to perform any actions, but it has the potential to be released and then consumed or converted to kinetic energy. On Earth, potential energy (KP) is measured by the equation KP = M*G*H, where M is the mass, G is the gravitational acceleration, and H is the height. Gravitation acceleration is simply the acceleration of an object caused by the force of gravity; the conventional standard value is 32.2 ft/s^2 (9.8 m/s^2).
4. Chemical – Chemical energy is the energy inside molecules and their bonds. For example, when cars burn gasoline, the bonds between the carbon molecules and the hydrogen molecules in the gasoline are broken. This break down of the molecule releases energy.
5. Electric – Electric energy is created by electric fields, which result from the existence of charged particles such as electrons or protons, either statically as an accumulation of charge or dynamically as a current. Electricity can be thought of as current flowing through a wire.

Work

Work occurs when a force has been applied to an object and that object moves some distance. One of the fundamental equations for work is W = F*D, where W is work, F is force, and D is distance. For example, if you push a car with 200 N of force, but the car doesn't move, you haven't performed any work. On the other hand, if you push against the same car, and the car moves 10 meters, then you have performed work. In fact, you've performed exactly 200 N * 10 m = 2,000 Joules of work (1 Joule is 1 Newton meter).

Power

Power is defined as the rate at which work is performed. Units of power are usually measured in Joules per second (J/s), and 1 J/s is equal to 1 Watt. Power is directly related to the concept of work. For example, a car that is accelerating is using power because it is performing work over time, which is the force operating on a mass and increasing its velocity over a specific amount of time. The term used to describe the power of motorized vehicles is horsepower, a unit of power equal to 550 foot-pounds per second, which equals 745.7 watts.

Mechanical Comprehension

Simple Machines

Simple machines are devices that are designed to change either the direction or magnitude of a force. They do not generate force, but allow force to be used in a manner that could not ordinarily be obtained. The basic utility of simple machines is that they provide mechanical advantage, which is the ratio of the output force to the applied force.

Mechanical Advantage

Mechanical advantage is defined as the amount of force amplification that can be achieved by a tool or simple machine. The idea here is that, by applying a force for an increased distance, the applied force will be drastically multiplied. The output force will be larger than the input force, but the output displacement will be smaller than the input displacement. The equation that governs mechanical advantage is:

$$MA = \frac{Fb}{Fa}$$

In this equation, MA is the mechanical advantage, Fb is the force produced and Fa is the force applied. All simple machines are designed to provide a positive mechanical advantage in some way.

Inclined Plane

An inclined plane is a flat surface tilted at an angle. This allows an object to be pushed up the inclined plane. The inclined plane provides mechanical advantage by reducing the amount of force required to lift an object. However, the tradeoff is that the object needs to be moved a greater distance to achieve the required height. The inclined plane provides an advantage in that a lower force is required to move an object, meaning that even a small person could move heavy objects onto a loading truck, for example.

How much of a difference does an inclined plane make? Well, to lift an object with a mass of 100 kg, it would normally require a force of 9800 N to overcome gravity. However, how much force is required to move an object up an inclined plane? If the plane has an angle of 10 degrees and a friction coefficient of 0.30, then a force of only 4641 N is required to overcome the gravitational and friction forces and begin moving the object up the plane. This means that by using an inclined plane, you can dramatically reduce the force required to move the object. Even better, if you are moving the object on wheels and the friction is largely negated, the required force is only 1700 N!

Wedge

A wedge is a simple machine composed of two inclined planes, as seen below.

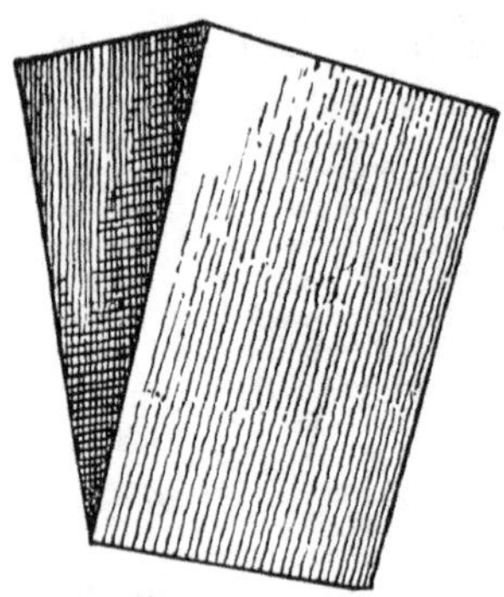

A wedge is designed to amplify force. A force applied at the wider part of the wedge is amplified through a reduction of applied surface area, which results in a wedge being able to split wood or cut vegetables. It's easiest to consider the performance of a wedge by comparing the pressure on the opposite ends of the wedge. Pressure is defined as force / area. If you apply a force to the wide face of the wedge above 50 N, with an area of 0.1 m^2, what is the corresponding pressure on the pointy side of the wedge, which has a surface area of 0.001 m^2? The original pressure is 50 N / 0.1 m^2, or 500 pascals. The ending pressure is 50 N / 0.001 m^2, or 50,000 pascals. The use of the wedge amplified the pressure felt at that area by 100 times. This is the basis on which a wedge works. Common wedges include knives, axes, log splitters and doorstops.

Lever

A lever is a simple machine that consists of a rigid beam that is pivoted about a hinge, also known as a fulcrum.

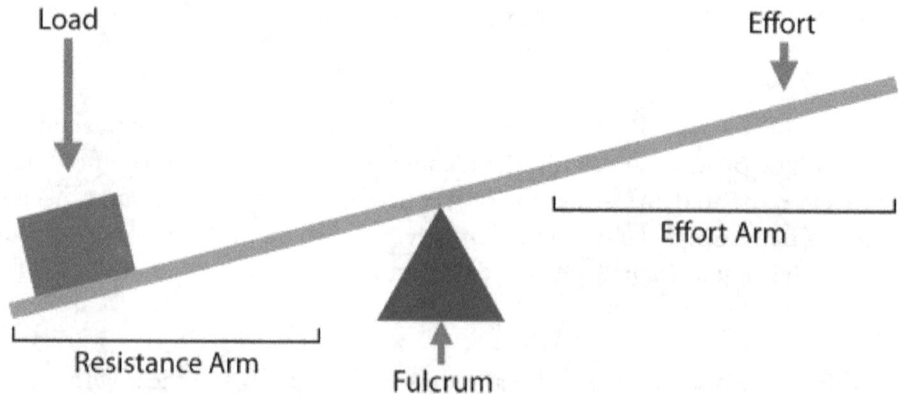

The location of the fulcrum changes the amount of torque that the effort can produce. If the effort arm is much longer than the resistance arm, then a very high torque is produced. This allows a small force to lift a large mass. Conversely, if the effort arm is much shorter than the resistance arm, then the same applied force cannot lift the same mass.

The mechanical advantage of the lever is that the effort force can be applied over a longer distance in order to reduce the amount of force needed to lift a heavy object.

Pulley

A pulley is a type of simple machine that is used to change the direction of an applied force. Pulleys work in tandem with a rope that is attached to one or more objects, and the rope is slung around a rotating disc, as seen in the figure below.

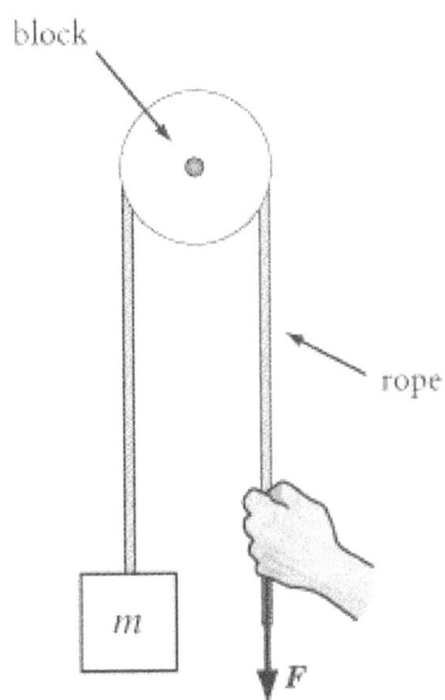

In this example, force is being applied in a downward direction, and the pulley is changing the direction of the force such that the mass is moving in an upward direction. In a case where it is not possible for you to lift an object a certain height, such as 10 meters, a pulley allows you to change the direction of the force applied so that you are able to lift the object much higher. However, in the example of the pulley above, the amount of force required is not reduced. In block and tackle pulley systems, as seen below, the addition of a 'block' (a rotating disc attached to the hook) and additional windings of rope, can create a mechanical advantage.

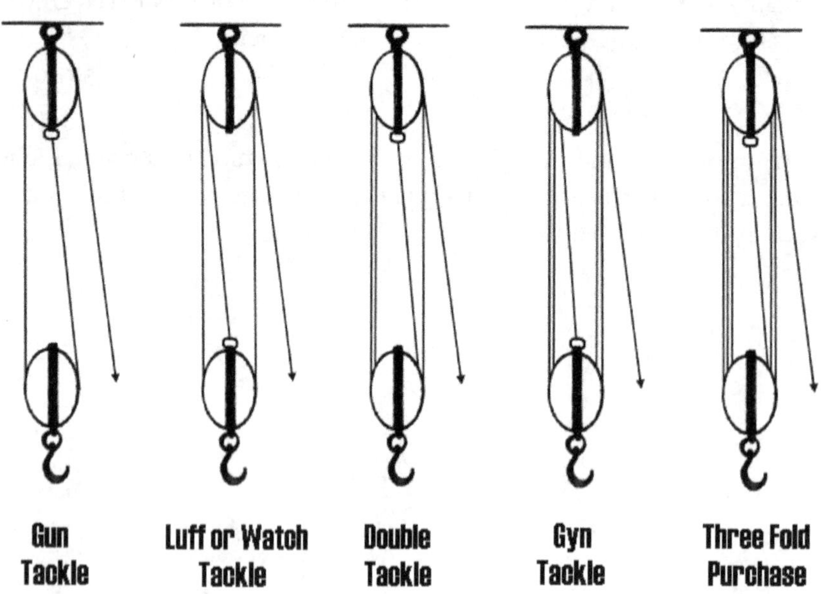

The block and tackle system produces mechanical advantage depending on the number of sections of supporting rope. For example, with a gun tackle, a mechanical advantage of 2 can be generated. With a Gyn tackle, a mechanical advantage of 5 can be generated.

Wheels

A wheel is not a simple machine by definition, but it reduces the friction force experienced when performing work. Ordinarily, a relatively high amount of friction exists between an object and the ground, with a friction coefficient normally between 0.4 and 0.6. This means that if you want to push a heavy object, you'll need to exert quite a bit of force to overcome the friction force. The wheel replaces the ground friction coefficient with a friction coefficient at the axle of the wheel. If the wheel is well greased and has proper bearings, the friction coefficient could be as low as 0.01, meaning that the force required to push an object is greatly reduced.

Gears

A gear is a machine that is designed to amplify force by increasing (or decreasing) the amount of torque applied at one of the gears in a system. Gears are machined parts that are typically made of metal and consist of cogs (teeth) arranged around a circular center part. The interaction of two gears and their teeth can be used to produce mechanical advantage.

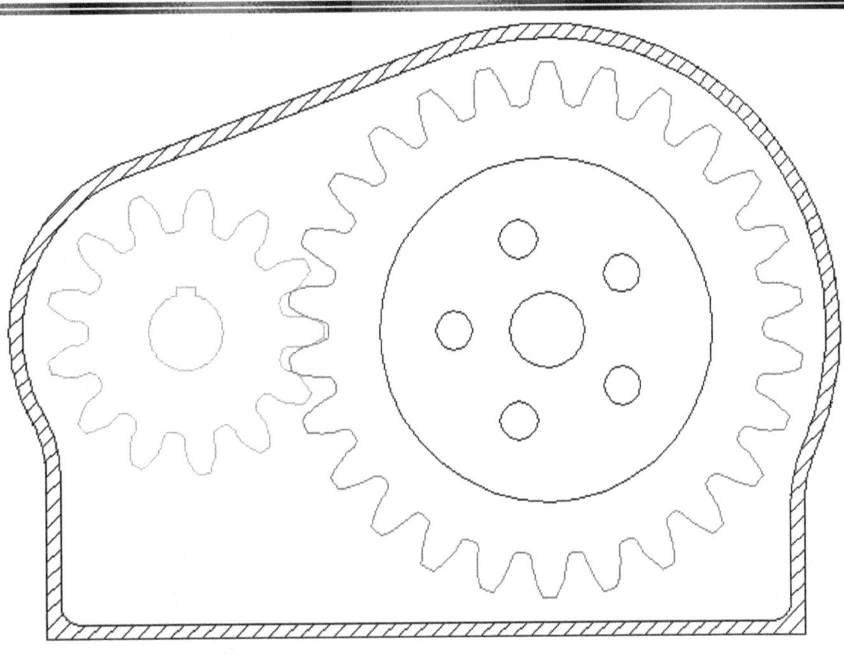

For example, in the gear system shown above, if you apply torque to the smaller gear, you will have to turn it several times in order to complete one rotation of the larger gear. If you apply torque to the larger gear, it will only require a partial turn in order to complete one rotation of the smaller gear. Due to the diameter of the two gears, you will need to apply more force to the larger gear than the smaller gear.

One of the best examples of gear use is in your bicycle. Say you want to maintain a speed of 20 mph. When using the smaller gear, you have to pedal very quickly. When using the larger gear, you don't need to pedal as quickly. However, to maintain your speed, the smaller gear requires less force, whereas the larger gear requires more force.

Fluid Power/Hydraulics

Hydraulics apply Pascal's law to generate mechanical advantage. Pascal's law states that "an increase in pressure at any point in a confined fluid will result in the same increase in pressure at every other point in the container". This principle can be applied to create mechanical advantage, as seen in the example of a hydraulic pump below.

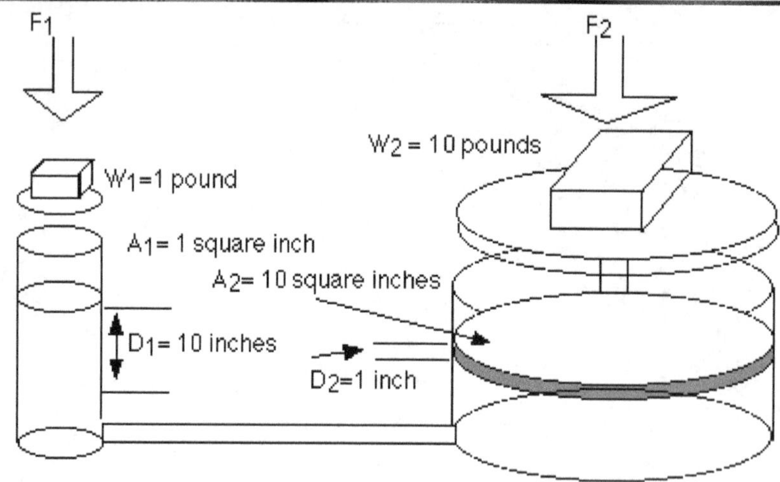

In this figure, a smaller force (F_1) can be used to lift a larger mass (W_2) due to the application of mechanical advantage in a hydraulic pump. The figure shows two cylinders, connected by a narrow pipe filled with liquid. As F_1 is applied, it increases the pressure of the fluid, which results in the upward movement of W_2. In this particular pump, W_1 must move 10 inches downward in order to move W_2 one inch upward.

In our world, hydraulic pumps can be found in many places. For example, you can find a hydraulic pump in a car jack. If you've ever used a car jack, you know that you must pump the hydraulic jack several times just to raise the car a few inches off the ground. The mechanical advantage of the car jack is that the force applied to the jack is much less than the force required to lift the car itself.

Electronics Foundations

The Atom

An atom is the smallest unit of an element of matter that retains a chemical identity. There are smaller (subatomic) units of matter, such as quarks, protons and electrons, but these units are fundamentally indistinct. However, an atom of gold has distinctly different properties compared to an atom of iron, copper or any other element.

Atoms are composed of a nucleus, which contains protons and neutrons, and electrons which orbit around the nucleus at the center of the atom.

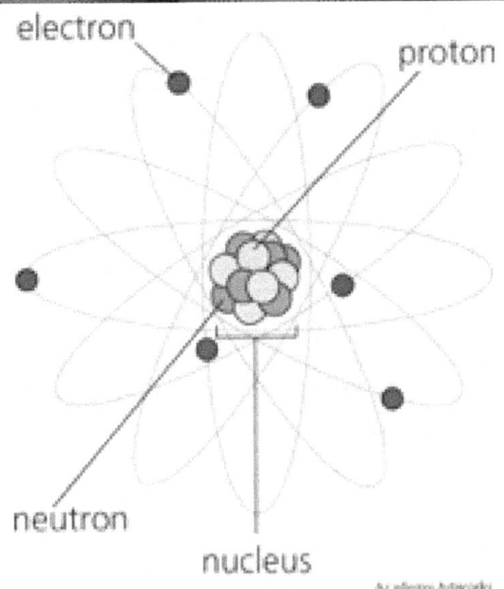

Protons are positively charged units that have a mass of 1 atomic mass unit (amu), and neutrons are non-charged units that also have a mass of 1 amu. Electrons are negatively charged units that have a mass of approximately 0.0005 amu. Elements that are not ionized have the same number of electrons as protons. For example, carbon, a non-ionized atom, typically has 6 protons and 6 electrons. The periodic table, a chart that contains the key information about all atoms, shows carbon has a mass of 12 amu per atom. Since the mass of the electrons are negligible, you can conclude that carbon also has 6 neutrons.

Electrical Charge

What exactly is an electrical charge, and how is it formed? The answer to this question requires an in-depth study of quantum physics and electrons. However, in general, an uncharged object consists of pairs of opposite charges: equal amounts of positive charge and negative charge. A charged object results when there is an excess of electrons (negative charge) or a shortage of electrons (positive charge). This condition produces ions, which are charged atoms. It is also the basis of charged objects, which can experience the same excess or shortage of electron charges.

Positive and negative charges interact with each another in a specific way:

1. Two positive charges will repel each other
2. Two negative charges will repel each other
3. One positive and one negative charge will attract one another

Charges are associated with particular units of mass. Protons found in an atom's nucleus have a positive charge, and electrons have a negative charge. Electrical charges and the movement of electricity are fundamentally about the movement of electrons. Movement of charge is a basic quality of metals, which allow electrons to move very easily.

Perhaps the best and most vivid example of charge in nature is when lightning storms occur. A lightning bolt occurs as a result of a very large charge imbalance between the air (which contains a large negative charge in a storm) and the ground (which contains a reservoir of positive charge). When this potential difference becomes too great, the negative charge's attraction force to the positive charge becomes very high. As a result, the electrons in the clouds travel down to the ground, causing a flash of lightning.

Electrical Components

Electrical components are very small pieces of equipment used to build circuits. The most common types of electrical components are:

Resistor

A resistor is a component made of material that is difficult for electrons to pass through. Resistors reduce the rate at which electrons can flow through a circuit. As a result, resistors can change the voltage and current in a circuit.

Capacitor

A capacitor is a component made of two parallel plates with a dielectric (non-conducting) material sandwiched between the two plates. Capacitors are capable of accumulating charge. A charged capacitor can be used to modulate the amount of current in a circuit or to store electrons for later use.

Transistor

A transistor is a semiconductor component that can hold information. Transistors typically operate as a kind of switch, and they turn on or turn off in response to the flow of current. In computer language, a single transistor corresponds to a single unit of binary code (either a 1 or 0, with 1 being on and 0 being off).

Inductor

An inductor (also known as a coil) is a component that is able to store voltage as a magnetic field. As electrons pass through an inductor or coil, a magnetic field is generated.

Diode

A diode is a two-terminal component that possesses high resistance in one terminal and low resistance in the other. Its primary purpose is to allow a uni-directional flow of current. In other words, current can pass through in one direction, but it cannot come back in the reverse direction. This behavior of electricity through a diode is called rectification. One of the more important uses of diodes is in the conversion from alternating current (AC) to direct current (DC).

Voltage and Current

Voltage (measured in volts) and current (measured in amperes) are two units of measurement used to describe the flow of electrons through an electrical circuit.

Voltage is best described as the potential difference between the start and end of a circuit. It is a form of potential energy. If no potential energy exists, then the electrons won't move from one end of the circuit to the other, and thus there is no electricity. If a great amount of potential energy exists, then the electrons are under a lot of pressure to move from one end of the circuit to the other.

Current can be thought of as the flow of electrons. A flowing river is a good way to consider the concept of current. The greater the current, the faster the flow of electrons/charge.

Again, using the analogy of a river, some of the key differences between voltage and current can be understood. Imagine a channel of water that is perfectly flat. There is no change in elevation from the beginning to the end of the river, and no new water flows into the river. In this situation, there can be no movement of water, and because there is no potential energy, the water will be stagnant. However, if one end of the river is at a higher elevation than the other, there is potential energy, and of course the water will flow. Again, voltage is the potential difference between the start and end of a circuit. It is a form of potential energy. There can be no voltage without current.

Voltage can be thought of as the driving force that pushes current through a circuit. However, most circuits have some form of resistance. As a result, the current flow is directly related to the voltage, but is reduced by the resistance.

AC/DC – What's the Difference?
Alternating current (AC) and direct current (DC) are both forms of electricity in that they both are based on the movement of electrons. The primary difference is the way in which the electrons move through the circuit. In direct current, the flow of electrons is constant and uni-directional. The best example of a direct current source is a battery. Alternating current can be thought of as a type of wave. The flow of electrons move back and forth. Because AC is a type of wave, the electrons can travel over a long distance. As a result, it is the type of current used in power lines that supply buildings and homes with electricity. The majority of household appliances use alternating current.

Resistance

Resistance (measured in Ohms) is caused by the friction within a circuit, which hinders or even prevents the flow of electrons through the circuit. Using the analogy of a river, the flow of water through a pipe with a rough interior surface is not nearly as easy as the flow of water through a pipe with a smooth interior surface. Because of this friction, the overall water flow is reduced or hindered. The same is true in an electrical circuit. The resistance within a circuit determines how smoothly the electrons will move through it.

Electrical resistance in a wire is a property of its material and thickness. The more conductive the material, the lower the resistance of the wire. The larger the diameter of the wire, the lower the resistance. For example, copper has very low resistance, and so it's commonly used as a material for wire and electric cables. Again, when you compare these two characteristics to the flow of water through a pipe, there are some clear similarities. The specific resistance of a wire can be calculated according to the following equation:

$$R = \frac{\rho L}{A}$$

ρ = resistivity
L = length
A = cross sectional area

When considering the relationship between voltage, current and resistance, it can be understood that the greater the resistance, the lower the current, and that the greater the voltage, the higher the current. Voltage is the driving force behind the flow of current. Ohm's Law puts this linear relationship into an equation:

V = I*R where V = voltage, I = current, and R = resistance

This formula says that current is directly proportional to the strength of the ratio of voltage divided by the resistance. This important equation allows you to calculate a missing variable if you are given two known values in an electrical system. For example, if you have a 1.5 V battery powering a radio that has an internal resistance of 35 Ohms, you can use Ohms Law (V = I*R or I = V/R) to find that I = 1.5V/35 Ohms = 0.043 Amperes or 43 milliamps.

Circuits

Most of the value of electricity in every day application comes about because of the flow of electrical charge. Television, computers, cell phones are all electrical devices that use circuits that are made possible by electrical charge movement. Like mechanical devices, without movement we only have potential energy. In order for electricity to do work for us, we must have motion. That motion is possible with circuits where the motion is the movement of electrical charge. To understand that process, we must understand the basics of electrical circuits.

Conductors

Whether the circuit uses printed circuit boards or wired circuits, the circuit is made up of conducting materials. A conductor is a material that has the property of charge mobility specifically to allow the flow of electrons. Our best examples are conductors like copper, brass, silver, gold and aluminum which are all good electrical and heat conductors as well. In these materials the electrons in the outer part of the atom are free to move around. The protons, the positive charged particles, are held in place in the nuclei so the protons have no mobility. The nuclei which are made up of protons and neutrons are fixed in a matrix surrounded by a sea of electrons that move easily in the presence of an electromotive force. Electrons will always flow in the direction of a positive electrical potential which is what we call voltage. It's the electrons that make up the charges in motion called current. Current is thus defined as the flow of electrical charge past a point in a circuit.

Insulators

The discussion of conductors would be incomplete without materials called insulators. Something as simple as a light bulb would be potentially dangerous if not for an insulating shield that prevents dangerous shocks to the people that need the light. As you may have guessed, an insulator is simply a material that does NOT have charge mobility. Because both the electrons and protons of the insulating material are fixed in a matrix, the presence of electrical potential has no effect and currents are not conducted through the material. Because of this property, an electrical cord carrying 110 volts and 15 to 20 amperes is something you can pick up without fear of getting a shock in an everyday house-hold example. The insulation covering that power cord is essential to the safety of electrical devices for everyone.

Current

In these examples we have already mentioned the basic electrical terms for measuring electricity in circuits. Current flow is the motion of electrons which have a unit charge of "e", that measures 1.6 x 10^{-19} coulombs. That exponent tells us that the charge is extremely small. The unit of current is called the ampere and it is defined as one coulomb of charge per second. One Coulomb per second means that an amazing number of electrons are moving to make that current. How many? Let N be the number of electrons per second:

$$1 \ ^{coulomb}/_{second} = N \text{ per second} \times 1.6 \times 10^{-19} \text{ coulombs}$$

$$N = 6.25 \times 10^{18} \text{ per second}$$

That is 6250 Quadrillion electrons per second. Don't worry they won't run out!

Voltage

I hope you're asking about what causes these electrons to be moving in the conductor. In the earlier discussion of conductors we said that charges would move under the influence of electric potential, sometimes called voltage (V). It can also be called "electromotive force" (EMF) which means exactly "the force that causes electric charge movement". What does it look like? If you've seen lightning, you've seen electricity discharge through the atmosphere due to an extreme electric potential. If you've ever gotten a shock after walking across the carpet, your shock was due to excess charge on your body. The excess charges increased their potential because they are like charges and repel each other. When packed close together they react like a coiled spring. They have to be discharged for the same reason as the lightning! For our purposes, voltage can be supplied by batteries or electrical power from a wall outlet. As common as these examples are, they are different and we will see later how different they are!

Ohms Law

The calculations associated with basic circuits are very simple. Ohms Law says that in a current flow situation, voltage is the product of the current times the resistance or

$$V = I * R$$

It also contains the relations of current and resistance as follows:

$$I = {}^{V}/_{R} \quad \text{or}$$

$$R = {}^{V}/_{I}$$

This relation also tells us about our units of measure in the circuit electricity that we may need to work with:

Voltage (V) in Volts = Current (I) x Resistance (R) and

Current (I) in Amperes = Voltage (V) / Resistance (R) and

Resistance (R) = Voltage (V) / Current (I)

When we discuss resistors we will look at the unit of measure for resistance. If we are looking at the power consumed by a circuit the calculations are as follows:

Power in Watts is $V \times I$ or $I^2 \times R$ or V^2 / R for simple circuit calculations. This unit of power is the same unit used in other areas of Physics and it provides a means to compare mechanical and electrical systems on the basis of energy.

Sources of EMF

Previously, we mentioned two sources of voltage or EMF. Batteries of all types are capable of providing direct current (DC) only. Direct current means that there is a positive terminal and a negative terminal and the electric potential between the two is a never changing constant. There are batteries in various potential outputs for a wide variety of uses. Common AAA, AA, C, and D cell batteries are designed to supply a constant 1.5 volts DC for an extended time. Car batteries are mostly rated at 12 volts DC offering high current outputs for starting automobiles in the most difficult conditions. Older cars may use 6 volt batteries. Future cars may use higher voltages for lighter weight and increased reliability. As many types of batteries as there are, they all have a DC output voltage as a common feature.

Alternating current (AC) is the electric potential source that we use in our homes and work. Most of these outlets are 110 to 120 volts that varies between a positive and negative polarity. Without an oscilloscope to visualize this variation AC has no apparent difference from the DC electricity. However the variation from positive to negative takes place 60 times per second. In practice, AC allows a significant amount of power to be applied for an extended amount of time.

Circuit Components

A resistor is possibly the most common of electric circuit components. The unit of electrical resistance is called the Ohm. By using the Ohms law equation

$$V = I \times R \qquad \text{then}$$

$$\text{Resistance (R)} = \text{Voltage (V)} / \text{Current (I)}$$

In this equation, the unit "Ohm" (Greek letter "omega" or Ω) is the ratio of volts per ampere. In circuits, resistors limit the flow of current. When part of a circuit, resistors exhibit a voltage drop equal to the product of the current and the resistance of the device itself. Because they function like an electrical form of friction, resistors must be able to dissipate heat.

Ohms law is used to calculate the current in a resistor when a potential is applied. We start with the ohms law equation, V = I x R. If a 20 Ω resistor is in a circuit with a 1.5 Volt battery a current is calculated as follows:

$$I = {}^{V}/_{R} \qquad \text{means}$$

$$I = 1.5\text{ V} / 20\,\Omega \text{ (Amperes)} \quad \text{or}$$

0.075 Amperes of direct current

This value would usually be written in terms of milli-amperes (1/1000 of an ampere) as 75 mA. The symbol for a resistor looks like this:

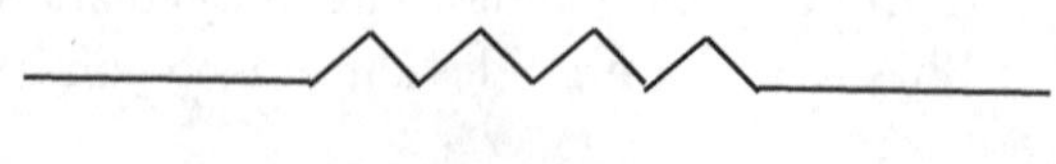

Resistor R

A capacitor is a device that stores electrical energy in a circuit. It stores energy in the form of electric charge that builds up on the parallel plates inside. In practice, the capacitor has an insulating layer between two conducting layers that are rolled into a cylindrical shape. The two leads of the capacitor each connect to one of the two conducting layers and the current that flows into the capacitor deposits charge on the conducting surfaces inside. The insulating layer lies in between the conductors and prevents the charge from passing from one plate to the other. As the charge is deposited on the conducting layers the potential builds just like the static charge that we talked about earlier. From this description, you may have guessed how the capacitor stores charge. Just like the shock of a static discharge from walking across the carpet, the capacitor will discharge if the leads are connected to a circuit path. Be careful, because that circuit path could be your fingers if you pick up while it is charged.

The calculations for the capacitor are once again very simple. The unit of the capacitance is the Farad. The capacitance is the ratio of the Charge Q divided by the potential V or:

$$C = Q / V$$

The potential of a capacitor is the ratio of the charge Q (coulombs) divided by the Capacitance (C) or

$$V = Q/C$$

You may be asking about the current? The current into the capacitor deposits charge (Q) that allows the Potential (V) to reach a certain value (V). That potential V is the voltage of the EMF supplied in the circuit. Once that EMF is reached there is no more "force" to push charge into the capacitor. The capacitor has a stored potential energy and is ready to discharge. Be careful if handling! The symbol for a capacitor looks like this:

Capacitance C

An inductor in a circuit looks like a coil of wire which is exactly what it is. The value of the inductor is in the unit of "Henrys". Since it is a coil of wire, you might think that a coil of wire will have no effect in a circuit and you would be right. In a DC circuit which is most of what we do at this level, the inductor just passes current with no change in voltage. The inductor does show a potential drop in an AC circuit since the potential drop V is equal to the inductance (called L) times the change in current per unit of time or:

$$V = L \times {}^{\Delta I}/_{\Delta t}$$

In a DC circuit there is a constant current so the Inductor has no effect. The effects in AC circuits are a little beyond our purpose in this study guide.

Our discussion of the circuit devices must also include switching devices which are used in many circuit applications. The Semiconductors are the Diodes and Transistors. The Diode allows only one-way flow of electrical current and blocks the current flow in the opposite direction. The device is controlled by the voltage applied in a positive or negative direction. If voltage is applied in a positive direction current flows but opposite voltage prevents current from flowing. If this sounds confusing, it is simply a switching device that is on or off. It is useful in converting AC voltage to DC voltage and a majority of devices use diodes to do this conversion.

The transistor also allows regulated flow of current with a third connection called the "base". The "collector" and "emitter" are like the leads of a resistor and its function is like a variable resistor in the circuit. While transistors are used in a large variety of ways, for our purposes the transistor will be used as a switch for turning off and on. The symbol looks like this:

Collector (V_{out})

Base (V_{in})

Emitter (Ground)

A relay will perform a similar switching function but it is a mechanical device instead of a semiconductor. The input supplies a small amount of current to a coil which activates a switch that is either on or off. A small applied current allows a much larger current to be switched. Relays are used in cars to switch 12 volt systems off and on with small amounts of current input.

Circuit Basics

The diagrams below show the two circuit configurations that are essentials of simple circuit understanding.

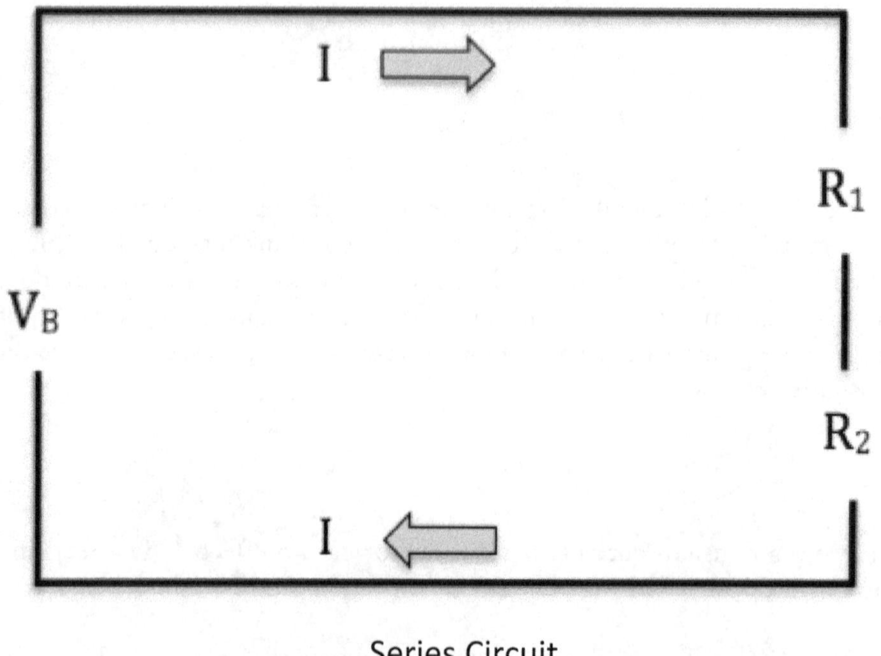

Series Circuit

Single current path circuits (called series) allow only one path for current to follow in the circuit. All of the series resistance voltages in the circuit must add up to the total of the applied Voltage in this case applied by a battery, V_B. The voltages have to add as follows

$$V_B = V_{R1} + V_{R2}$$

If the single value of the current is called I, then the Ohms law equations says:

$$V_B = I \times R_1 + I \times R_2$$

So $$V_B = I \times (R_1 + R_2)$$

And $$V_B = I \times (R_{equivalent})$$

This says the equivalent resistance of a series circuit is equal to the sum of the resistors in the circuit:

$$R_{equivalent} = R_1 + R_2$$

That math is easy for us to remember!

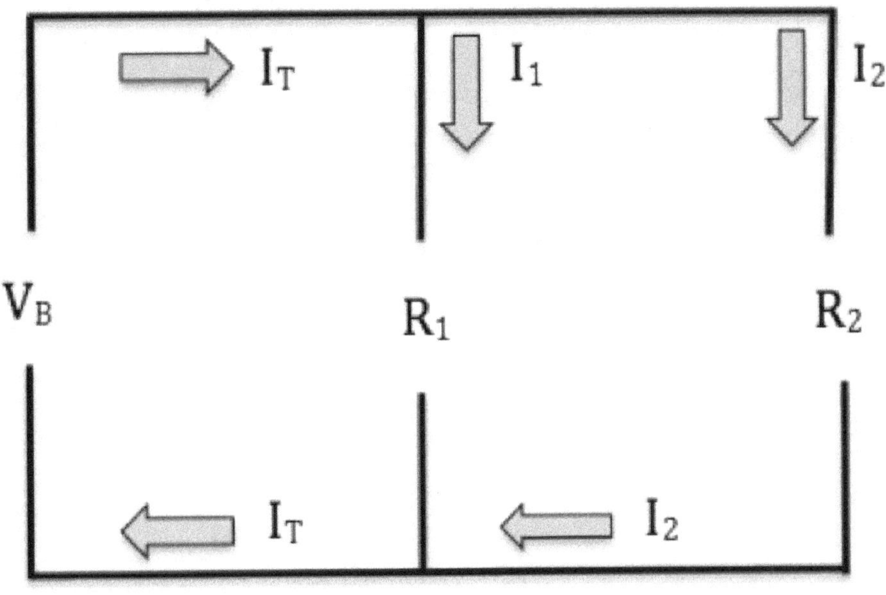

Parallel Circuit

The multiple current paths (called parallel) are slightly more complex. In the battery and the two resistors are connected in parallel so they all see the same electric potential. Notice that the current, I, that leaves the battery branches into two paths with a separate current for each resistor. Thus the current adds:

$$I = I_{R1} + I_{R2}$$

Applying Ohms law again (three times):

$$V_B / R_{equivalent} = V_B / R_1 + V_B / R_2$$

Since the battery voltage is the same for each component the equivalent resistance for the parallel circuit is simplified as:

$$1/ R_{equivalent} = 1/R_1 + 1/R_2$$

That may seem unusual but remember the currents add, not the voltages. The most important outcome is that a parallel circuit can have a significantly higher current than a series circuit. It also means that an additional resistor does not necessarily that the current is decreased! Adding that extra resistor in series will often times increase the current. It means that you need to check the numbers with a calculation of the equivalent resistance.

Let's look at some circuit examples.

1. A 1.5 volt battery is connected to a short piece of wire between the positive and negative terminals. How much current will be produced if the resistance of the wire is 0.01 Ω ?

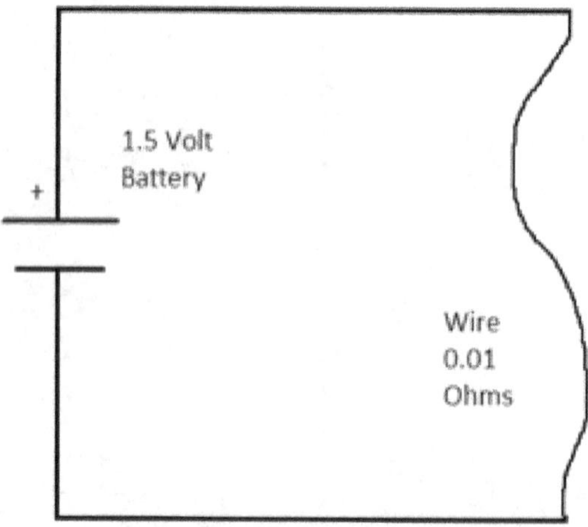

2. A 12 volt battery is connected with a 100 Ω and a 50 Ω resistor in series. What is the potential drop (measured voltage) across each individual resistor?

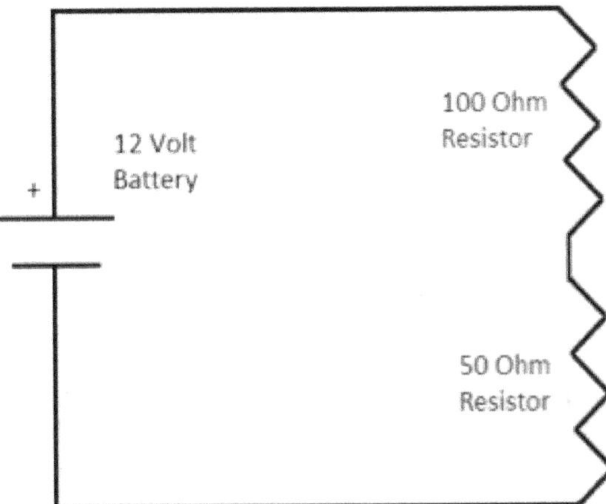

3. A 25 Ω and a 150 Ω resistor are both connected in parallel to a car battery with 12 volts potential. What is the total current and the current in each of the resistors.

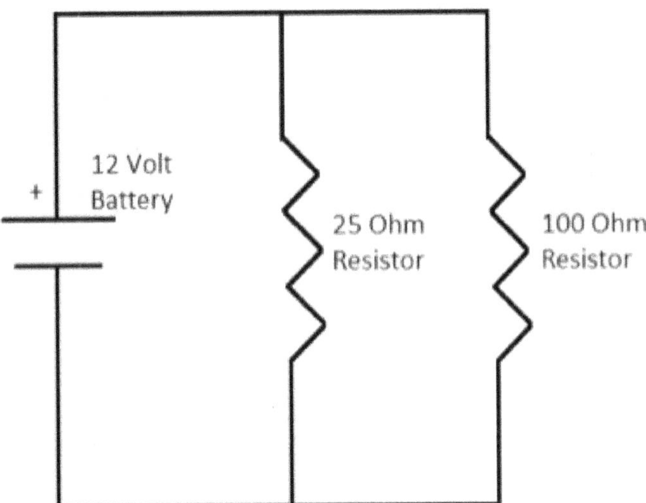

Solutions

1. Answer is 150 amperes. If I = V / R, then the current would be 1.5 volts/0.01Ω. The current would be 150 amperes. This may seem like a lot and it is. Connected this way, the wire which is a small diameter wire would be too hot to hold in just matter of a second or so. Using our equations for power, the heat would come because this current and voltage (V x I) is making 225 watts. In circuits the combination of high current and small wires will produce large amounts of heat. Larger diameter wires have less resistance and will handle higher currents successfully.

2. Answer is 8 volts for the 100Ω resistor and 4 volts for the 50 Ω resistor. The total resistance for the series resistor pair is $R_{equivalent} = R_1 + R_2$ or 150 Ω. The current is 12 / 150 or .08 amperes (80 milliamperes) so the potentials are:

$$100 \times 0.08 \text{ and } 50 \times 0.08 \quad \text{or}$$
$$8 \text{ volts and } 4 \text{ volts respectively.}$$

3. Answer is Total current is 560 mA, $I_{25\Omega} = 480mA$ and $I_{150\Omega} = 80mA$. Since both resistors see the same 12 volts, the two currents are calculated as:

$$I_{25\Omega} = 12 \text{ volts} / 25\ \Omega = 480mA \quad \text{and}$$
$$I_{150\Omega} = 12 \text{ volts} / 150\ \Omega = 80mA \quad \text{so}$$
$$\text{Total current is } 480mA + 80\ mA \text{ or } 560\ mA$$

Chemistry Foundations

The periodic table contains a great deal of information about the atoms of each known element. The figure below is for the element Molybdenum. The atomic number of an element is equal to the number of protons contained within the element.

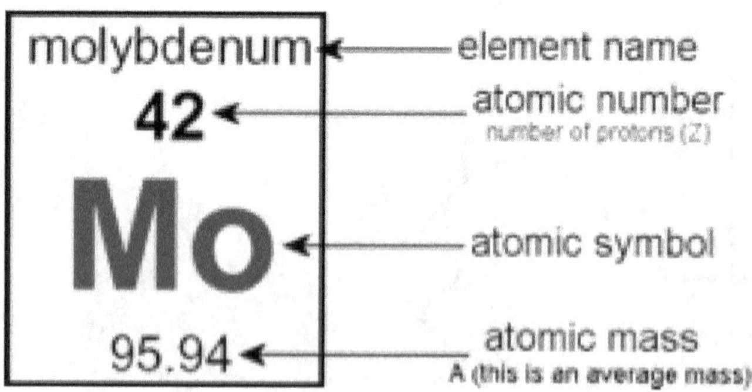

The atomic mass is an average mass that indicates approximately how many neutrons are contained within the atom. The location of the element in the periodic table indicates its electronic structure and the location and behavior of its electrons.

In 1869, Dimitri Mendeleev conceptualized the idea of a periodic table. At that time, only about 40 elements had been discovered, compared to the 118 known elements of today. When Mendeleev first created the periodic table, many scientists thought he was fundamentally wrong or even crazy. Only after he correctly predicted the existence of several elements (elements that would "fill in a hole" in Mendeleev's periodic table) did scientific opinion turn his way. Now, the scientific community universally accepts his invention as the best way to describe the elements and their specific relationships.

Prior to this invention and with only 40 elements discovered, scientists lacked the ability to organize the elements, understand their properties, and determine their relationships. They also did not understand where new elements might be found or comprehend the electronic structure of the various elements. When Mendeleev proposed his early version of the periodic table, he organized the elements using two key factors: number of protons and number of electrons.

Atomic Number & Mass

The number of protons within an element is known as its atomic number. This number is located in the upper right corner of the element's square on the periodic table. For example, on the table below, you can see that Nickel has an atomic number of 28 and Oxygen has an atomic number of 8. This is the number of protons that Nickel and Oxygen have in their nucleus.

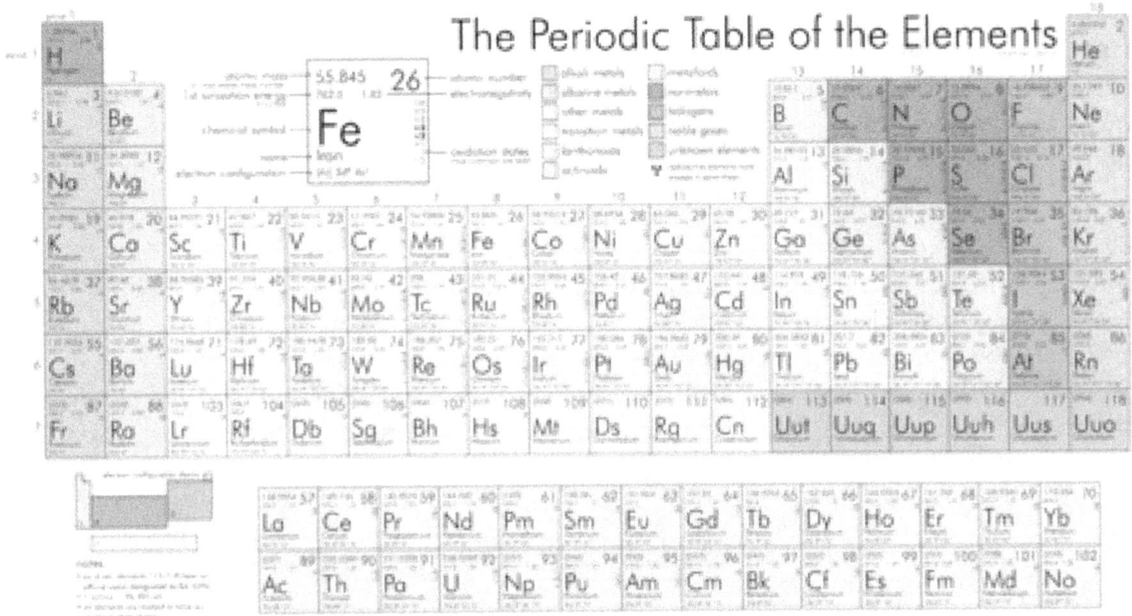

Another item that you can find on the periodic table is the number of electrons within an element. In its ground state, the number of electrons is equal to the number of protons for that element. Based on its atomic number, you know that Oxygen should also have 8 electrons in its ground state. But Oxygen is listed as having an atomic mass of 16 — what's up with that?

A third item that you can identify on the periodic table is the atomic mass of an element. One atomic mass unit is equal to the mass of a proton or a neutron. This atomic mass denotes the number of atomic mass units that one atom of an element weighs. This number is located in the upper left corner of the element's square on the periodic table.

A neutron is a neutral particle (hence the name), and it doesn't serve any specific purpose other than to add mass to the atom. While the mass of a neutron and proton are essentially the same, the mass of an electron is so small that it is considered to be without any mass. As a result, it is easy to calculate the number of protons and neutrons in an element. If you know the atomic number and atomic mass of an element, you can always determine the number of neutrons in that element. For example, Calcium, which has an atomic number of 20 and an atomic mass of 40, has a total of 20 neutrons.

If you look at the periodic table, you may notice that some of the elements have an atomic mass that isn't a whole number. For example, Iron has an atomic mass of 55.845. Here's why: elements have a variety of isotopes that result from the variations of the element with either more or fewer neutrons. For example, less than 1% of Iron (abbreviated as Fe) atoms have 32 neutrons while about 92% of Iron atoms have 30 neutrons. Because the different isotopes exist, scientists take a weighted average of the different isotopes of each element and calculate an average atomic mass based upon the amount of that isotope that occurs naturally on earth. Therefore, to be more accurate, it can be said that considering a large number of Iron elements, the average Iron atom has an atomic mass of 55.845. From that number, subtract the atomic number (26, the number of protons), and you get an average of 29.845 neutrons. The range is from 19 to 46 neutrons including radioactive and unstable isotopes.

Electrons & Elements

The next method of organization on the periodic table involves the electrons of each element. Each column has a number, called a group number. These numbers run from 1 to 18 based on the 18 columns of the table.

Electron Shells

The concept of electron shells is essential to understanding basic chemistry. The electrons in each atom are organized into layers called shells, and these shells are organized much like an onion. The following are the four types of electron shells: S-shell, P-shell, D-shell, and F-shell. These first three shells are the most important since F-shells are seen only in rare-earth elements, located on the bottom two rows of the periodic table. Rare-earth elements are less understood by scientists and are likely to be less relevant to most scientific work at this introductory level.

The following describes the distinguishing feature of each of the first three types of shells:

S-shells: They hold two electrons, and each electron has a circular orbit.

P-shells: They hold six electrons, and each electron has a double elliptical orbit (dumbbell-shaped, like a stretched-out number 8).

D-shell: They hold 10 electrons, and each electron has a quadruple elliptical orbit (like two P-shell orbitals connected together at the mid-points and at right angles in all dimensions of space — Don't worry, this won't be on the test!).

Therefore, the maximum number of electrons that can be held by the three major shells (ignoring the F-shell) are exactly 18 electrons, corresponding to the 18 groups in the periodic table. These groups are organized as columns in the irregular grid of the periodic table, and each group corresponds to the same number of total electrons in the outer shell. For example, Iron and Ruthenium both have 10 total electrons in their outer shell. However, Ruthenium has an extra shell of electrons, since it's in a lower period — organized as 7 rows — on the periodic table. The 8th and 9th rows of the periodic table are the Lanthanide and Actinide series, which include the elements with electrons in the F shells that were mentioned previously.

Electrons & Properties

The periodic table explains the chemical properties of elements and their interaction, and this explanation focuses on electrons. Electrons react, form bonds, and oxidize or reduce when they are transferred from one atom to another during bonding.

Electrons tend to remain in their shells. If the electron shell of an atom is full, there is a stable state in the completed shell. In this stable state the full shell means that the electrons have a "buddy", and they are unlikely to react. If the electron shell is even partially empty, and some electrons don't have a "buddy", they are much more likely to react.

For example, Chlorine is a highly reactive gas in group 17 (the 17th out of 18 columns), and in period 3 (the 3rd out of the 9 rows.) Therefore, Chlorine has a total of 7 valence electrons: 2 in the S-shell and 5 in the P-shell. A valence electron in an atom is an electron that can participate in the formation of a chemical bond. A valence electron can only be in the outermost shell (because the inner shells are "full"). The outer shell in chlorine is a P-shell, which can hold up to 6 electrons but only has 5. An electron dot diagram illustrates the bonding between atoms of a molecule and the lone pairs of electrons that may exist in the molecule. Therefore, a dot diagram to describe Chlorine, would look like this:

The 7 dots represent the 7 valence electrons in the S and P shells. The diagram is an example of a Lewis Electron Dot Diagram and as you can see, the 7th electron is "all alone," indicating that the outer shell isn't full. This 7th electron needs a "buddy", one more electron to fill the P-shell of electrons. Remember, the S-shell holds 2 electrons and the P-shell holds up to 6 electrons. As a result, the Chlorine atom is quite reactive. The outer P-shell is very much in need of a "buddy" to complete itself; i.e. it wants to gain another electron to fill its P-shell and as a result become stable!

Based on this example of the Chlorine element, there are several general rules to determine an element's reactivity:

1. The closer an atom is to filling its outer (valence) shell, the more reactive it is. For example, if you carefully examine the periodic table, you can conclude that Fluorine is more reactive than Oxygen, and that Oxygen is more reactive than Nitrogen.

2. If an atom's outer shell is filled, it will not be very reactive. For example, all of the so-called noble gases located in group/column 18 — from Helium and on down the rest of that column — are examples of atoms with the completed outer shell.

There are also other generalizations you can make about some properties of the elements in the periodic table. For example, the elements in group 1 and 2 — such as Hydrogen (H) and Magnesium (Mg) — are very reactive, but in the opposite way. Instead of gaining electrons to fill up an incomplete outer shell, these elements are looking to donate electrons, i.e. to "empty" their outer shells. As a result, Group 1 elements are said to form a positively charged ion of +1, and Group 2 elements are said to form a positively charged ion of +2. In both cases, these groups will formulate these ions because the electrons are loosely bound and can be readily ionized due to the loss of the electron(s).

Some additional general properties that can be inferred from a careful examination of the periodic table include the following:

1. electronegativity — the chemical property that describes the tendency of an atom or a molecule to attract electrons toward itself. This property increases in elements located in the upper right of the periodic table and decreases for elements located in the lower left of the table (not including the noble gasses).

2. atomic radius — a measure of the size of an atom from the center of the nucleus to the boundary of the surrounding cloud of electrons. This increases from the right to the left of the periodic table. The atomic radius also increases from the top to the bottom of the groups on the periodic table.

3. atomic mass — this increases along with an element's atomic number

Advanced Chemistry

Chemical Bonding

Earlier, we took a look at the chemical elements, so the next step is to understand what happens between elemental atoms when two or more of them are bonded together. When an atom is arranged by itself, it is called an element. When atoms of two or more different elements are bonded together, it is called a compound. The properties of a compound depend both on the compound's composition (the number and type of elements bonded within the compound) and the types of bonding that occur among the atoms in the compound.

What is a bond?

There are two basic types of bonds that occur between atoms in a compound: ionic and covalent. In an ionic bond, one or more electrons are stripped away from one atom by another atom, resulting in a positive charge on one atom (a cation) and a negative charge on the other (an anion). Objects with the same charge repel each other, while objects with opposite charges attract each other. The force responsible for this attraction or repulsion is electromagnetic force. The electromagnetic force between the positively charged cations and negatively charged anions in an ionic compound keep the compound tightly bound together in a 3-dimensional crystalline structure of alternating positive and negative ions.

An example of an ionic bond is the compound sodium chloride (NaCl), also known as table salt. If you look closely at table salt, you'll see that it is composed of crystals. In table salt crystals, every chlorine atom has stripped one electron from every sodium atom, creating negatively charged chlorine ions and positively charged sodium ions. The positive and negative ions strongly attract each other to form a sodium/chloride ion lattice or crystal.

In a covalent bond, electrons are shared between two atoms, such that both atoms are able to fill their valence shell of electrons as much as possible. The atomic nuclei in both atoms are attracted to these shared bonding electrons. This attraction keeps the two atoms connected as a unit.

A good example of a covalent bond is the methane molecule (CH_4), which consists of carbon and hydrogen atoms. Carbon has four valence electrons and needs four more to fill its valence shell. Each hydrogen atom has 1 valence electron and needs 1 more to fill its valence shell. As a result, when they share electrons, it looks like this:

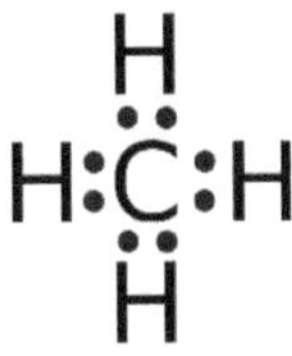

The carbon atom now has a full valence shell and is stable, and each of the hydrogen atoms also has a full valence shell and is stable.

Have you noticed a trend at this point about the nature of bonds? Both the ionic bond and covalent bond end up with a similar "product". The atoms involved in both of these types of bonds end up with a full valence shell. Since bonding occurs with the purpose of generating a full valence shell, you can predict the bonds that will occur between different elements. For example, how many hydrogen atoms will bond to a nitrogen atom? You can answer this by looking at the nitrogen atom, which has five valence electrons. As a result, the nitrogen atom will need three more valence electrons to fill its valence shell. This means that nitrogen can share a bond with three hydrogen atoms to create a NH_3 molecule (also known as ammonia).

Here are some examples of compounds with ionic and covalent bonds:

- Ionic: NaCl, KCl, $MgBr_2$, NaOH, FeO
- Covalent: N_2, CH_4, SO_3, NO_2

Ionic, Covalent or Ionic-Covalent?

Although you typically characterize bonds as either ionic or covalent, most ionic bonds have some covalent characteristics, and most covalent bonds have some ionic characteristics. The ionic character of a bond is determined by the difference in electronegativity between two binding atoms. For example, in ferrous oxide (FeO), the oxygen atom has a much higher electronegativity compared to the iron atom. The oxygen atom attracts bonding electrons more strongly than the iron atom. As a result, the electrons in the oxygen-iron bond are unequally shared, spending more time close to the

oxygen atom. Although this is still a predominantly covalent bond, there is some separation of electron charge: the oxygen atom has a partial negative charge, and the iron atom has a partial positive charge. This separation of charge causes the iron-oxygen molecule to have a partial positive pole and a partial negative pole. Such molecules are called dipoles.

Weak Bonding Types

Aside from the two primary types of bonds, there are also some weaker bonds that exist due to intramolecular interactions. In ionic and covalent bonds, the bond occurs directly between the two atoms. In bonds such as hydrogen bonds or Van der Waals interactions, the weak bond comes from the interaction between two molecules.

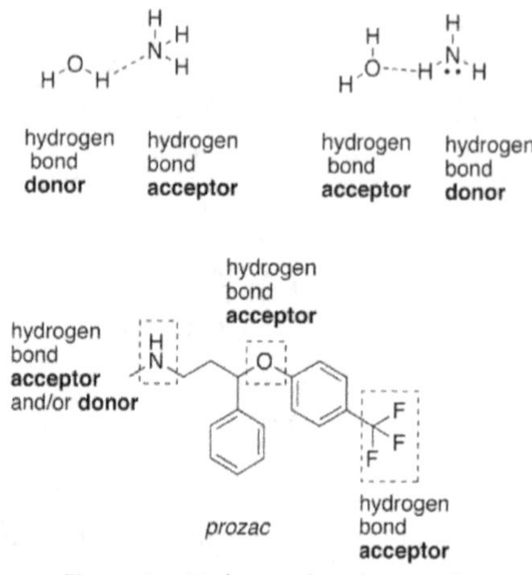

Figure 1 – Hydrogen bond examples

In the diagram above, you can see some examples of the most common intermolecular bond: the hydrogen bond. The hydrogen bond occurs when a molecule has a dipole (as mentioned above), meaning that one end of the molecule is partially positively charged while the other end is partially negatively charged. In the case of the water molecule (H-O-H), the electronegativity of the oxygen atom pulls more electrons toward it, which results in a negative charge on the oxygen atom and a positive charge on both hydrogen atoms. In this case, the water molecule is not a dipole, but a tripole with one negative end and two positive ends, as represented in the diagram below.

δ^-

δ^+ O δ^+

H H

As a result of this positive and negative charge, the positive poles of a water molecule are attracted to the negative pole of other water molecules. The intermolecular attraction between oxygen and hydrogen atoms in water molecules is called hydrogen bonding. As a result of hydrogen bonding, water has much stronger cohesive properties than most other substances composed of molecules with similar molecular weight. These relatively strong cohesive forces give liquid water a very high surface tension. This high surface tension allows water to move up plant stems through capillary action. The strong cohesive force also gives water a high heat capacity, making it an excellent thermal buffer. One of the major functions of Earth's oceans is to serve as a large heat sink. This heat sink effect tends to smooth out temperature variations, reducing the range of extreme heat and cold on the surface of the planet. All of these properties of water are extremely important in creating and maintaining life on Earth, and all of these properties are the result of the hydrogen bonding that occurs among water molecules.

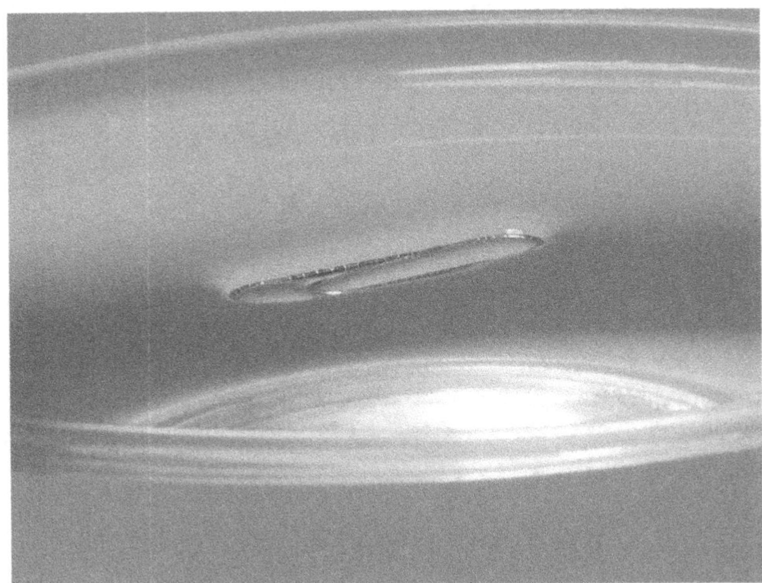

Figure 2 – A paperclip floating on top of water as a result of surface tension caused by hydrogen bonds.

Bond Structures: What's a VSEPR?

When bonds form, they do so with a particular geometry. This geometry is designed to minimize the interaction forces between any two atoms in the molecule. As a result, there is a standard set of geometries predicted by a concept called Valence Shell Electron Pair Repulsion Theory (VSEPR). This theory states that, because valence electrons have a negative charge and repel each other, they will arrange themselves as far apart from each other as possible.

This means that a molecule with one central atom and two bonded atoms, such as CO_2 (O=C=O), should be perfectly linear since the electron distribution is equal. This is called a linear bond, and its geometry is shown in the diagram below.

X—A—X

However, this geometry is not true for all molecules with a central atom and two bonds. After all, the water molecule is not linear. Why does this happen? Because of the presence of extra electrons around the oxygen atom, which act equivalently to a third atom. As a result, the configuration for water is a bent configuration, shown in the diagram below.

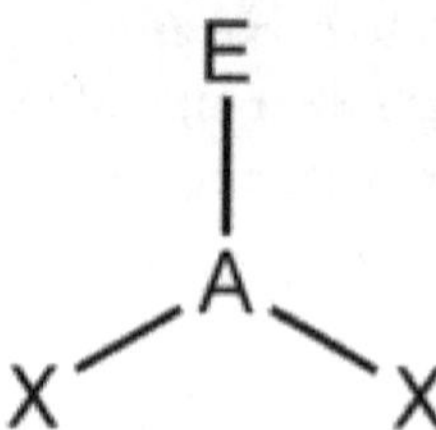

Molecules with three atoms attached to it, such as BCl_3, result in a trigonal planar configuration, shown in the diagram below.

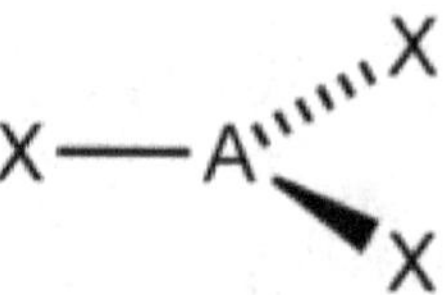

The last common configuration is known as a tetrahedral configuration. This occurs when four atoms are attached to a central atom, such as in the CH_4 or PO_4 molecules. The tetrahedral configuration is shown in the diagram below.

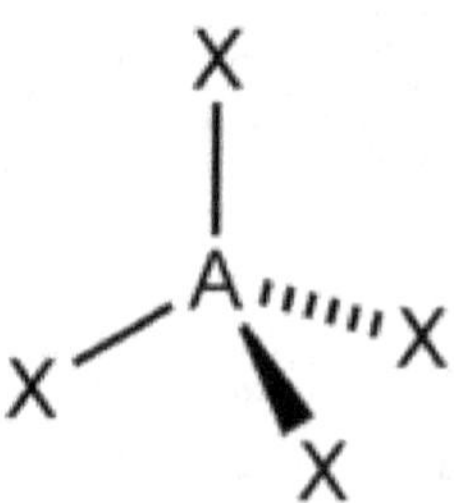

There are quite a few additional configuration types, depending on the number of free electron pairs and atoms that are attached to the central atom. Some of the other possible configuration options include octahedral, seesaw and trigonal bipyrimidal. When determining the geometric structure of a given molecule, always count the number of atoms attached to the central atom, as well as the number of free electron pairs that the central atom possesses in its valence shell. From this, you can determine a rough geometry for the molecule.

pH

When you measure the pH of a solution, you are measuring the concentration of the hydronium ions in the solution. pH represents the amount of available hydrogen in a solution. To calculate pH, which is a logarithmic term, all you need to know is the concentration of hydronium ions.

$$pH = -\log{(H_3O^+)}$$

The pH scale, (shown below), is a visual representation of the color responses to a pH test. The lower the pH is, the higher the concentration of hydronium ions and the more acidic the solution. The higher the pH is, the lower the concentration of hydronium ions and the more basic (or alkaline) the solution.

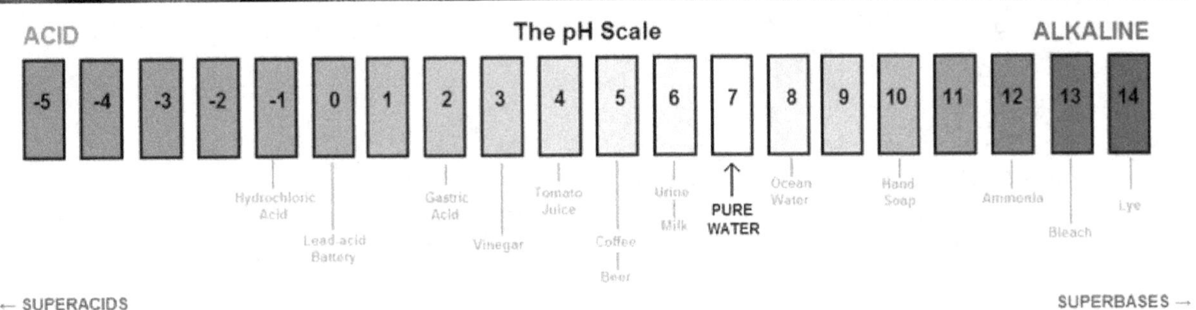

The pH scale runs from -5 to 14, although you'll rarely work with solutions with a pH lower than zero. Solutions less than 7 are considered acids, and solutions greater than 7 are considered bases (or alkalines). Pure water is neutral and is not considered an acid or a base.

Let's look at an example of how to calculate the pH of a solution.

A scientist has a solution of 0.5 M hydrochloric acid. What is the pH of the solution?

Answer: First, write the reaction equation to make sure you know the concentration of hydronium ions:

$$0.5\ HCl + 0.5\ H_2O \rightarrow 0.5\ H_3O^+$$

You conclude that a 0.5 M solution of HCl will result in a 0.5 M concentration of hydronium ions. Now, use the pH equation to solve for the pH:

$$pH = -\log(0.5) = 0.301$$

Thus, the pH of this solution is 0.301.

Now, you may be thinking, "Wait! The figure above shows that hydrochloric acid has a pH of -1. That doesn't match the answer I just calculated." There's an answer to that. The pH of a solution largely depends on the concentration of the hydrochloric acid. The figure is likely comparing solutions that are all 1 M. If you use a small amount of hydrochloric acid, say 0.01 M, the pH will be more like 2. Moreover, the more diluted the acid is, the higher the pH will be.

Acids and Bases

Acids and bases are common substances that, when combined with water, result in reactions known as acid-base reactions.

Acids

Although there have been several definitions of acids over the years, the most common definition today is the Bronsted-Lowry definition. According to Bronsted and Lowry, an acid is any substance that is able to release an H+ ion, resulting in the formation of a hydronium ion in water. For example, sulfuric acid will dissociate in water to form:

$$H_2SO_4 + H_2O \leftrightarrow H_3O^+ + HSO_4^-$$

You can see that the sulfuric acid molecule released an H^+ ion to the water, which resulted in the formation of a hydronium H_3O^+ molecule.

Strong and Weak Acids

At this point, you should know that the strength of an acid is directly related to the concentration of hydronium ions in a solution. So, for an acid that dissociates completely, it is quite simple to calculate the total strength. But what if the acid does not dissociate completely? In that case, it would be more difficult to determine the pH.

This is the difference between a strong acid and a weak acid. A strong acid dissociates completely. A weak acid dissociates only partially, according to its acid dissociation constant (with the abbreviation of pKa).

The pKa of an acid is determined according to the following equation:

$$\mathrm{p}K_\mathrm{a} = -\log_{10} K_\mathrm{a}$$

The function to find the Ka, the acid constant, is:

$$K_\mathrm{a} = \frac{[\mathrm{A}^-][\mathrm{H}^+]}{[\mathrm{HA}]}$$

This means that the acid dissociation constant is equal to the concentration of the conjugate base (A-) multiplied by the acid (H+) and then divided by the amount of remaining acid. If you rearrange this equation, you get the Hendersen-Hasselbalch equation:

$$\mathrm{pH} = \mathrm{p}K_\mathrm{a} + \log \frac{[\mathrm{A}^-]}{[\mathrm{HA}]}$$

This equation can be used to calculate the dissociation of a weak acid. For this calculation to work, you must know the pH of a solution and the pKa of the acid.

You can also calculate the dissociation of a weak acid using the acid dissociation equation. However, this requires some relatively complex math and is not covered under the scope of the exam. The major takeaway from this section is that strong acids dissociate completely and weak acids do not.

Bases

When working with bases, you use slightly different terminology. Instead of pH, you use the term "pOH", and instead of pKa or Ka, you use the terms "pKb" and "Kb" (where "b" represents the base). According to Bronsted and Lowry, a base is any substance that is able to accept an H+ ion. The primary base reaction is:

$$OH^- + H_3O^+ \leftrightarrow 2\,H_2O$$

That's right. If you neutralize an acid with the hydroxide (a Bronsted-Lowry base), the end product is water. Like with acids, you can calculate the pOH of a base by calculating the negative logarithm of the concentration of base substance in the solution.

$$pOH = -\log (A^-)$$

One thing to remember about bases is that you are not always considering only the OH^- concentration. Although hydroxide (OH^-) is one of the best H^+ ion acceptors, many other bases are able to accept an H^+ ion. For this reason, the equation for calculating pOH shows A^- as the base. Almost any negative ion is able to accept an H^+ ion to some degree.

Relationship between Acids and Bases

At this point, you may have noticed that when an acid is formed, a base is also formed. For example, when HCl dissociates in water, you get the hydronium ion, which is acidic, but you also receive a Cl^- ion, which can potentially absorb an H^+ ion.

So, if the dissolution of HCl creates both an acid and a base substance, then why is it considered an acid and not a base? The reason it's considered an acid is because chlorine is a very poor H^+ ion acceptor. In its ionized state, chlorine has a full valence shell and is unwilling to share any of those electrons with an H^+ ion. As a result, even though chlorine is indeed a base, it is a very weak base. As a general rule of thumb, a strong acid produces a weak conjugate base, and a strong base produces a weak conjugate acid. According to this rule, you can write the following:

$$pH + pOH = 14$$

The sum of the pH and the pOH of the same solution will always equal 14. Thus, for 0.5 M HCl, which we found has a pH of 0.3, the corresponding pOH is 13.7. This means that you have a very weak base and a very strong acid. You can test this with a variety of other acids and bases to determine what conjugate acids and bases are formed.

Real Connection

Many foods and beverages are more acidic or basic than you might think. In fact, to human taste buds, acidic foods taste sour or tart and basic foods taste bitter. Knowing the pH of food and beverages can help you maintain a healthy diet. Research has proven that a highly acidic diet can cause long-term stomach problems such as ulcers or acid reflux, while a highly basic diet can cause digestion problems, due to an increased pH in your stomach. In addition, acidic foods and beverages can have a slow, but dangerous effect on your teeth. Your teeth are composed of a form of calcium phosphate, which can melt under acidic conditions. A list of acidic and basic foods is provided below.

Food	pH
Cake, bread, rice	7.0 -7.5
Vegetables (peas, cabbage, etc.)	6.0 – 6.5
Onions, mushrooms, eggplant	5.3 – 5.8
Peaches, apples, oranges	3.8 – 4.3
Grapes, strawberries	3.4 – 3.7
Soda (Coca-Cola, Sprite, Mountain Dew)	2.8 – 3.0

Chemical Reactions vs. Physical Reactions

Chemical reactions result in a change in the molecular structure of a substance, usually forming a new chemical. Physical reactions result in the rearrangement of atoms or molecules of a substance, resulting in a change in the appearance or state of the substance. In physical reactions, the chemical composition does not change.

Chemical reactions include oxidation (rust), precipitation reactions or fermentation (where yeast converts sugar into ethanol). For example, if you leave a wrench out in the rain, the chemical composition will change. The atoms in water molecules will combine with the metallic atoms, which will eventually weaken the surface metal and cause it to disintegrate.

Physical reactions include dissolving, boiling or other changes of state. For example, when you dissolve salt in water, the physical structure changes. The salt is no longer a crystal and is now an ionic aqueous form in the water. If you whip cream or eggs, you turn the cream or eggs into a frothy, thick substance. This is a physical change, but the chemical composition of the cream and eggs has not changed.

The most common physical reactions are changes of phase. The three phases are solid, liquid and gas, and a majority of substances can exist in all three of these phases. A great example is water at the atmospheric pressure of sea level. Below 32°F, water is a solid. Between 32 and 212°F, water is a liquid. Above 212°F, water is a gas. When water changes between each of these phases, a physical reaction occurs. Other substances may require much higher or lower temperatures before a phase change can occur.

Instrument Comprehension

Select the diagram that matches the corresponding altimeter heading and compass direction.

1.

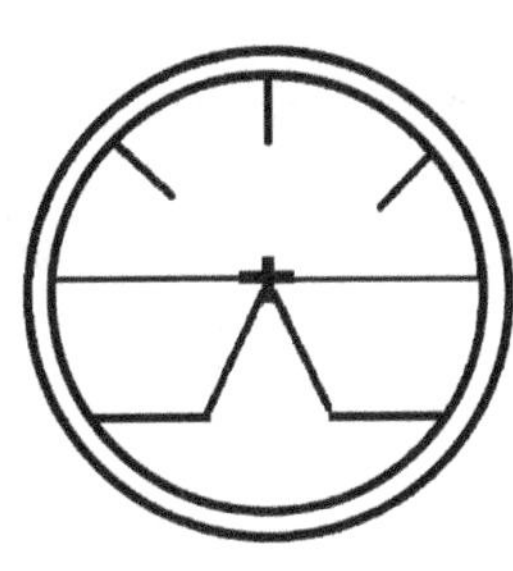

Artificial Horizon

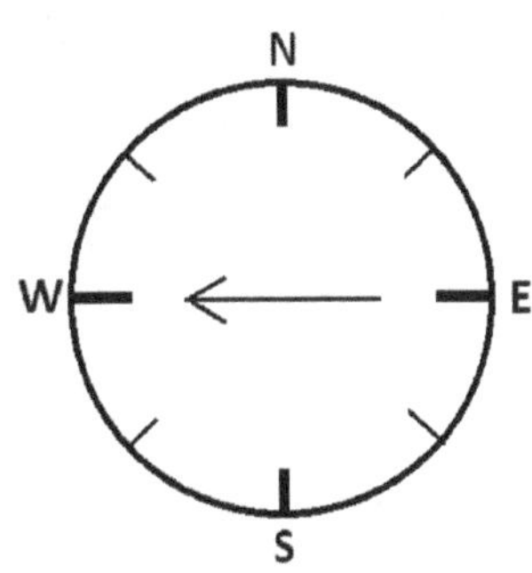

Compass

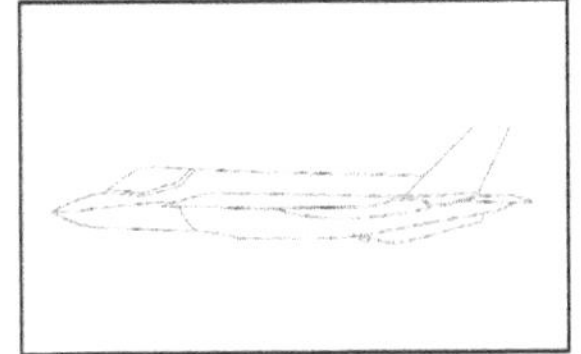

A

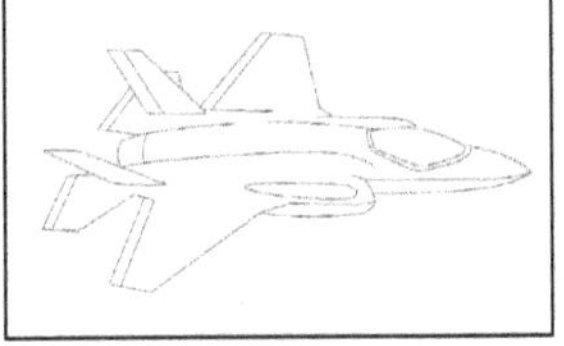

B

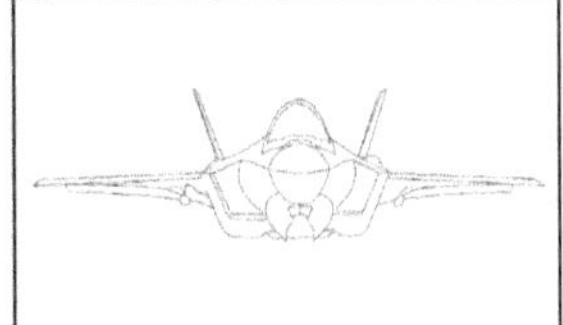

C

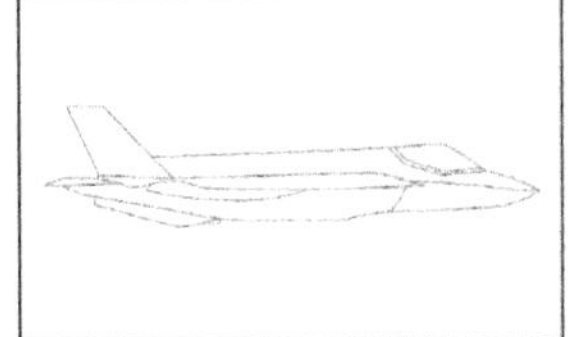

D

2.

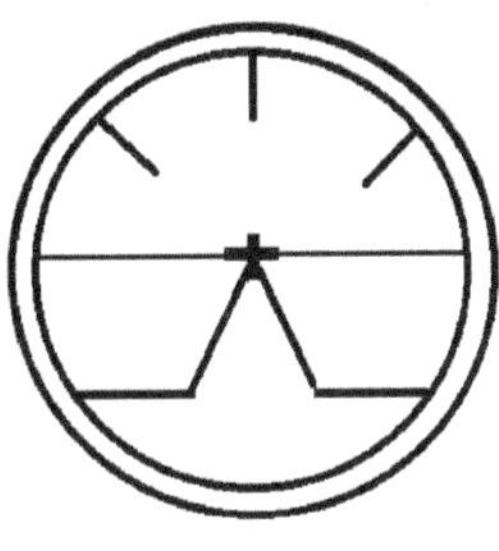

Artificial Horizon

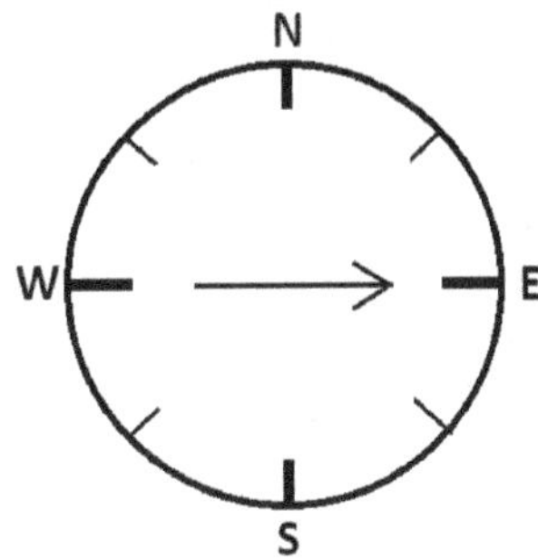

Compass

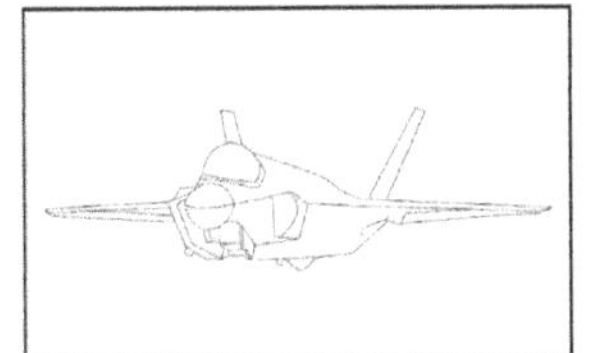

A

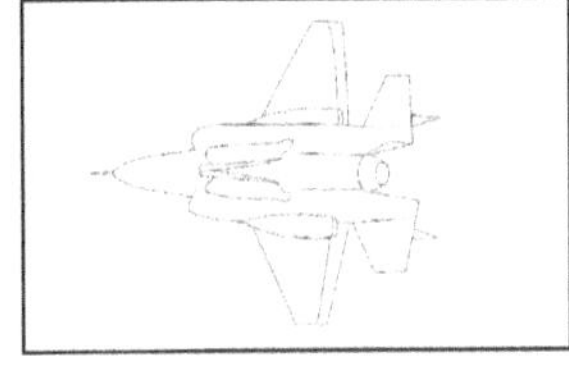

B

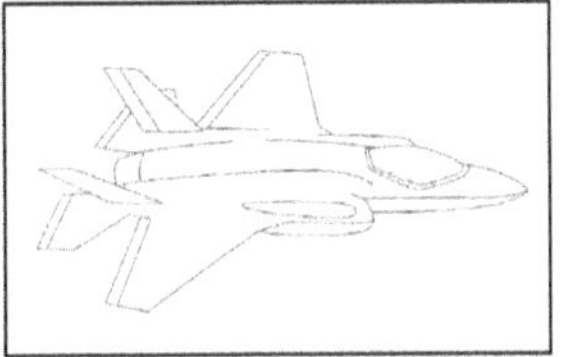

C

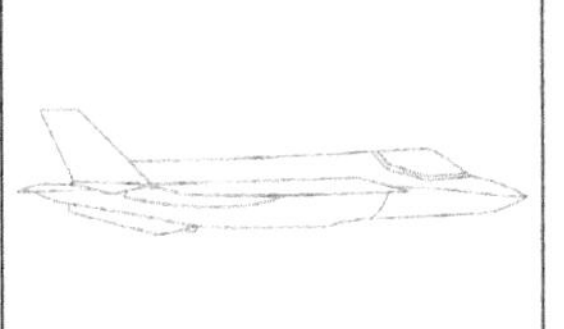

D

3.

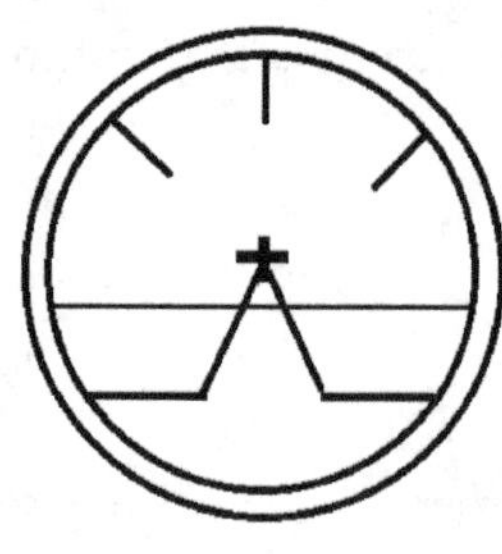

Artificial Horizon

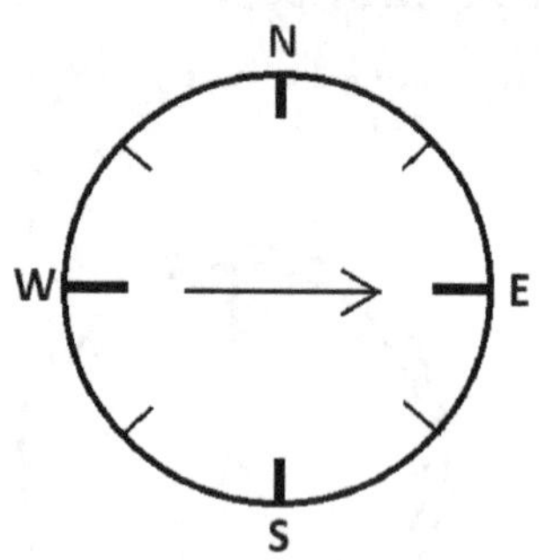

Compass

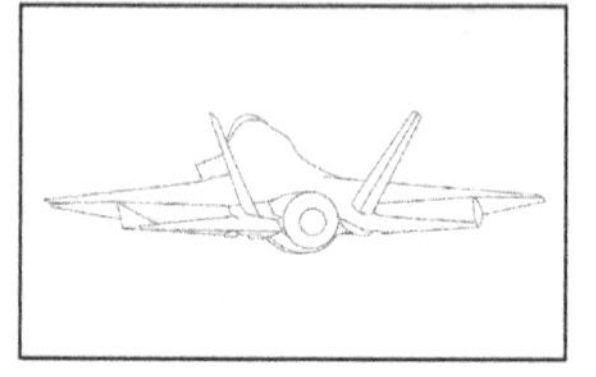

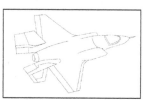

A

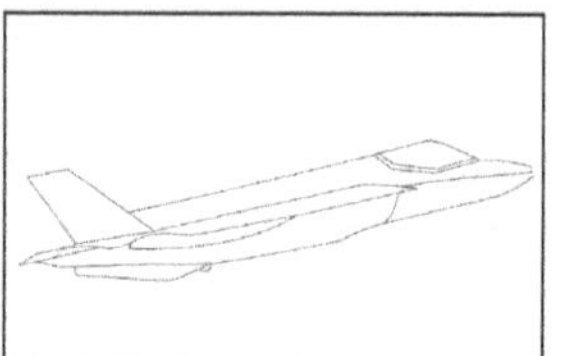

B

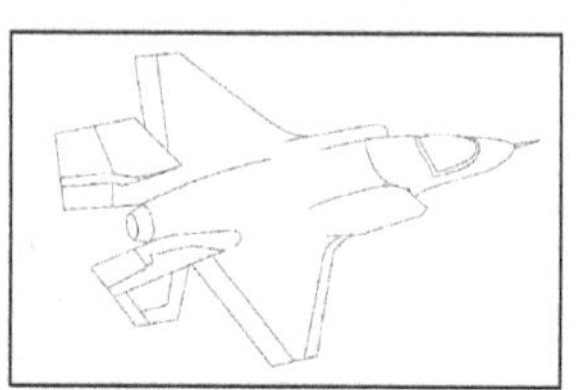

C

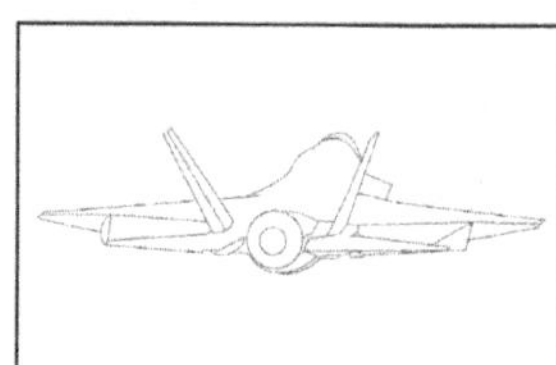

D

4.

Artificial Horizon

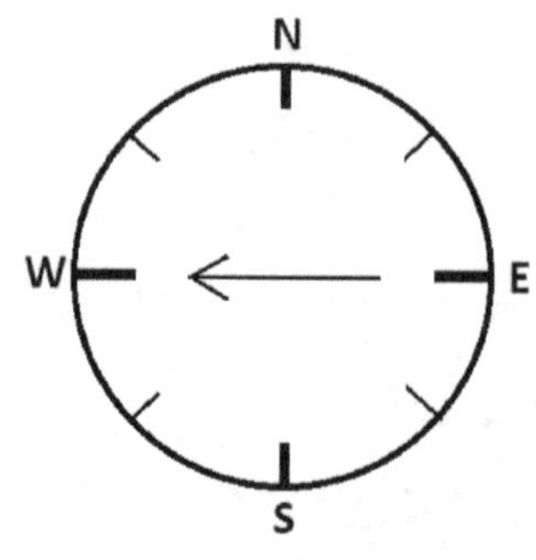

Compass

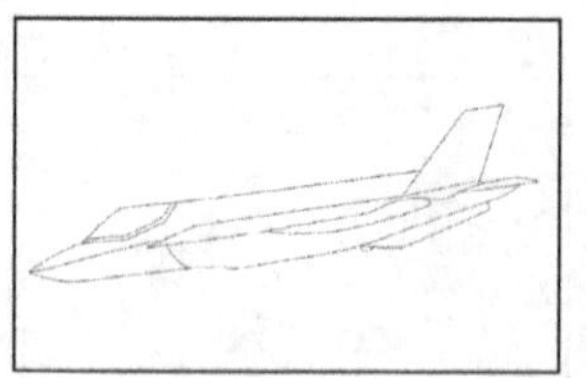

A

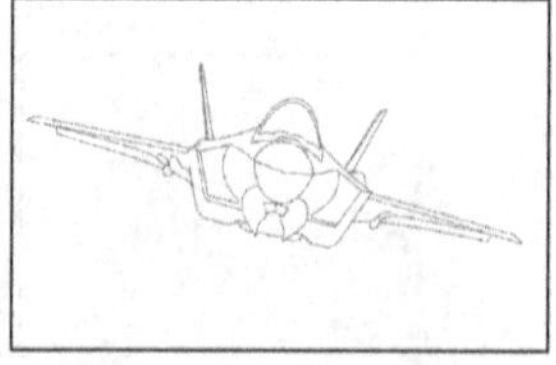

B

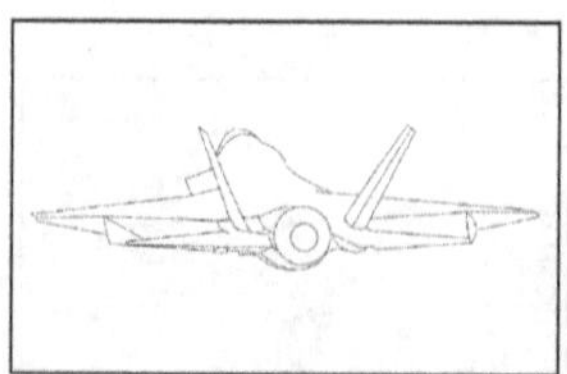

C

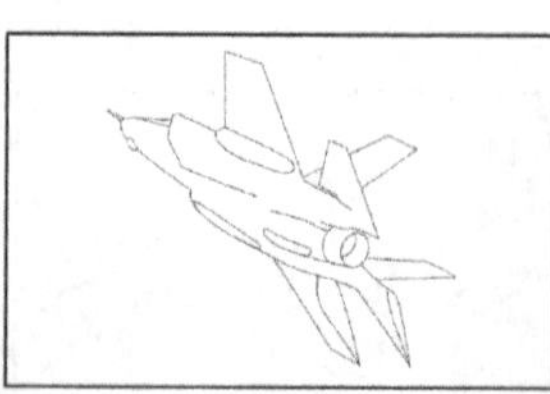

D

5.

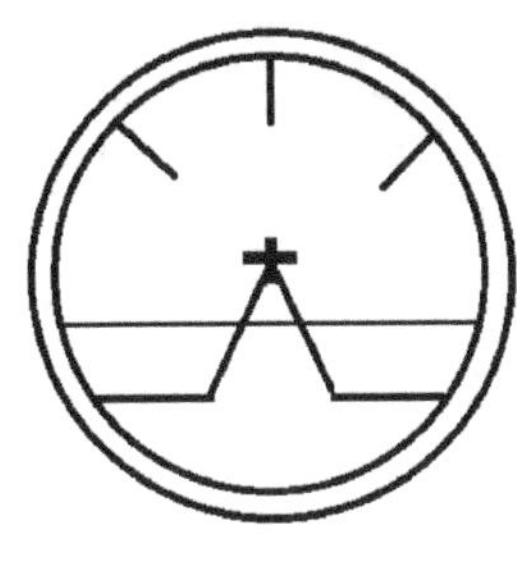

Artificial Horizon

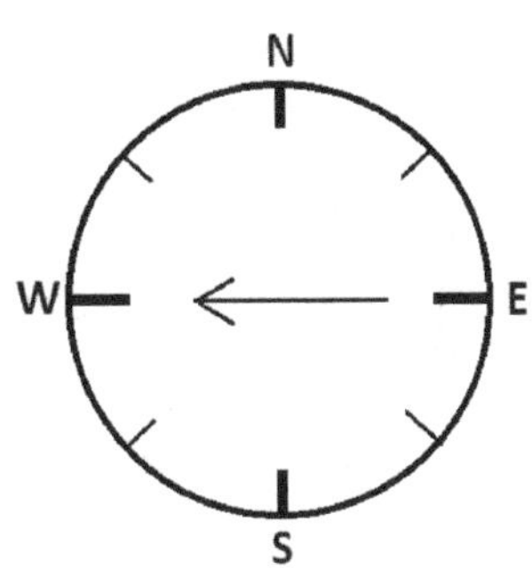

Compass

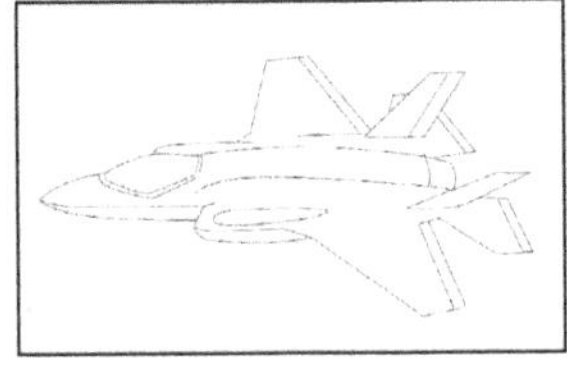

A

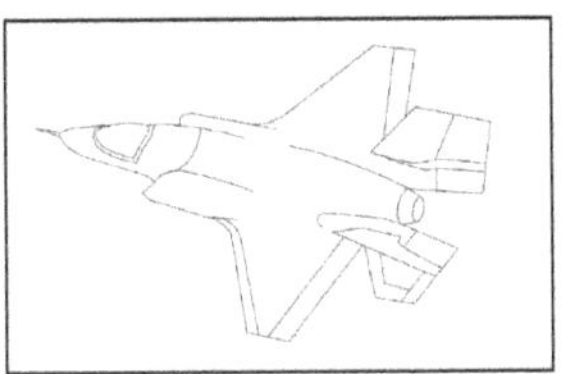

B

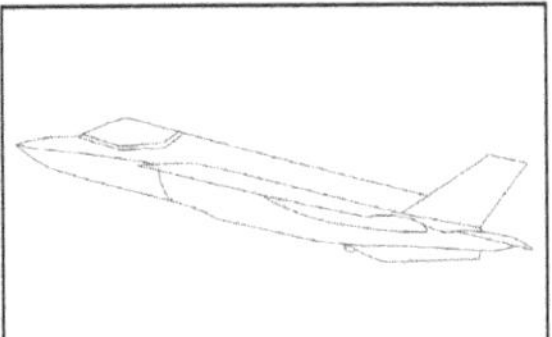

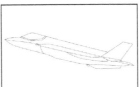

C

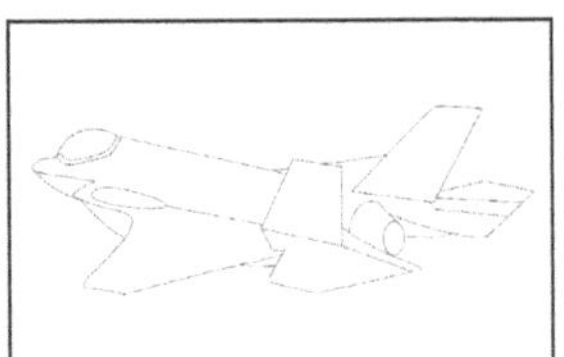

D

6.

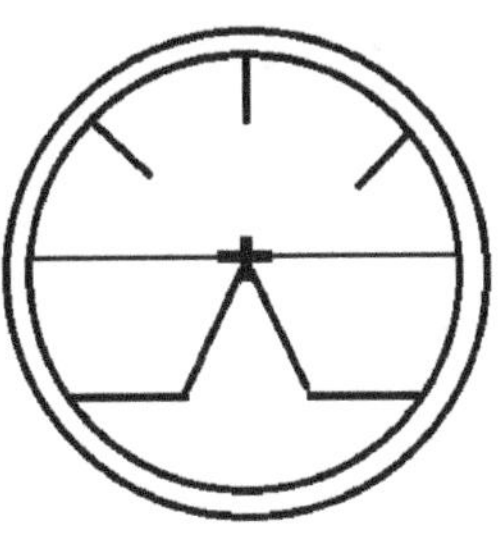

Artificial Horizon

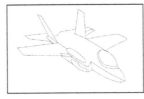

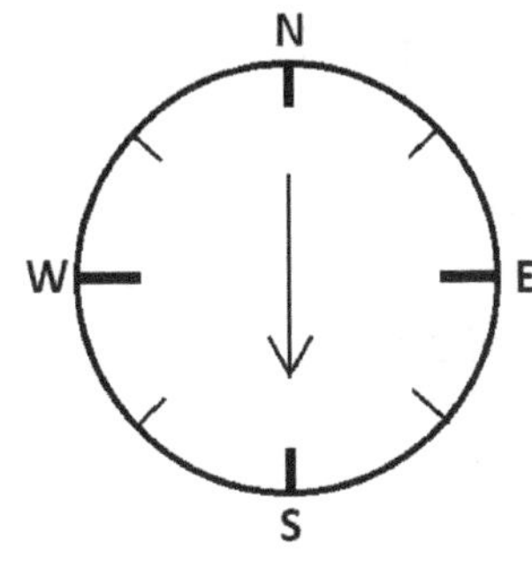

Compass

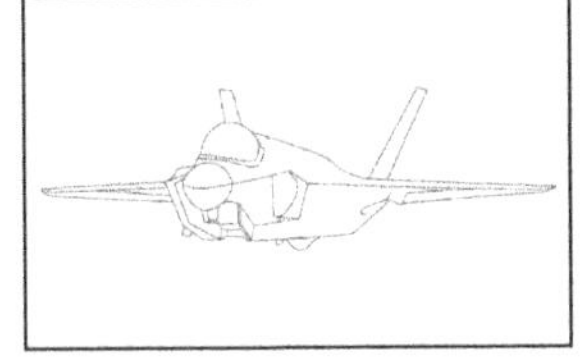

A

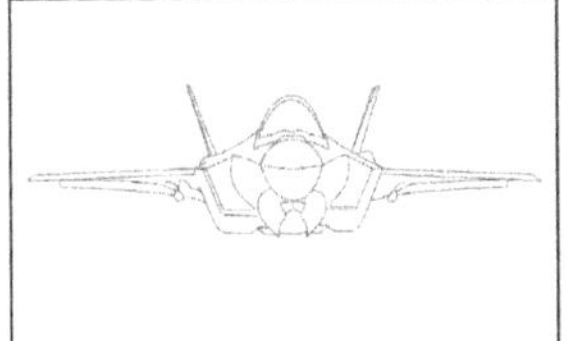

B

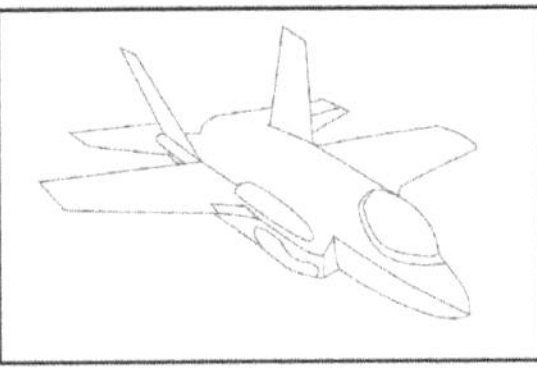

C

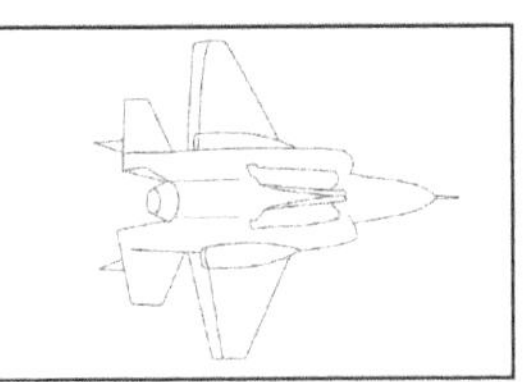

D

7.

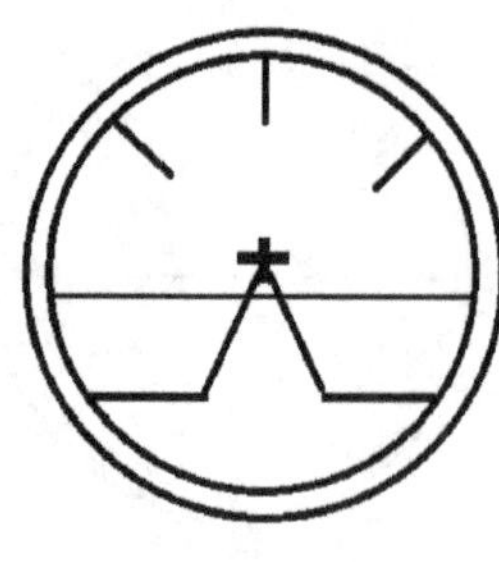

Artificial Horizon

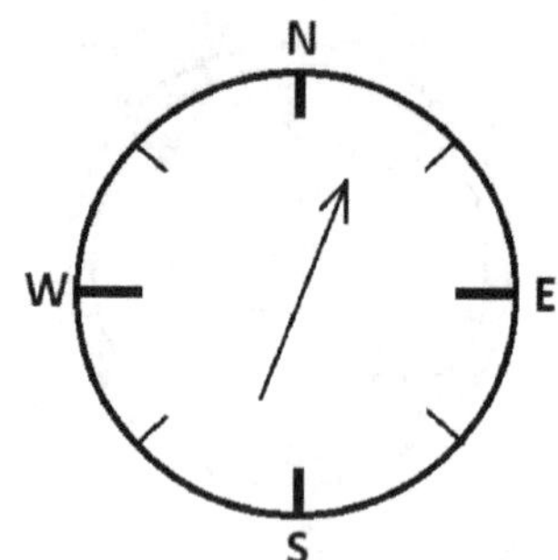

Compass

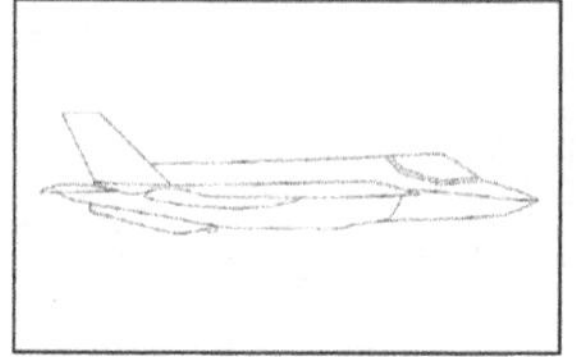

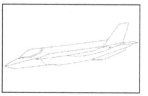

A

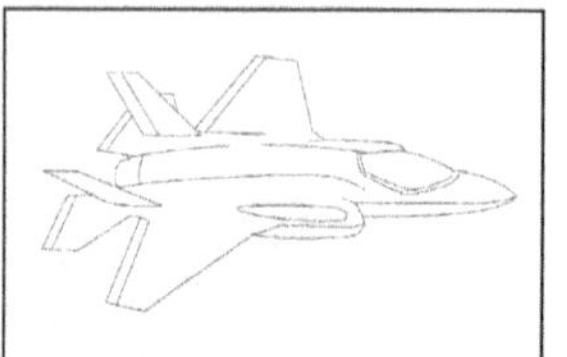

B

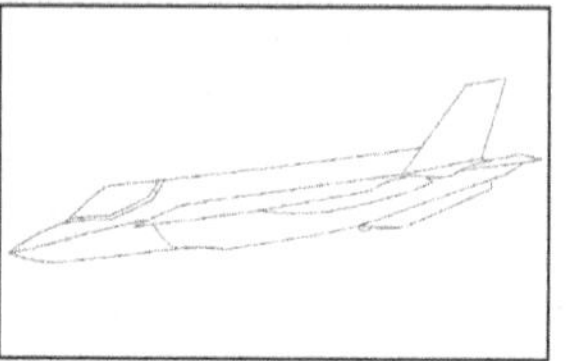

C

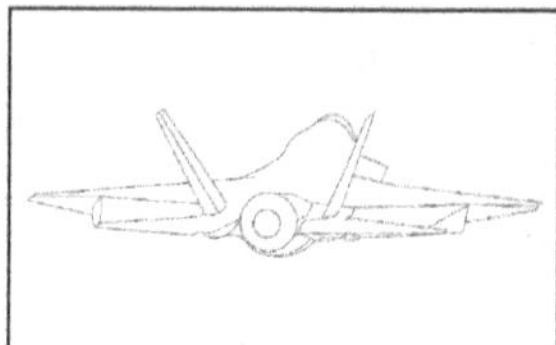

D

8.

Artificial Horizon

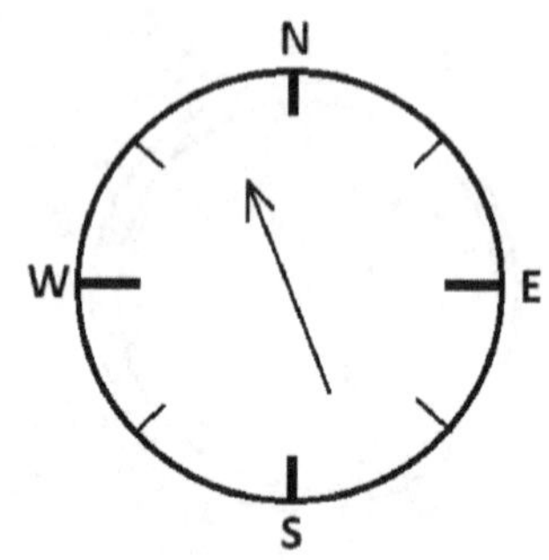

Compass

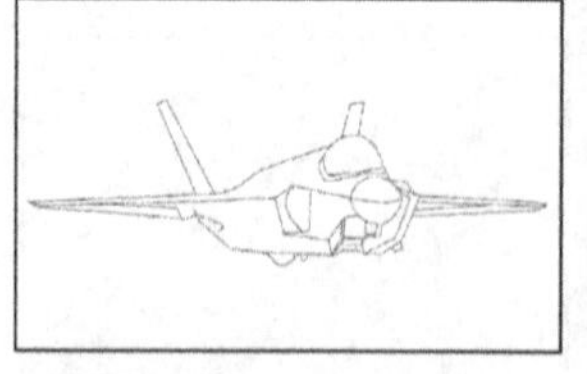

A

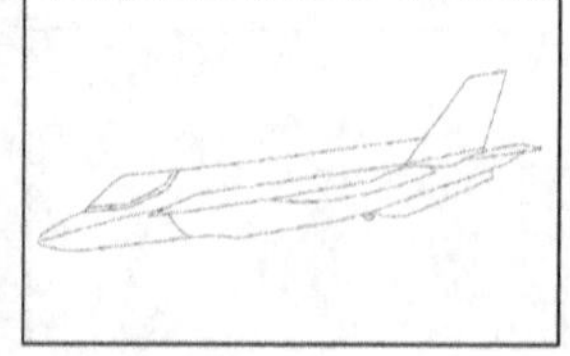

B

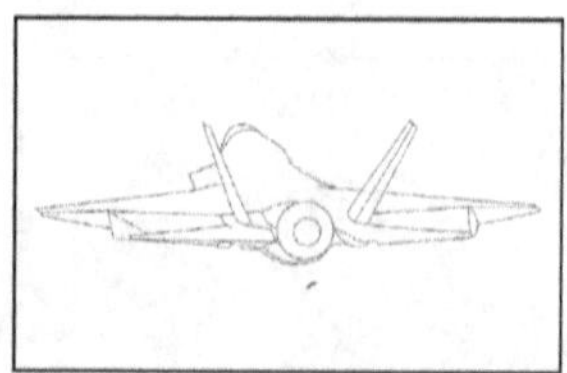

C

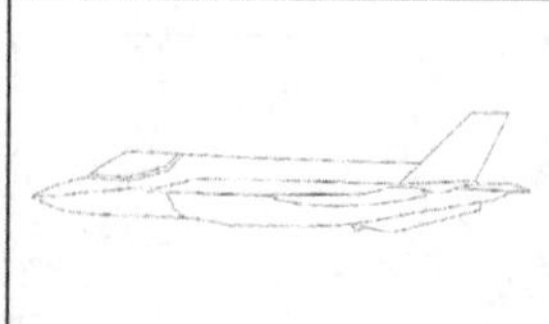

D

9.

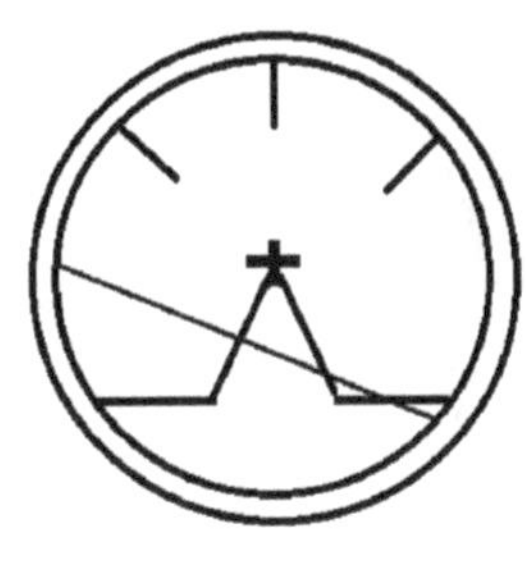

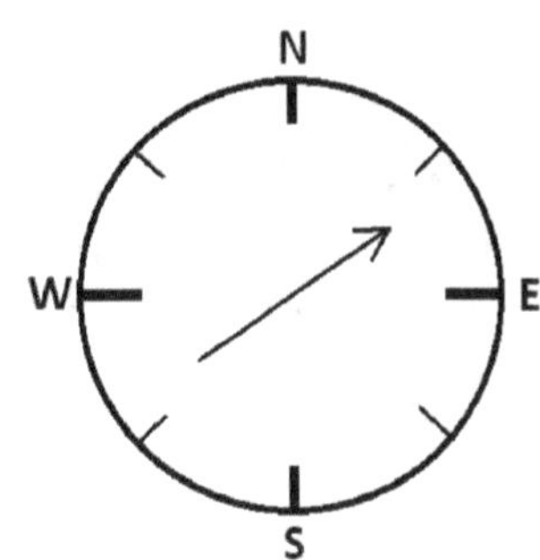

Artificial Horizon Compass

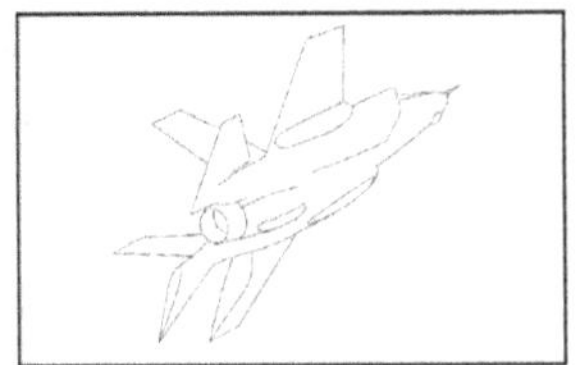 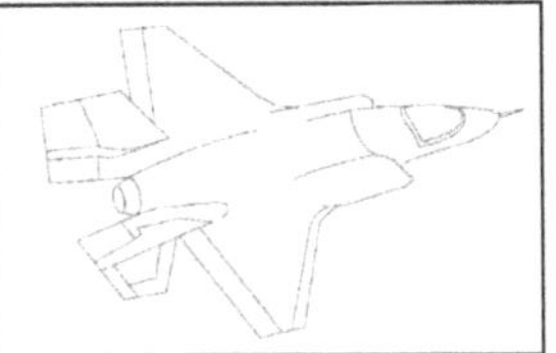 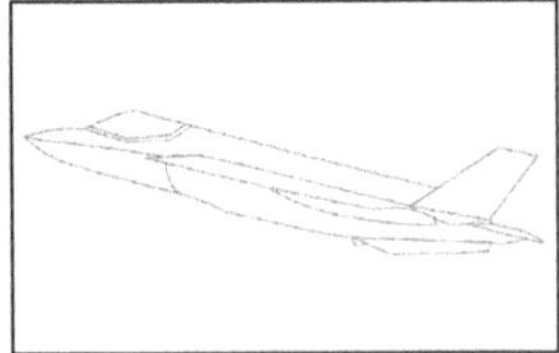 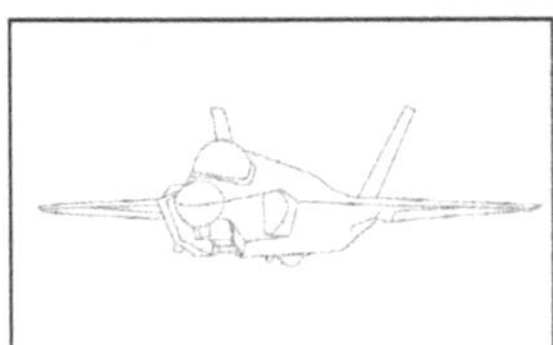

A B C D

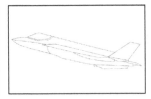

10.

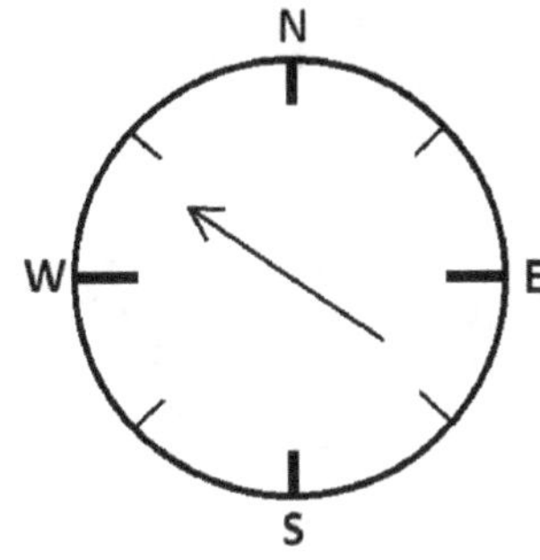

Artificial Horizon Compass

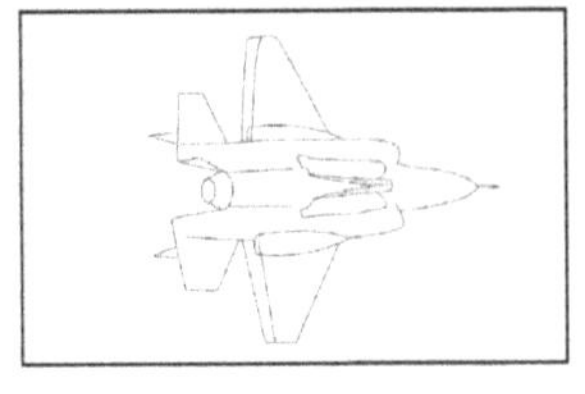 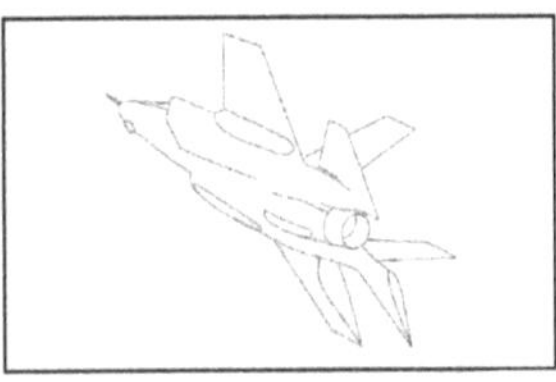 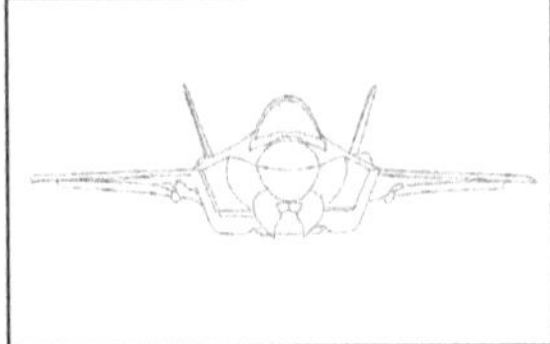 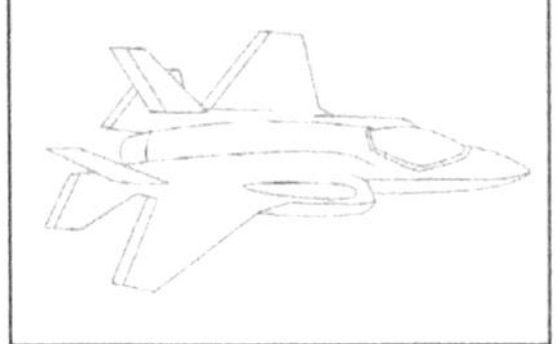

A B C D

11.

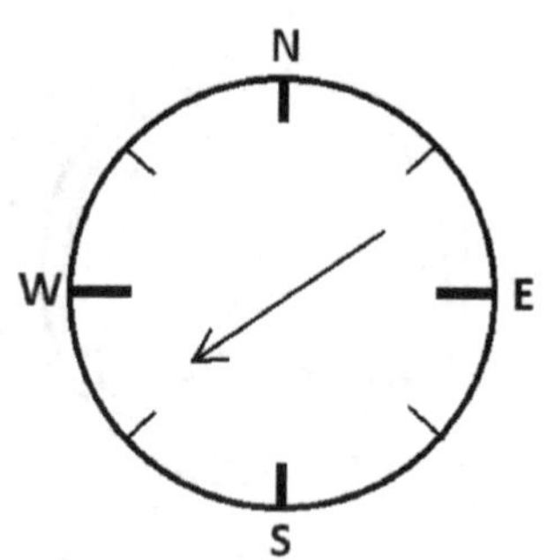

Artificial Horizon

Compass

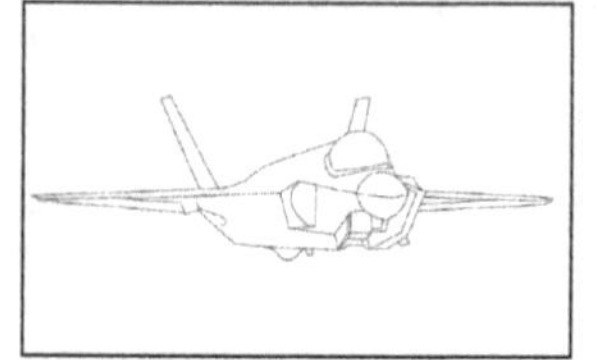

A

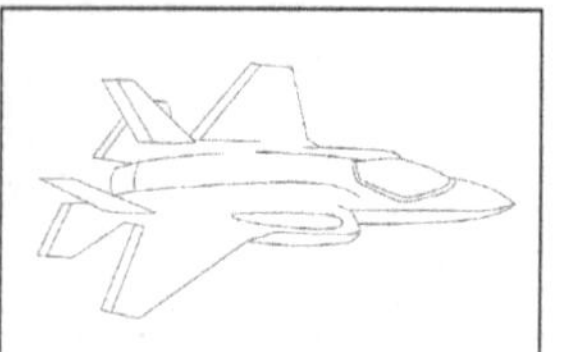

B

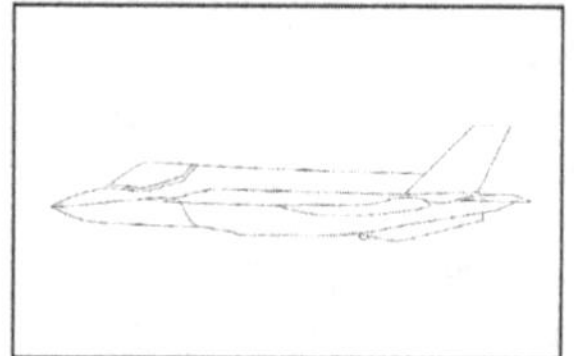

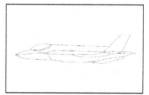

C

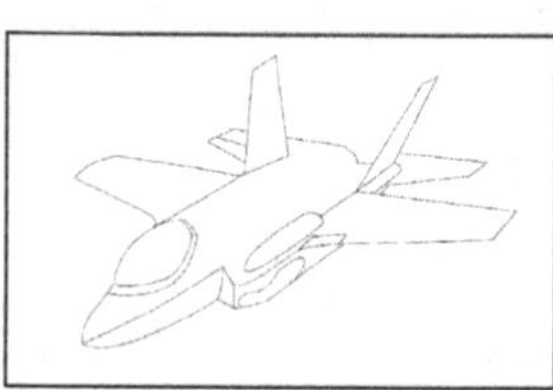

D

12.

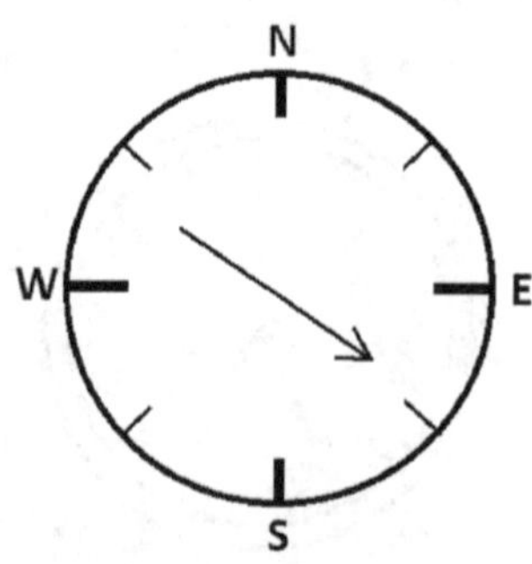

Artificial Horizon

Compass

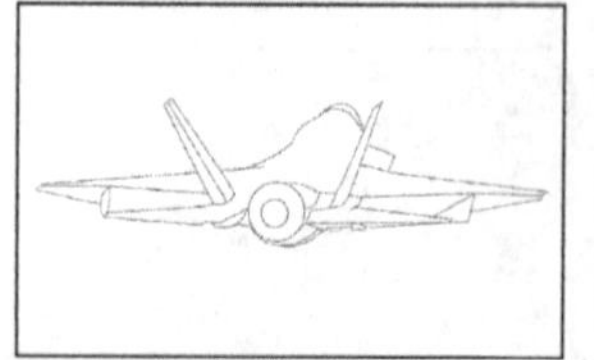

A

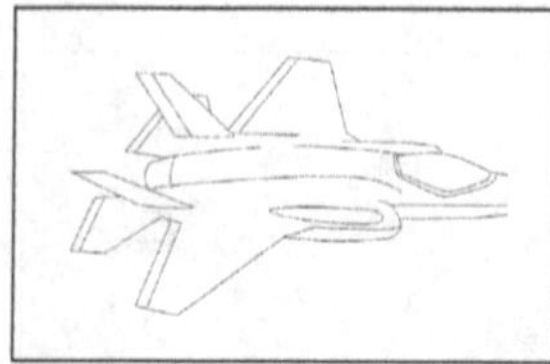

B

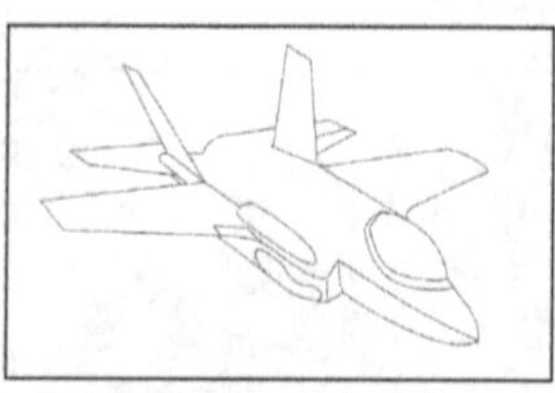

C

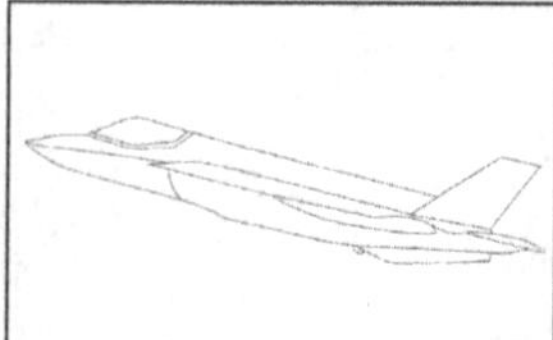

D

13.

Artificial Horizon

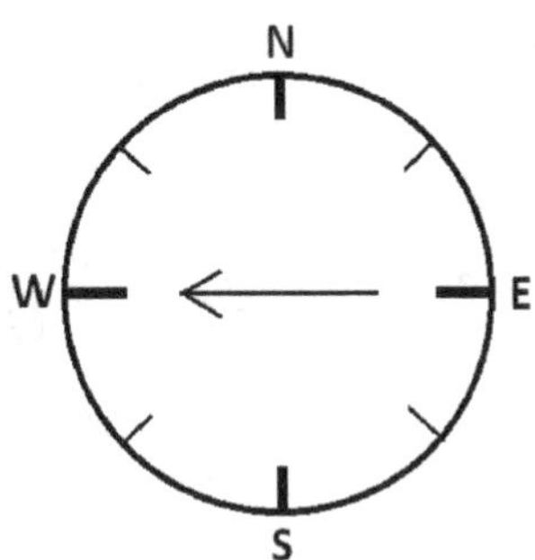

Compass

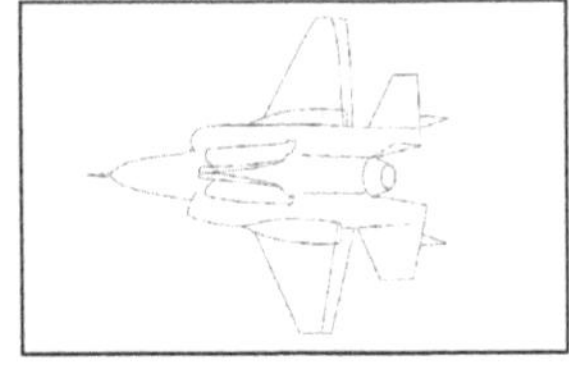

A

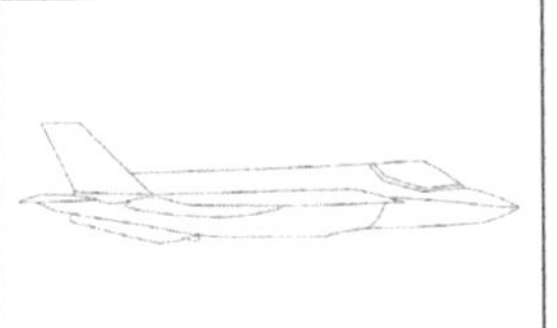

B

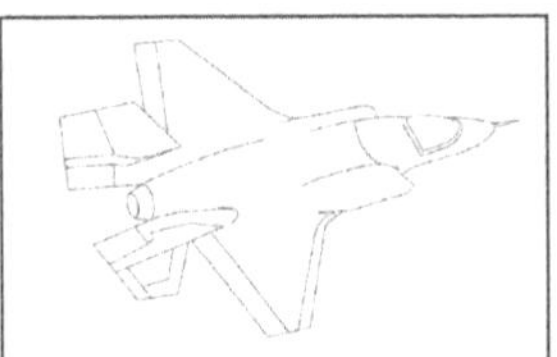

C

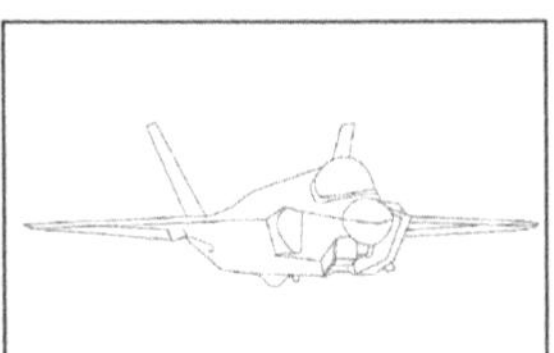

D

14.

Artificial Horizon

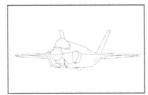

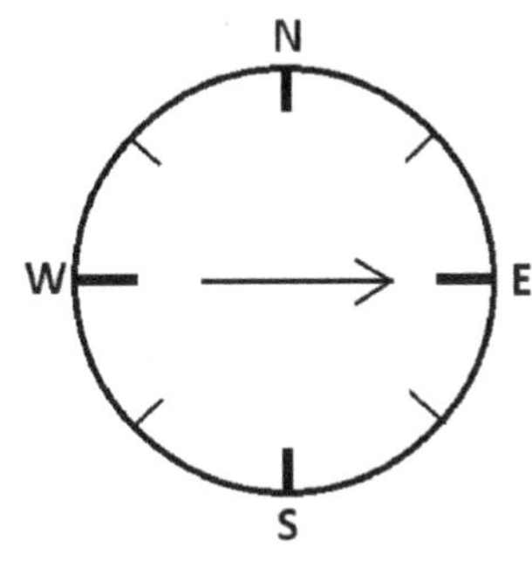

Compass

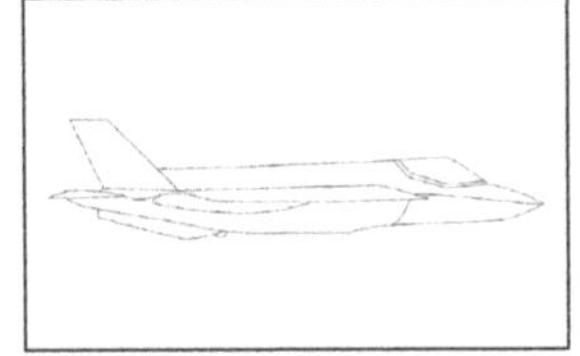

A

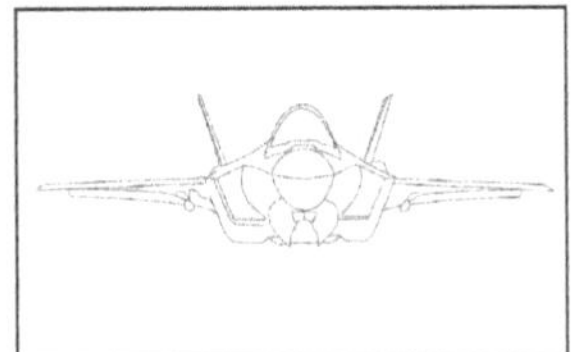

B

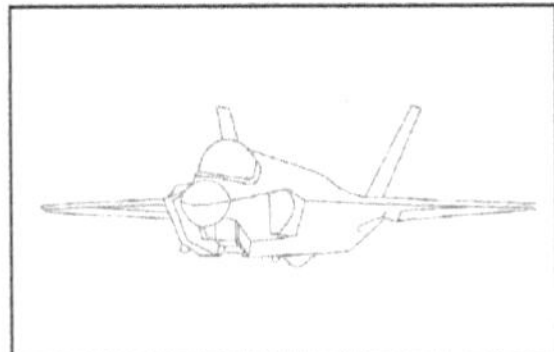

C

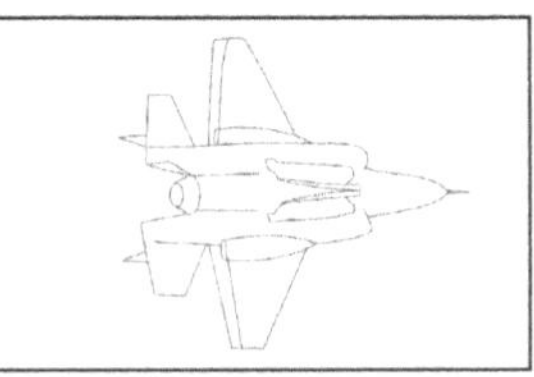

D

15.

Artificial Horizon

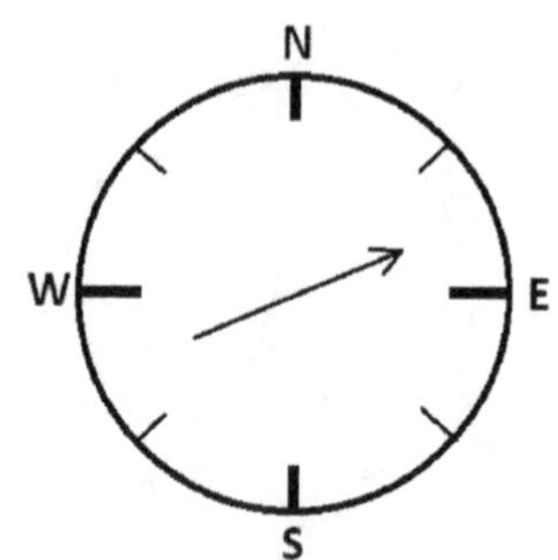

Compass

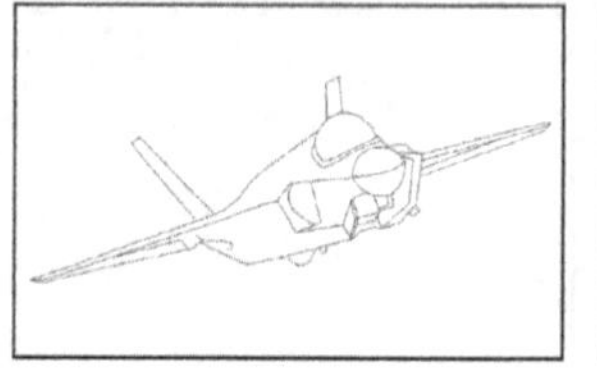

A

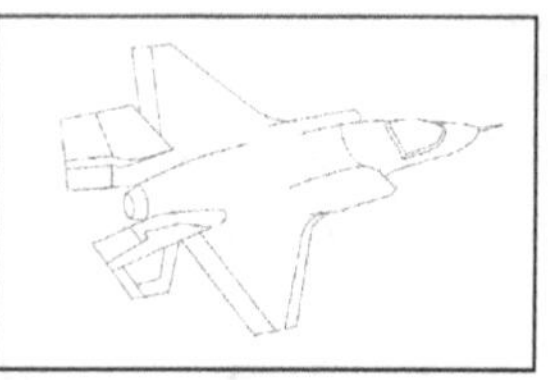

B

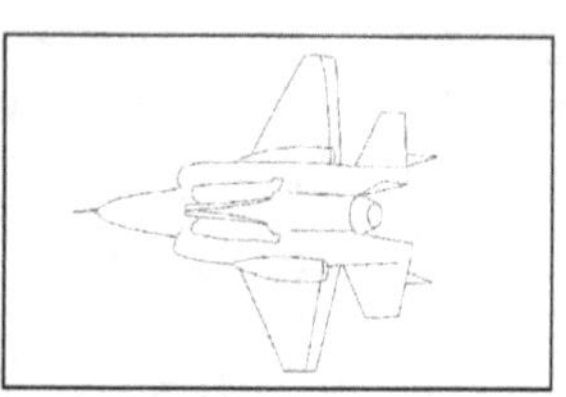

C

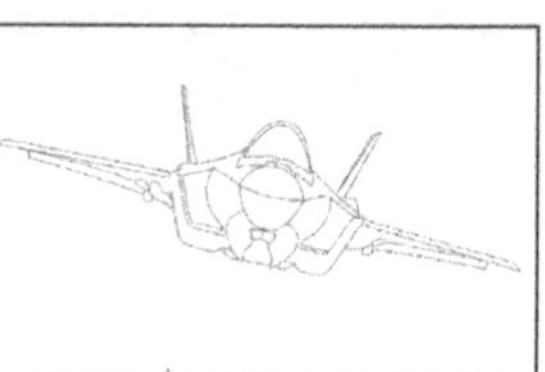

D

16.

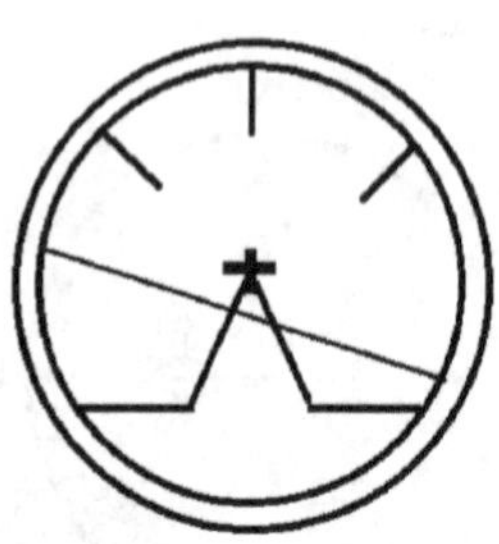

Artificial Horizon

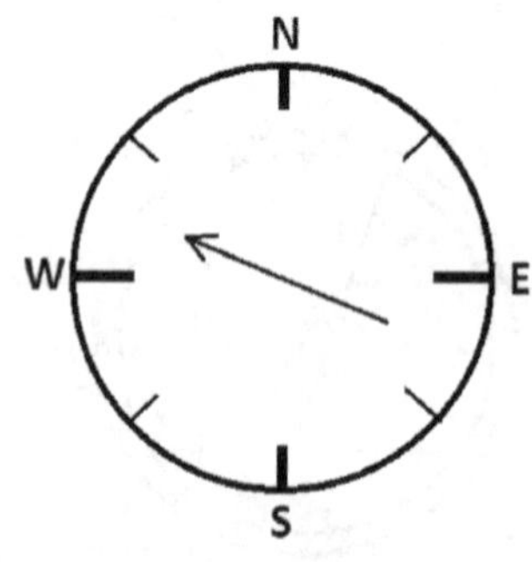

Compass

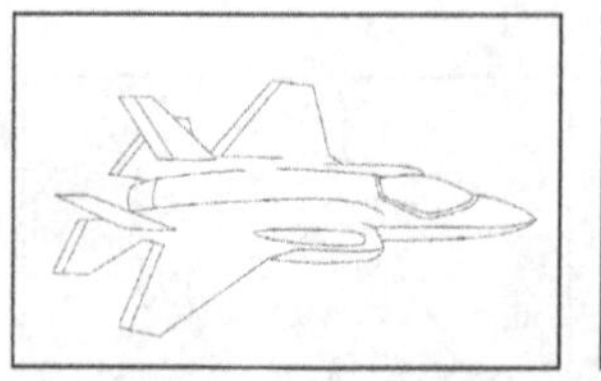

A

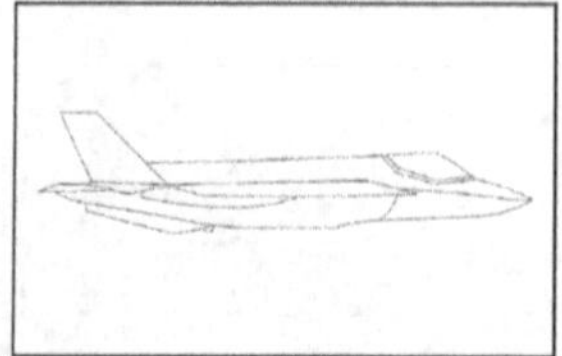

B

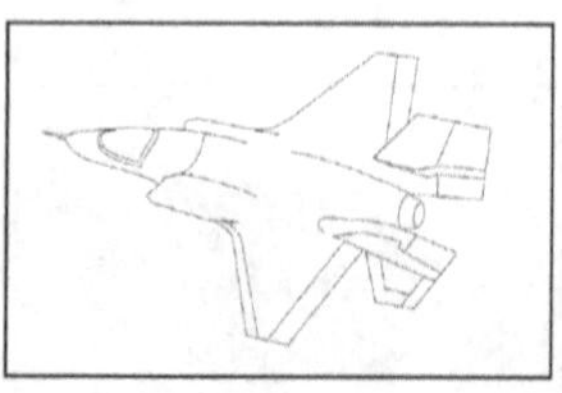

C

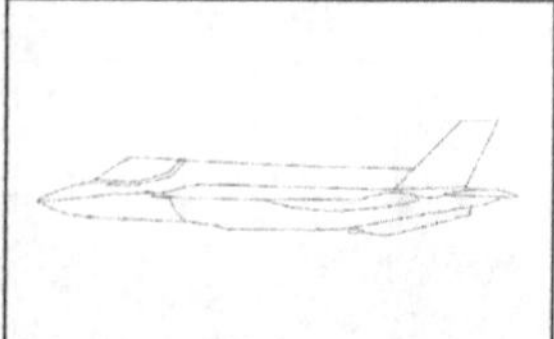

D

17.

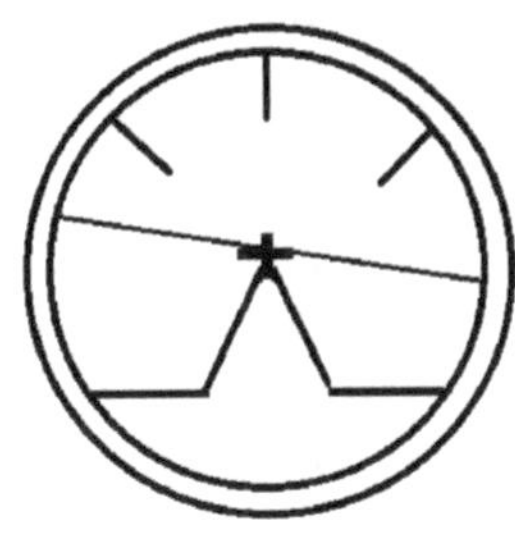

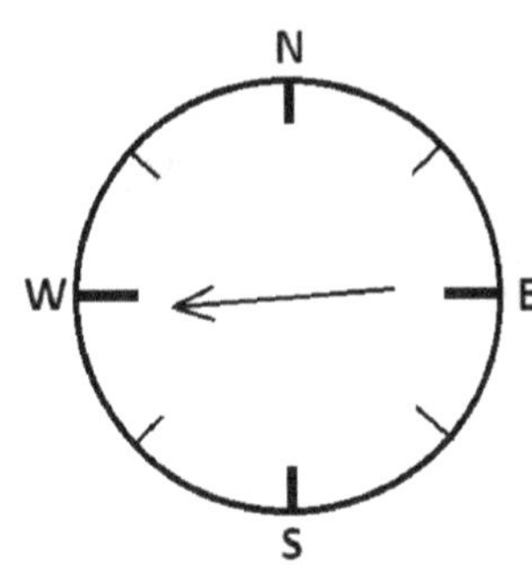

Artificial Horizon

Compass

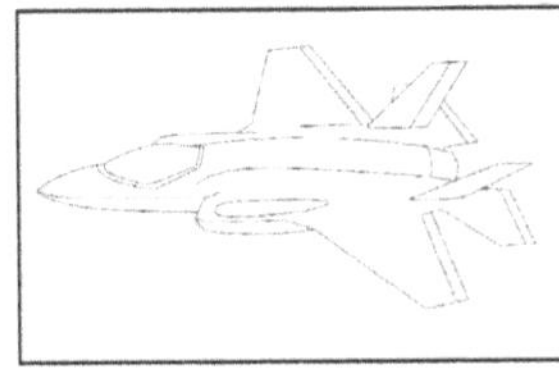

A

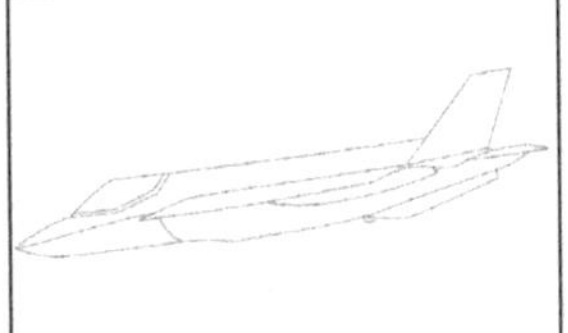

B

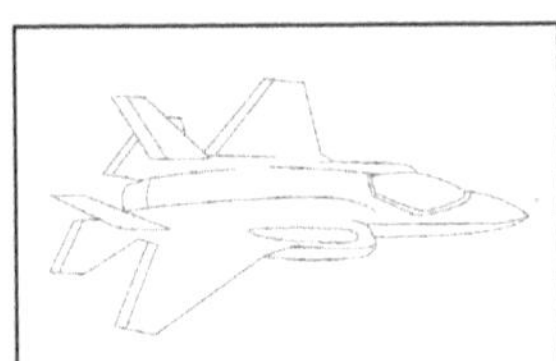

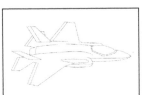

C

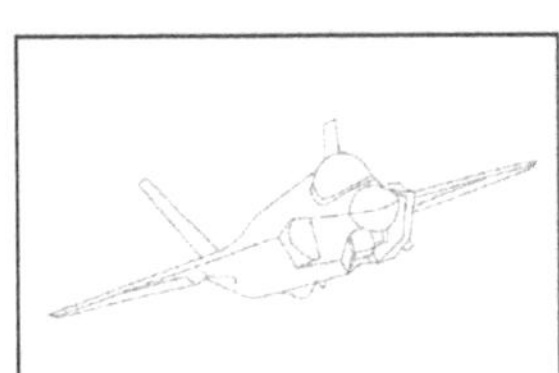

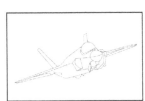

D

18.

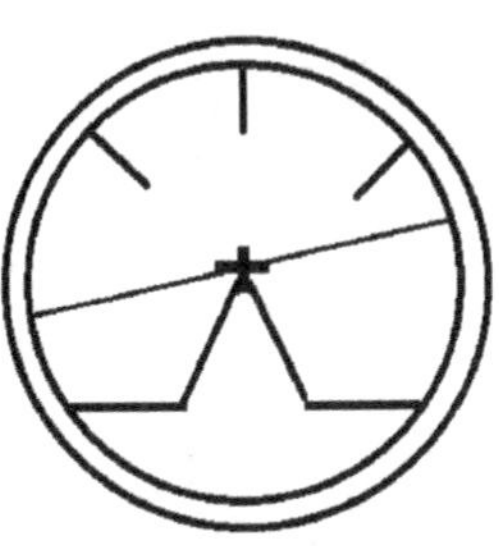

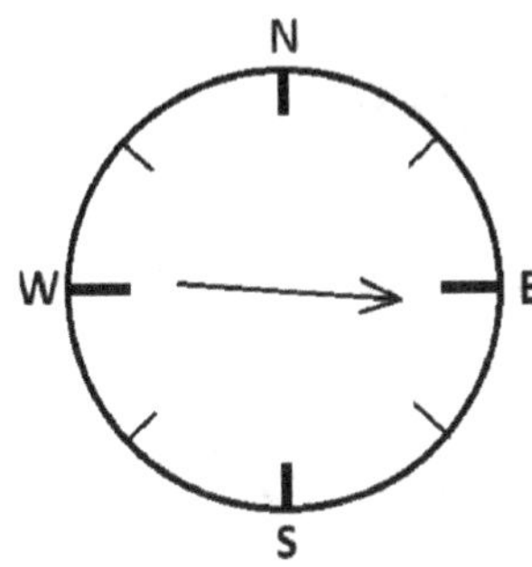

Artificial Horizon

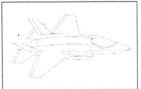

Compass

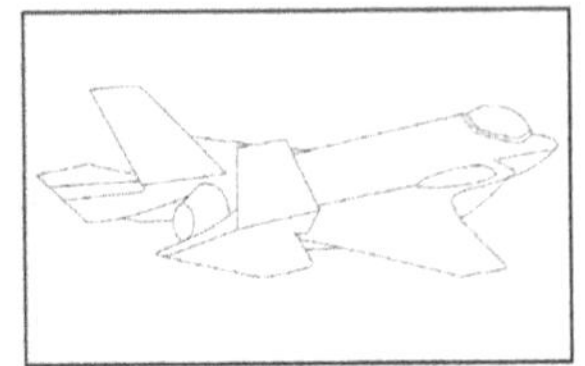

A

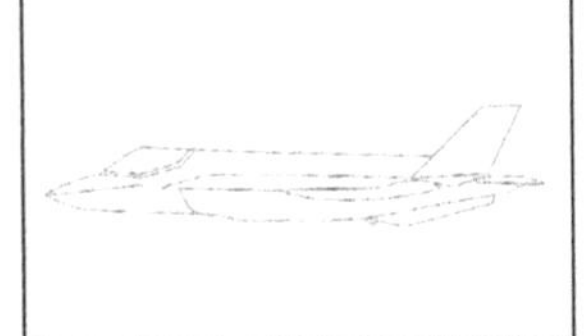

B

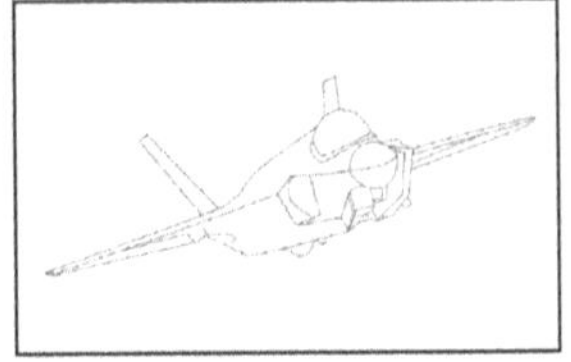

C

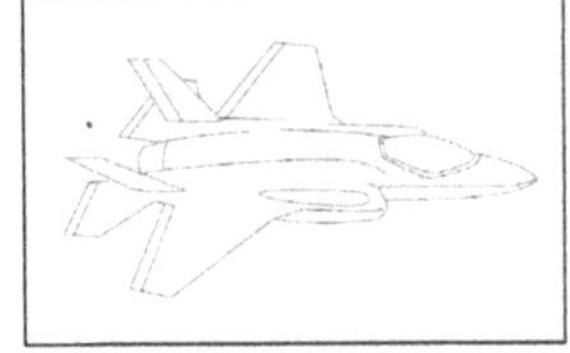

D

19.

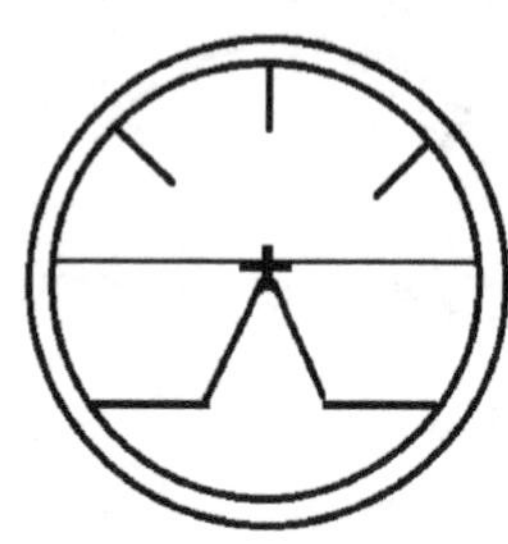

Artificial Horizon

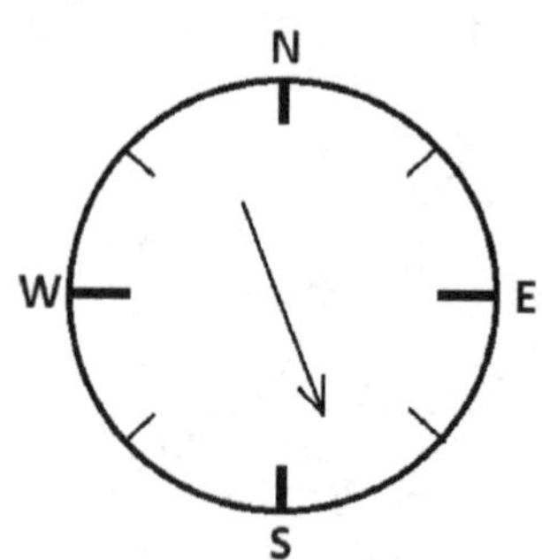

Compass

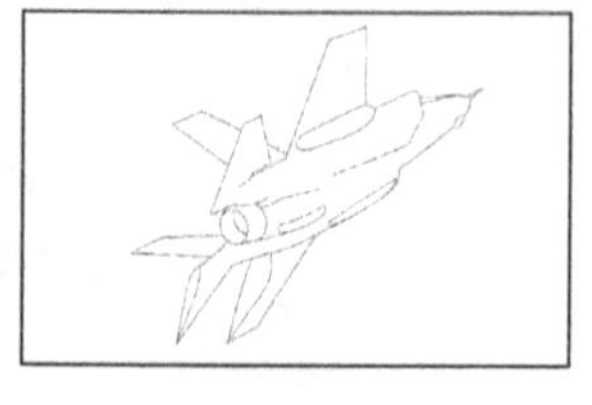

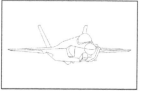

A

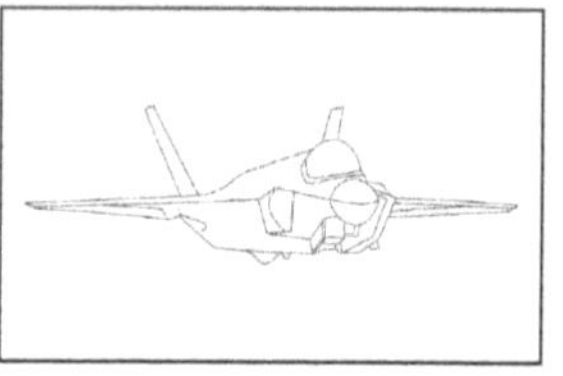

B

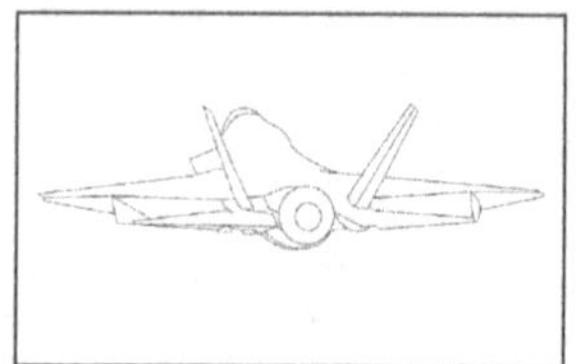

C

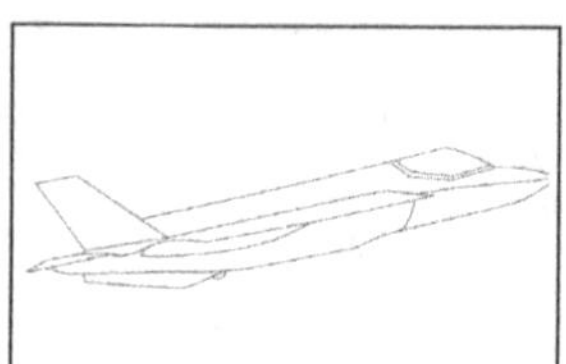

D

20.

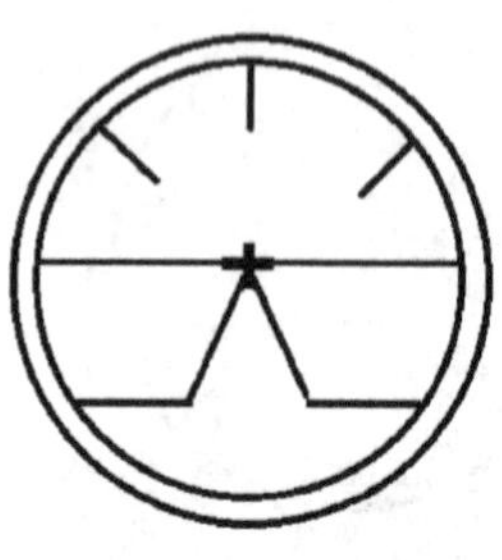

Artificial Horizon

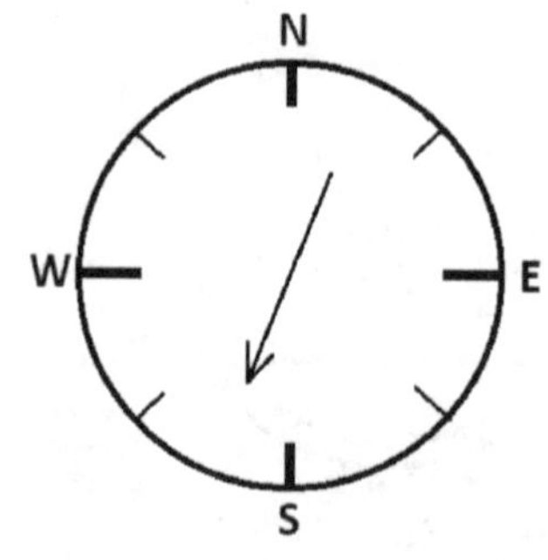

Compass

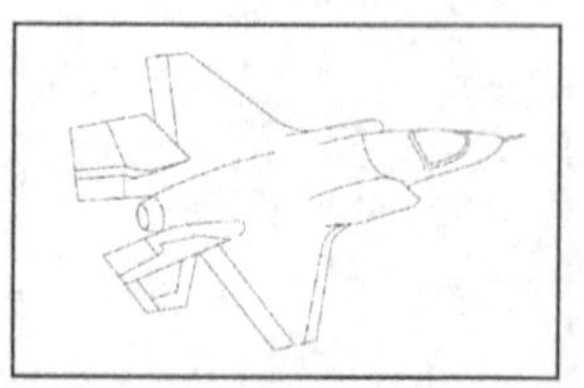

A

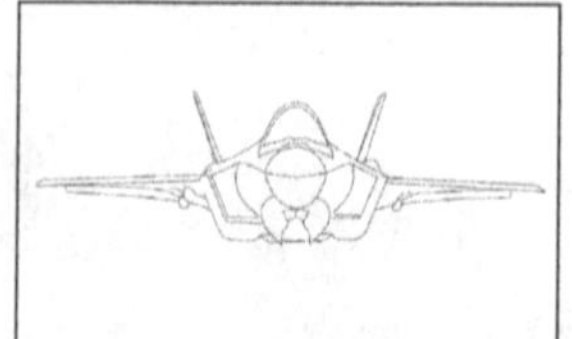

B

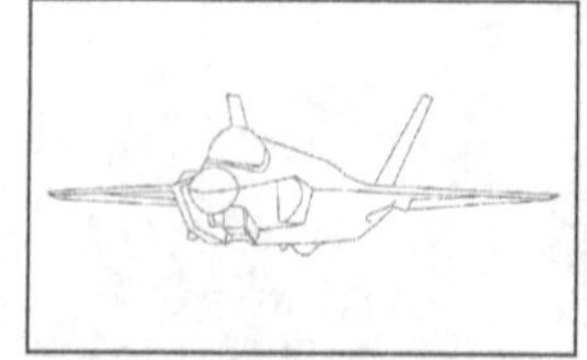

C

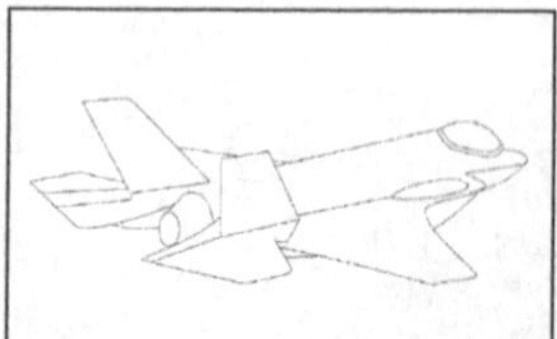

D

21.

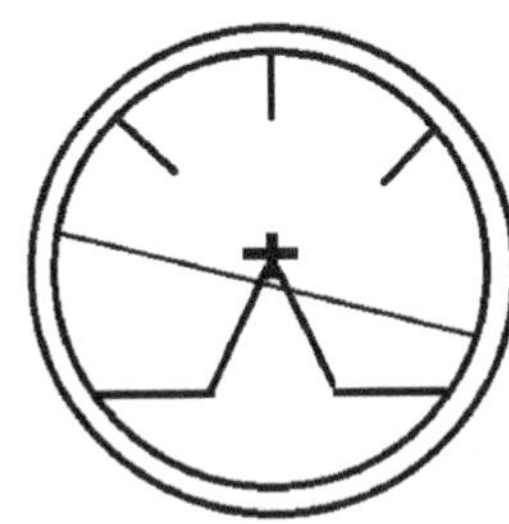

Artificial Horizon

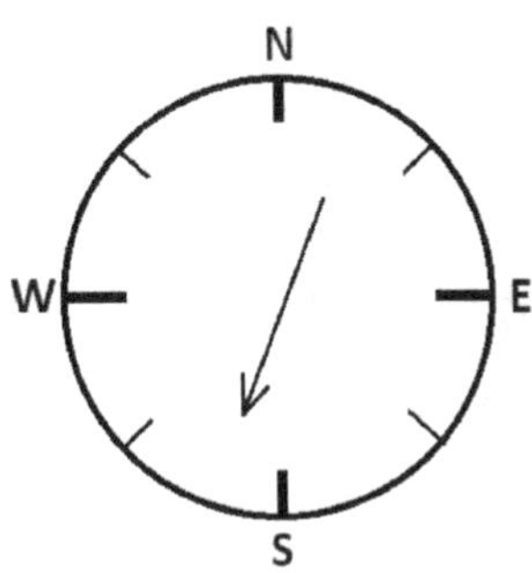

Compass

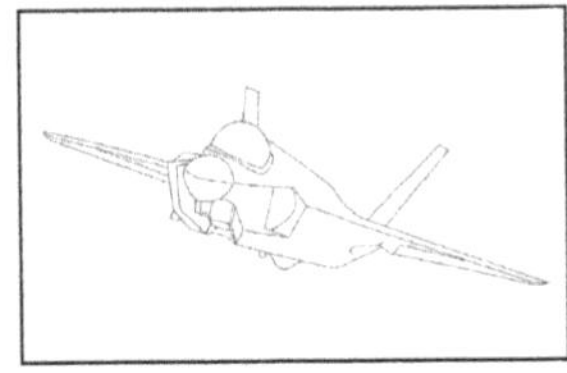

A

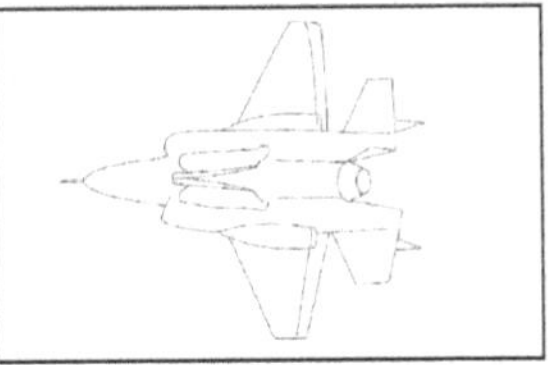

B

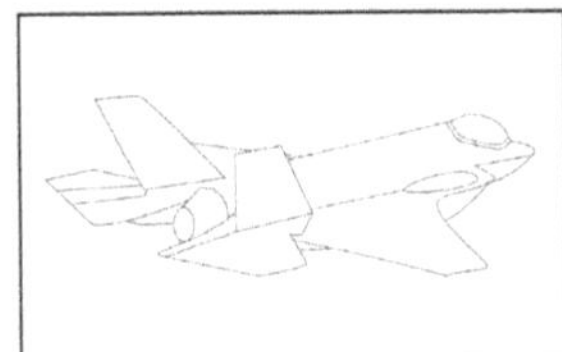

C

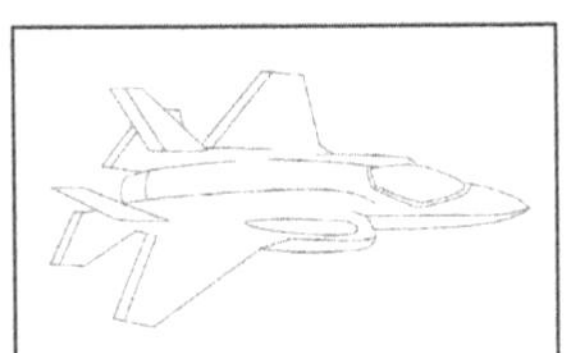

D

22.

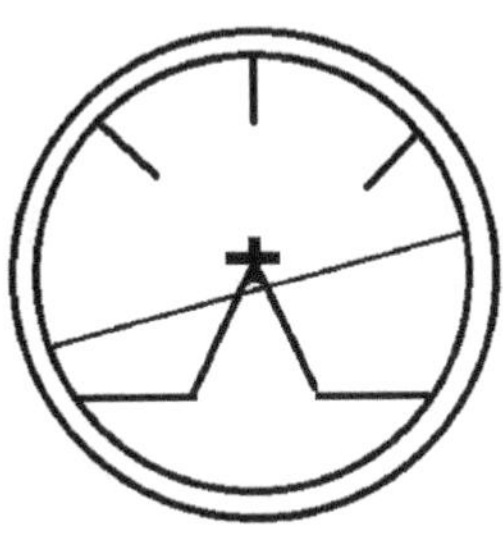

Artificial Horizon

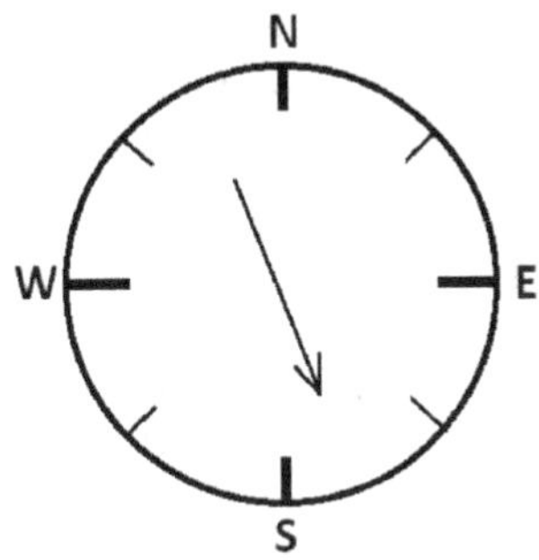

Compass

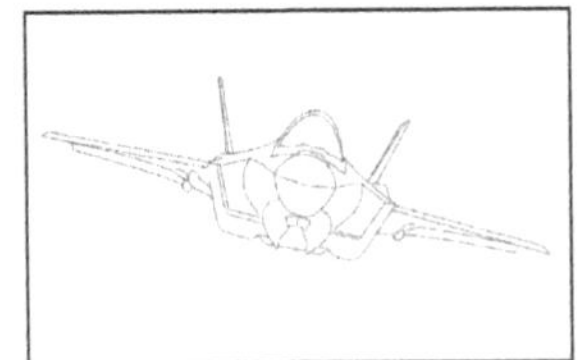

A

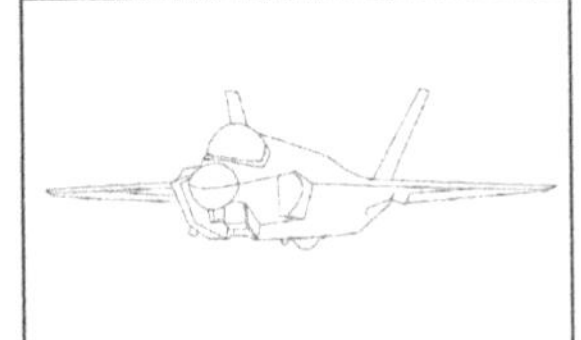

B

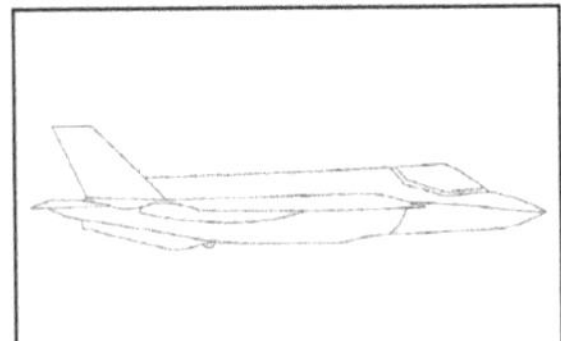

C

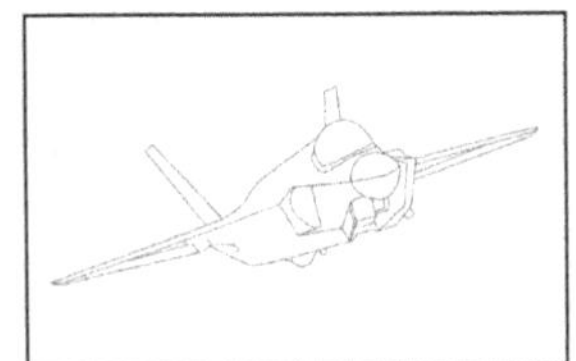

D

23.

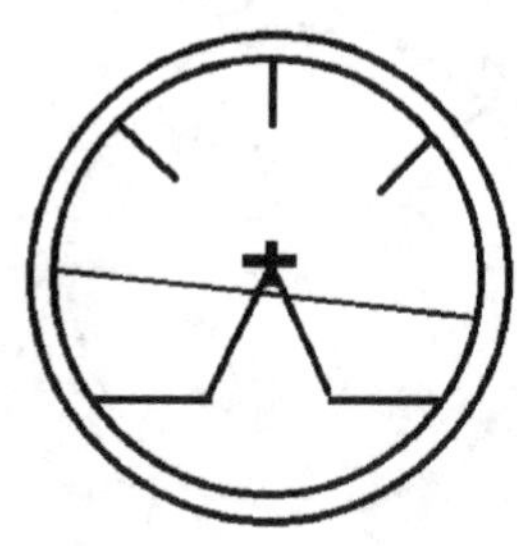

Artificial Horizon

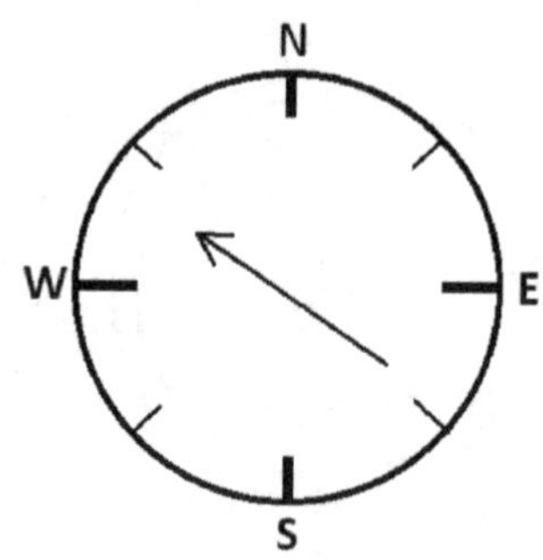

Compass

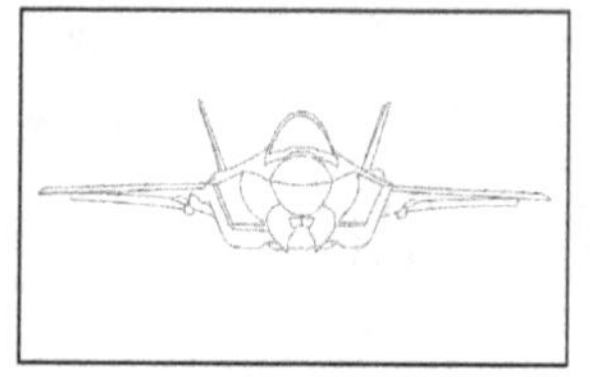

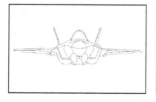

A

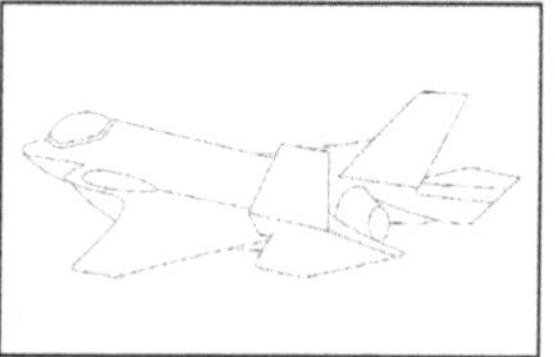

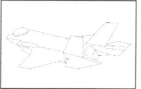

B

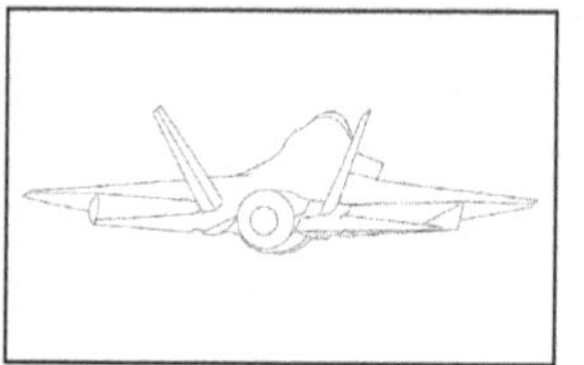

C

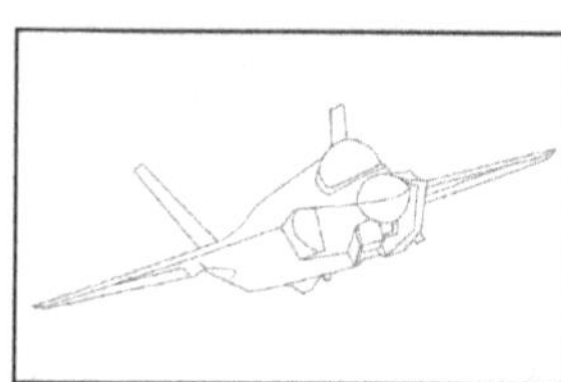

D

24.

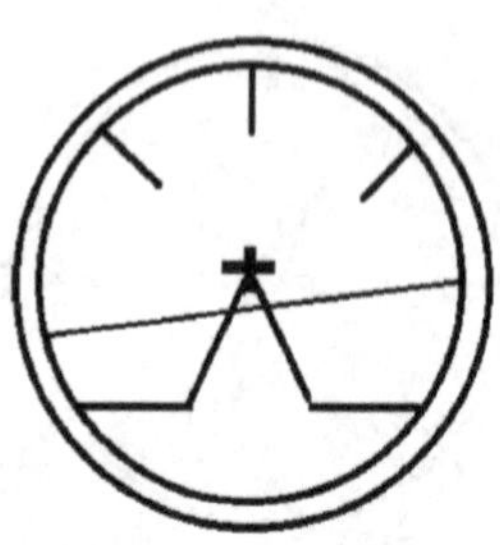

Artificial Horizon

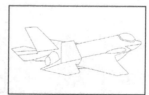

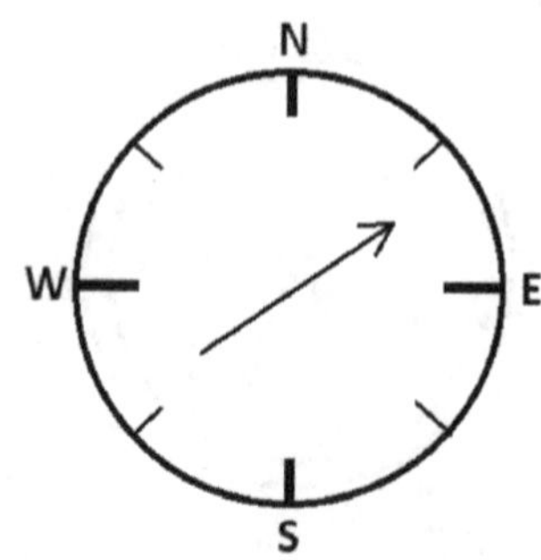

Compass

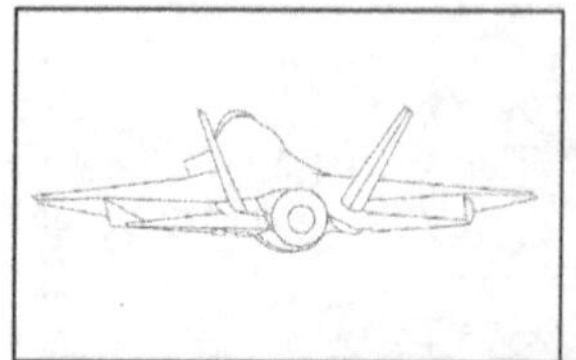

A

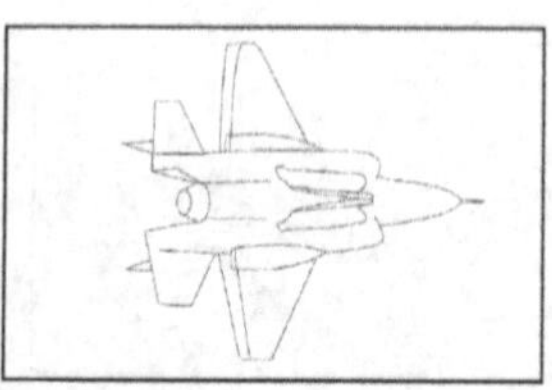

B

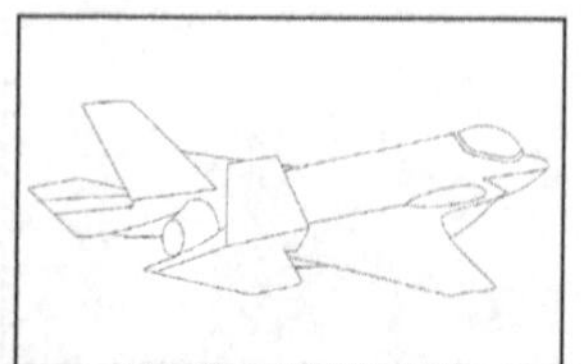

C

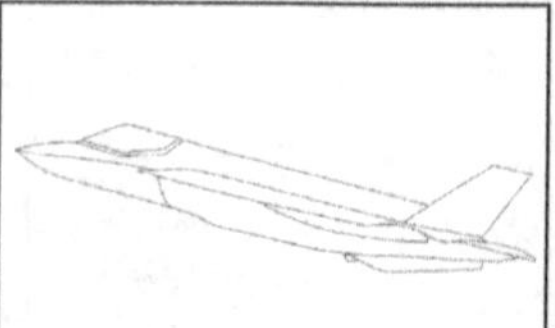

D

25.

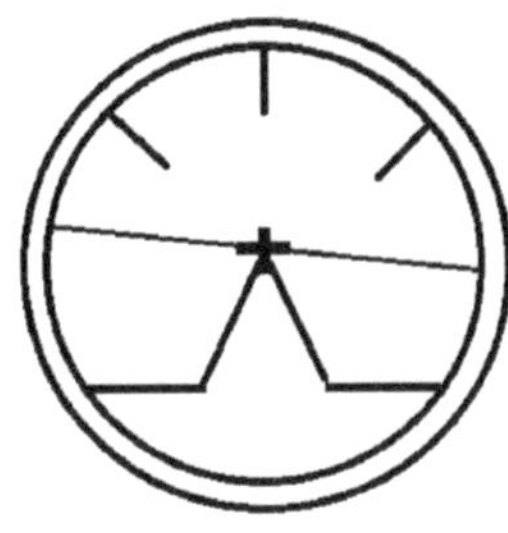

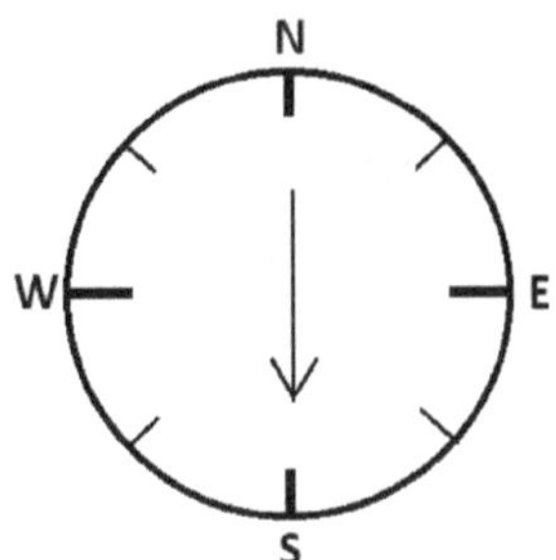

Artificial Horizon

Compass

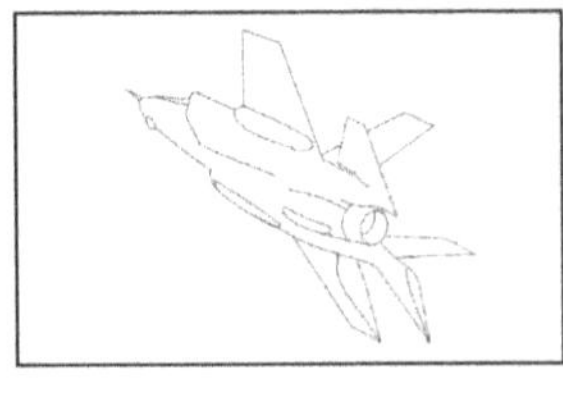

A

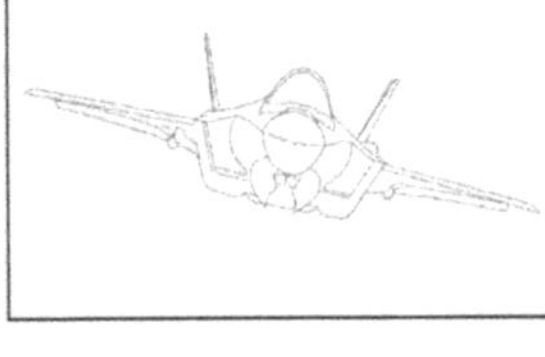

B

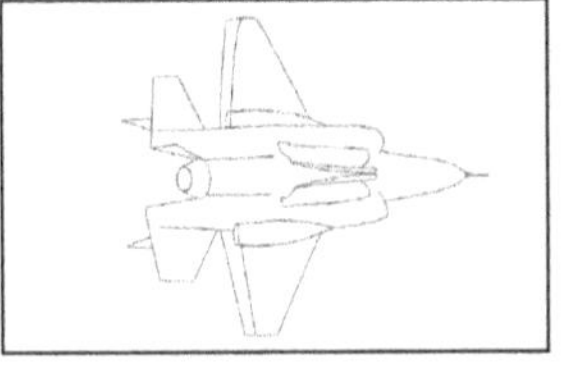

C

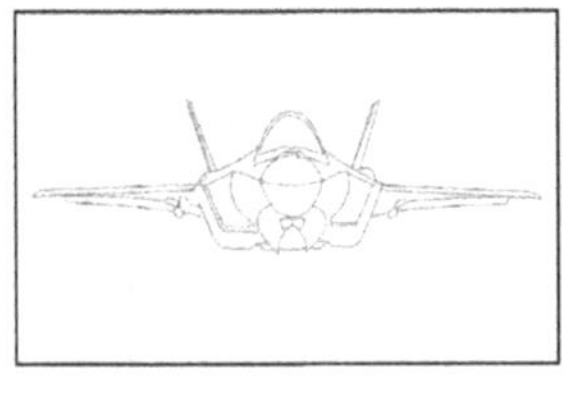

D

Verbal Analogies

Select the answer choice that most closely completes the analogy.

1. DOLL is to TOY as BASEBALL CAP is to
   a. Baseball
   b. Hat
   c. Head
   d. Sports

2. LEMON is to FRUIT as
   a. Peel is to potato
   b. Potato is to peel
   c. Carrot is to vegetable
   d. Apple is to vegetable

3. PLANE is to PILOT as CAR is to
   a. Chauffeur
   b. Cashier
   c. Telemarketer
   d. Doctor

4. SHOES are to FEET as
    a. Feet are to legs
    b. Glasses are to eyes
    c. Feet are to dancing
    d. Glasses are to seeing

5. NOTE is to MUSIC as
    a. Dancing is to music
    b. Flute is to music
    c. English is to language
    d. Letter is to writing

6. TWO is to FOUR as EIGHT is to
    a. Sixteen
    b. Twelve
    c. Seven
    d. Twenty

7. CAT is to KITTEN as
    a. Bee is to larva
    b. Caterpillar is to butterfly
    c. Dog is to wolf
    d. Larva is to bee

8. CUBA is to HAVANA as RUSSIA is to
    a. Japan
    b. Dublin
    c. Moscow
    d. Seattle

9. MOUSE is to CAT as
    a. Cat is to bear
    b. Fly is to spider
    c. Goat is to sheep
    d. Dog is to wolf

10. ONION is to TEARS as
    a. Pepper is to sneeze
    b. Salt is to taste
    c. Salt is to pepper
    d. Pepper is to spice

11. GLOVES are to COLD as SUNGLASSES are to
    a. Rain
    b. Summer
    c. Spring
    d. Sun

12. SOFT is to TOUCH as
    a. Music is to dancing
    b. Sound is to song
    c. Noise is to hearing
    d. Hearing is to noise

13. VACUUM is to DYSON as COMPUTER is to
    a. Mouse
    b. Phone
    c. Dell
    d. Laptop

14. TRIED is to TRY as
    a. Climbed is to climb
    b. Write is to wrote
    c. Fish is to fishing
    d. Thought is to thinking

15. LAMP is to LIGHT as AIR CONDITIONER is to
    a. Electricity
    b. Cool
    c. Heat
    d. Gas

16. ADDITION is to MATH as
    a. Subtraction is to division
    b. Language is to English
    c. Spanish is to English
    d. Painting is to Art

17. SALMON is to FISH as PARAKEET is to
    a. Rodent
    b. Bird
    c. Tree
    d. Flower

18. CLOTH is to DRESS as
    a. Second is to minute
    b. Needle is to thread
    c. Hour is to minute
    d. Thread is to needle

19. ONE HUNDRED is to TEN as FORTY-NINE is to
    a. Twelve
    b. Seven
    c. Six
    d. Two hundred

20. COW is to CALF as
    a. Kitten is to cat
    b. Goose is to gander
    c. Chicken is chick
    d. Fish is to lake

21. THUNDER is to LIGHTNING as
    a. Rain is to snow
    b. Spark is to flame
    c. Bud is to leaf
    d. Heat is to fire

22. WISCONSIN is to MINESOTA as TEXAS is to
    a. Maine
    b. California
    c. Oklahoma
    d. Florida

23. CHEF is to KNIFE as
    a. Carpenter is to hammer
    b. Plumber is to hatchet
    c. Screwdriver is to carpenter
    d. Car is to mechanic

24. MOTORCYCLE is to VEHICLE as NECKLACE is to
    a. Wear
    b. Neck
    c. Locket
    d. Jewelry

25. TULIP is to BULB as
    a. Leaf is to branch
    b. Oak is to acorn
    c. Blossom is to flower
    d. Pinecone is to pine tree

26. PIG is to BACON as is to COW is to
    a. Mutton
    b. Eggs
    c. Ham
    d. Steak

27. SPICE is to PEPPER as
    a. Organ is to heart
    b. Grapes are to wine
    c. Water is to life
    d. Soda is to drink

28. SWIM is to SWAM as CATCH is to
    a. Catching
    b. Caught
    c. Has caught
    d. Did catch

29. SPAGHETTI is to PASTA as
    a. Bird is to Robin
    b. Batman is to Robin
    c. Bird is to Batman
    d. Robin is to bird

30. SCREEN is to TELEVISION as HINGE is to
    a. Chair
    b. Table
    c. Door
    d. Window

31. FIVE is to TWENTY-FIVE as
    a. Seven is to forty-nine
    b. Four is to forty
    c. Six is to twelve
    d. Ten is to fifty

32. CAIRO is to EGYPT as LONDON is to
    a. France
    b. England
    c. Ireland
    d. Spain

33. KITCHEN is to COOK as
    a. Pool is to swim
    b. Hot dog is to grill
    c. Slide is to park
    d. Hair is to cut

34. CAR is to ROAD as BOAT is to
    a. River
    b. Pilot
    c. Water
    d. Sky

35. FLU is to FEVER as
    a. Pneumonia is to lungs
    b. Tumor is to cancer
    c. Brain is to stroke
    d. Cold is to congestion

36. BOUGHT is to TAUGHT as RUNNING is to
    a. Will hold
    b. Playing
    c. Ran
    d. Jumps

37. DAISY is to FLOWER as
    a. Maple is to tree
    b. Mind is to body
    c. Song is to music
    d. Dance is to song

38. COLD is to SHIVER as HEAT is to
    a. Fire
    b. Spark
    c. Sweat
    d. Warm

39. BANK is to RIVER as
    a. Ocean is to beach
    b. Beach is to coast
    c. Ocean is to waves
    d. Coast is to ocean

40. LEAF is to BUD as TREE is to
    a. Seed
    b. Acorn
    c. Oak
    d. Root

41. PERSIAN is to CAT as
    a. Dolphin is to whale
    b. Dalmatian is to dog
    c. Tree is to elm
    d. Flower is to seed

42. HURRICANE is to OCEAN as
    a. Bird is to owl
    b. Tornado is to land
    c. Lightning is to thunderstorm
    d. Hail is to snow

43. RIDDLE is to SPHINX as SONG is to
    a. Dance
    b. Sound
    c. Singer
    d. Music

44. HARP is to INSTRUMENT as
    a. Smartphone is to phone
    b. Phone is to cell phone
    c. iPhone is to Android
    d. Android is to iPhone

45. HAMMER is to NAIL as SCREWDRIVER is to
    a. Philips
    b. Screw
    c. Bolt
    d. Chisel

46. OVEN is to BAKER as
    a. Salon is to stylist
    b. Plumber is to sink
    c. Jack is to mechanic
    d. Electrician is to wires

47. SIX is to EIGHTEEN as TWELVE is to
    a. Seventeen
    b. Forty
    c. Five
    d. Thirty-six

48. MONTANA is to UNITED STATES as
    a. Ontario is to Canada
    b. Canada is to Alberta
    c. Montreal is to Canada
    d. Montreal is to Quebec

49. CHINESE is to FOOD as PITBULL is to
    a. Cat
    b. Poodle
    c. Fight
    d. Dog

50. APPLE is to CORE as
    a. Petal is to stem
    b. Peach is to pit
    c. Peel is to banana
    d. Pork is to beans

Table Reading

Select the correct coordinates from the table values.

X-Value (columns), Y-Value (rows)

Y \ X	-15	-14	-13	-12	-11	-10	-9	-8	-7	-6	-5	-4	-3	-2	-1	0	1	2	3	4	5	6	7	8	9	10	11	12	13	14	15
15	64	2	8	74	64	46	42	74	74	95	60	97	68	25	10	43	84	44	87	89	9	52	71	45	1	78	13	69	25	13	62
14	55	13	14	42	43	44	82	15	46	93	53	78	47	56	77	83	40	89	5	4	71	15	80	86	51	48	2	95	93	51	32
13	92	72	18	4	51	90	22	14	79	27	53	53	3	86	78	94	59	76	30	39	97	94	3	64	8	20	86	30	37	89	60
12	80	25	12	67	14	78	27	16	19	47	99	61	50	61	75	78	3	62	72	59	37	85	83	85	13	45	31	50	75	19	50
11	62	44	78	54	54	95	76	5	66	83	52	81	93	83	24	89	53	32	29	37	12	4	85	16	39	32	38	19	90	79	66
10	41	90	35	57	35	97	22	24	58	16	88	17	4	29	51	18	37	5	45	42	28	45	2	25	37	43	97	28	20	99	54
9	41	49	26	43	50	56	60	21	72	74	95	7	50	52	45	1	37	23	68	98	25	86	3	37	67	80	53	15	35	92	15
8	53	50	6	44	7	75	16	78	23	49	33	47	7	55	60	50	61	82	72	6	74	61	11	75	76	75	9	16	91	81	56
7	14	48	60	22	6	33	46	79	48	72	29	89	76	56	14	81	35	7	53	55	49	60	56	92	45	10	62	52	64	71	33
6	90	94	52	80	34	26	96	1	22	45	29	96	50	70	71	8	37	10	33	47	13	26	29	48	57	58	74	34	10	77	92
5	3	60	89	47	90	85	49	56	1	44	10	93	31	19	69	52	34	20	91	65	44	93	40	37	59	99	92	86	10	85	23
4	37	50	90	83	64	18	69	28	40	53	24	77	16	10	19	54	70	47	72	5	70	10	77	14	93	63	42	61	76	49	29
3	43	77	16	73	18	30	51	70	2	82	87	39	47	72	90	38	21	61	95	34	57	60	72	99	76	17	64	67	4	98	36
2	6	71	36	70	14	88	8	18	19	38	56	24	13	52	70	79	26	76	16	91	71	8	9	44	95	76	43	94	9	86	87
1	69	4	27	63	68	3	55	3	33	16	6	16	4	52	26	82	71	6	11	18	79	30	55	35	37	3	47	15	68	4	18
0	47	83	5	48	91	37	71	83	82	93	68	42	74	6	44	26	64	76	16	74	22	6	84	70	34	42	11	29	38	64	34
-1	99	46	76	95	43	6	50	70	87	72	89	60	23	28	41	88	23	17	43	4	48	73	59	53	89	81	77	84	86	17	44
-2	55	50	16	85	61	41	10	79	36	46	90	13	21	60	98	72	20	55	66	37	22	41	12	13	1	26	18	44	78	74	78
-3	81	85	56	82	8	56	87	84	23	47	49	59	90	53	99	65	15	83	78	32	77	97	40	18	90	65	18	5	25	62	9
-4	28	89	83	14	17	75	56	51	14	77	41	57	10	82	9	94	21	89	35	70	48	18	17	13	64	63	31	74	12	98	43
-5	62	92	9	4	49	17	86	90	75	8	48	75	86	45	54	60	86	6	47	62	34	36	98	38	69	47	66	93	61	14	60
-6	14	14	26	91	50	23	66	23	29	39	17	38	72	44	8	95	13	36	90	45	44	18	36	88	3	11	76	61	74	58	86
-7	12	93	94	72	38	95	12	51	56	88	9	71	76	99	10	23	78	2	76	85	97	19	69	19	21	30	72	66	66	16	70
-8	71	97	45	37	62	4	93	81	47	43	40	83	90	92	59	84	96	84	51	61	47	67	65	6	72	71	37	75	67	80	78
-9	24	89	81	46	85	18	52	25	10	97	26	20	49	70	46	11	94	70	86	96	97	3	27	63	31	9	53	72	60	53	25
-10	41	97	4	15	33	79	37	74	38	93	56	8	86	3	55	93	28	41	96	67	7	16	65	89	82	5	36	18	76	2	94
-11	27	95	94	82	20	30	31	81	59	94	95	99	45	8	7	94	11	59	23	62	3	36	62	90	79	71	13	4	64	83	7
-12	19	5	84	33	76	11	17	5	11	35	85	3	49	23	1	35	71	42	42	55	85	63	47	98	75	82	98	71	55	55	5
-13	11	62	19	31	92	61	12	66	12	72	99	75	87	13	10	39	37	3	52	49	41	8	95	92	75	45	30	86	91	96	28
-14	20	33	24	76	89	51	80	14	29	55	7	13	59	66	72	30	52	26	59	59	94	44	91	1	24	89	14	60	51	5	62
-15	72	25	55	75	16	98	73	85	77	21	39	84	85	78	59	24	47	32	65	74	13	58	55	90	35	9	43	5	9	28	63

	X	Y	A	B	C	D	E
1.	1	-9	94	3	19	1	98
2.	0	-6	8	37	77	95	91
3.	13	3	67	98	4	14	45
4.	-8	-7	14	51	56	78	22
5.	1	-12	71	33	97	47	76
6.	-13	10	12	31	55	18	35
7.	10	-2	24	73	26	52	17
8.	15	-7	14	41	75	90	70
9.	-4	10	17	81	73	7	1
10.	2	-3	14	4	99	83	15
11.	-3	6	51	50	8	14	77
12.	-14	13	19	15	72	11	10
13.	-10	-4	77	75	81	22	34

14.	8	4	21	52	97	35	14
15.	7	-7	66	1	69	34	25
16.	0	-9	4	65	33	11	41
17.	5	-8	47	99	28	79	17
18.	10	11	11	32	33	14	15
19.	15	8	55	42	56	13	37
20.	9	-3	14	17	15	87	90
21.	-7	7	48	88	74	84	2
22.	-11	-10	45	86	43	33	41
23.	-4	-11	53	23	73	84	99
24.	-13	12	3	12	53	22	64
25.	-9	-6	66	4	9	19	67
26.	-4	9	65	7	53	74	27
27.	4	5	15	77	65	31	12
28.	8	-1	9	12	33	77	53
29.	6	-10	69	29	48	54	16
30.	0	0	26	11	2	42	79
31.	-7	-2	18	99	36	3	61
32.	-15	2	15	6	21	29	45
33.	15	-4	27	55	43	83	87
34.	9	-14	13	15	89	92	24
35.	-7	-11	5	59	27	39	43
36.	9	-2	97	39	64	18	1
37.	2	1	6	29	4	13	81
38.	10	-7	59	15	33	30	65
39.	12	14	13	95	47	62	59
40.	1	5	63	14	34	78	86

Aviation Information

1. What altitude is displayed on the aircraft altimeter?
   - A. Radar
   - B. Density
   - C. Calibrated
   - D. Above Ground Level
   - E. Pressure

2. What occurs as a result of a forward center of gravity?
   - A. Difficulty applying downward pitch
   - B. Decreased stability
   - C. Longer range
   - D. Difficulty applying upward pitch
   - E. Decreased roll responsiveness

3. What type of environmental condition(s) yields the greatest aircraft performance?
    - A. Sea level and cold
    - B. High altitude and cold
    - C. High altitude and hot
    - D. Sea level and hot
    - E. Humid

4. Describe how to recover from a stall…
    - A. Decrease power and increase pitch
    - B. Increase power and increase pitch
    - C. Decrease pitch and increase power
    - D. Decrease pitch and decrease power
    - E. Increase power and add left or right rudder

5. Dead Reckoning navigation involves…
    - A. Using landmarks to pinpoint position
    - B. Using VORs and TACANs to pinpoint position
    - C. Utilizing a previously known position and using time and distance equations to estimate present position
    - D. GPS to estimate position
    - E. Determining position by only using a compass

6. In flight, the rudder controls…
    - A. Pitch
    - B. Yaw
    - C. Roll
    - D. Power
    - E. Speed

7. What effect do flaps have on landing distance?
    - A. Decrease
    - B. None
    - C. Increase
    - D. Decrease on wet runways only
    - E. Increase on wet runways only

8. When the aircraft yoke or control wheel is moved to the right, what happens to the right aileron?
    - A. Remains neutral
    - B. Moves upward
    - C. Moves downward
    - D. Initially moves upwards then downwards
    - E. Initially moves downwards then upwards

9. How does ice accumulated on the aircraft's wings affect the stall speed?
   A. No effect
   B. Decrease
   C. Decrease at high altitude
   D. Decrease at low altitude
   E. Increase

10. What conditions are conducive to fog formation?
   A. High temperature-dew point spread and high winds
   B. Dry desert areas and high winds
   C. Thunderstorms nearby and calm winds
   D. Low temperature-dew point spread and calm winds, especially in low lying valleys and coastal areas
   E. Hurricanes and high winds

11. In straight and level flight with the autopilot disengaged, after adding power or thrust the aircraft will…
   A. Descend
   B. Remain level
   C. Climb
   D. Roll to the right
   E. Roll to the left

12. What type of aircraft has the most severe wake turbulence?
   A. Heavy, slow, gear up, flaps up
   B. Light, slow, gear up, flaps up
   C. Heavy, fast, gear down, flaps deployed
   D. Light, fast, gear down, flaps deployed
   E. Heavy, fast, gear down, flaps up

13. What must be done to maintain altitude in a turn?
   A. Nothing
   B. Decrease pitch
   C. Decrease power
   D. Add rudder
   E. Increase pitch

14. What flight control is used to mitigate adverse yaw in a turn?
   A. Aileron
   B. Spoilers
   C. Flaps
   D. Rudder
   E. Aileron trim

15. Air Traffic Control orders a pilot discretion descent from 12000′ to meet a 3000′ crossing restriction. Using a 3 degree descent profile, how far away from the 3000′ constraint must the descent be initiated?

A. 5 miles
B. 10 miles
C. 20 miles
D. 30 miles
E. 38 miles

16. In calm winds, what happens to fuel consumption as the aircraft climbs?

A. No change
B. Decreases
C. Increases
D. Increases up to 10,000′ then decreases
E. Decreases up to 5,000′ then increases

17. What effect does a tailwind have on takeoff distance?

A. None
B. Decreases
C. Increases
D. Decreases on contaminated runways only
E. Increases on contaminated runways only

18. What is the best airspeed for maximum fuel endurance?

A. Maximum lift and lowest drag known as L/D Max
B. Minimum lift and highest drag known as L/D Max
C. Maximum lift and highest drag known as Vne
D. Just above aircraft stall speed

19. When is the magnetic compass most accurate?

A. Climb
B. Descent
C. Straight and level flight
D. Right turn
E. Left turn

20. An aircraft has a ground speed of 120 knots. How long will it take to travel 20 nautical miles?

A. 1 minute
B. 2 minutes
C. 5 minutes
D. 10 minutes
E. 30 minutes

Block Counting

GROUP 1

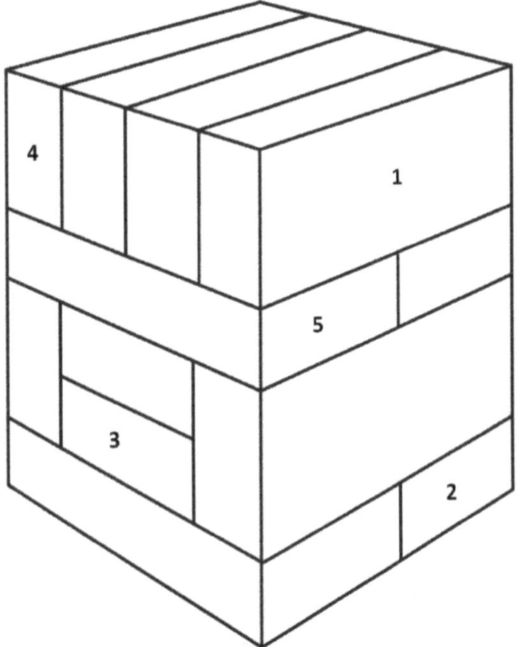

1. Block 1 is touched by ___ blocks.
    A. 1
    B. 2
    C. 3
    D. 4
    E. 5

2. Block 2 is touched by ___ blocks.
    A. 4
    B. 2
    C. 6
    D. 3
    E. 1

3. Block 3 is touched by ___ blocks.
    A. 4
    B. 5
    C. 1
    D. 3
    E. 2

4. Block 4 is touched by ___ blocks.
   A. 2
   B. 4
   C. 6
   D. 2
   E. 3

5. Block 5 is touched by ___ blocks.
   A. 7
   B. 8
   C. 3
   D. 4
   E. 5

GROUP 2

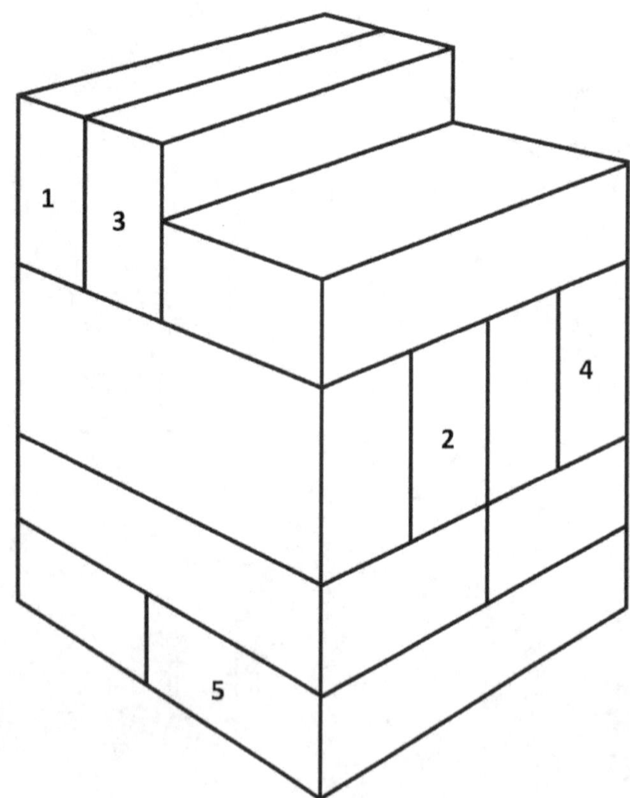

1. Block 1 is touched by ___ blocks.
   A. 2
   B. 3
   C. 4
   D. 5
   E. 6

2. Block 2 is touched by ___ blocks.
   A. 5
   B. 8
   C. 2
   D. 1
   E. 6

3. Block 3 is touched by ___ blocks.
   A. 5
   B. 6
   C. 3
   D. 2
   E. 7

4. Block 4 is touched by ___ blocks.
   A. 5
   B. 4
   C. 1
   D. 8
   E. 6

5. Block 5 is touched by ___ blocks.
   A. 1
   B. 2
   C. 3
   D. 5
   E. 6

GROUP 3

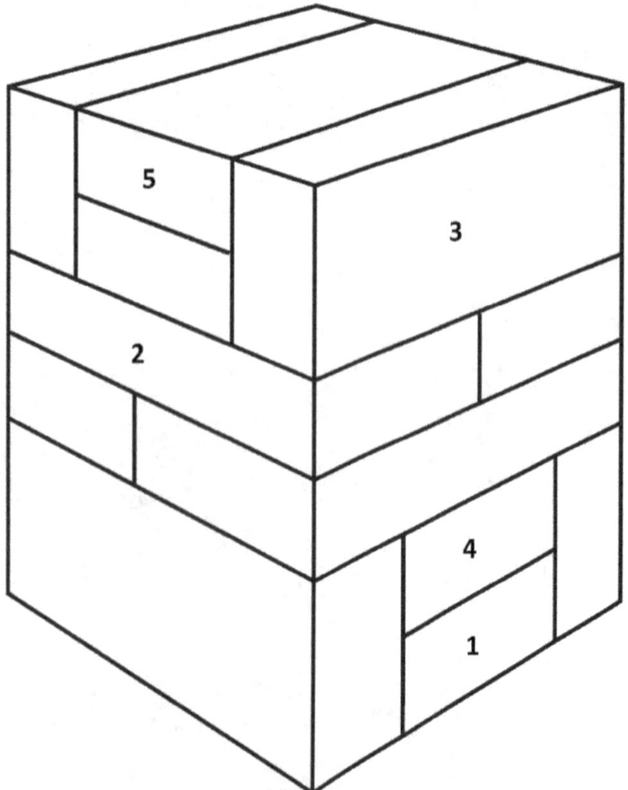

1. Block 1 is touched by ___ blocks.
   A. 4
   B. 3
   C. 1
   D. 2
   E. 5

2. Block 2 is touched by ___ blocks.
   A. 5
   B. 7
   C. 6
   D. 2
   E. 3

3. Block 3 is touched by ___ blocks.
   A. 4
   B. 3
   C. 2
   D. 1
   E. 5

4. Block 4 is touched by ___ blocks.
    A. 4
    B. 3
    C. 5
    D. 1
    E. 7

5. Block 5 is touched by ___ blocks.
    A. 1
    B. 2
    C. 3
    D. 4
    E. 5

GROUP 4

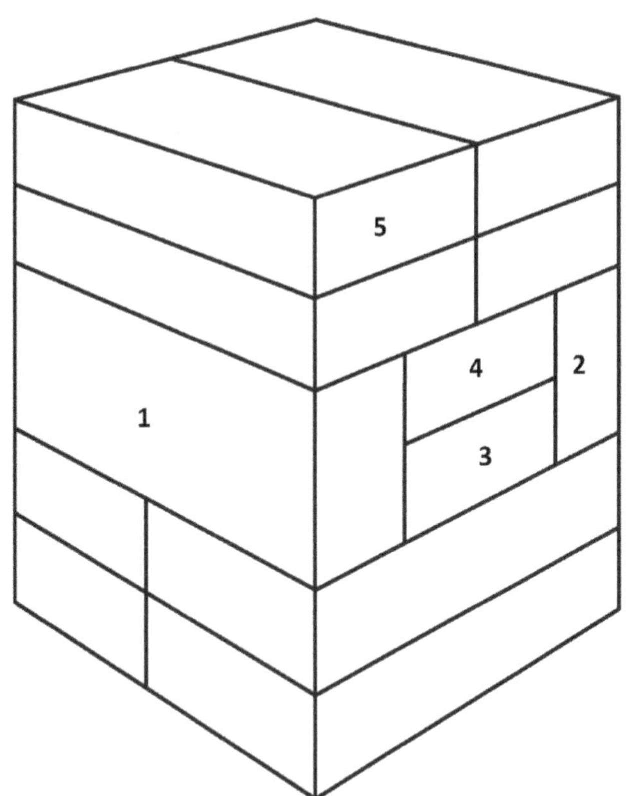

1. Block 1 is touched by ___ blocks.
    A. 5
    B. 3
    C. 4
    D. 7
    E. 2

2. Block 2 is touched by ___ blocks.
    A. 3
    B. 4
    C. 5
    D. 6
    E. 2

3. Block 3 is touched by ___ blocks.
    A. 4
    B. 6
    C. 3
    D. 5
    E. 2

4. Block 4 is touched by ___ blocks.
    A. 1
    B. 2
    C. 4
    D. 6
    E. 5

5. Block 5 is touched by ___ blocks.
    A. 4
    B. 6
    C. 8
    D. 1
    E. 2

GROUP 5

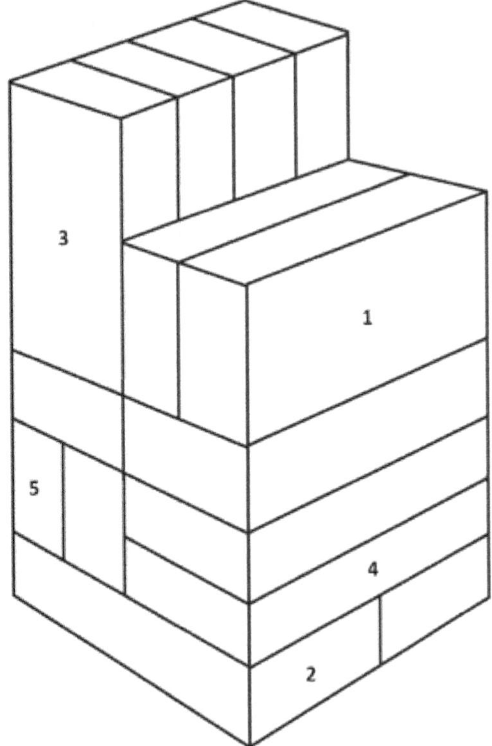

1. Block 1 is touched by ___ blocks.
   A. 1
   B. 3
   C. 2
   D. 4
   E. 5

2. Block 2 is touched by ___ blocks.
   A. 4
   B. 3
   C. 5
   D. 1
   E. 2

3. Block 3 is touched by ___ blocks.
   A. 2
   B. 6
   C. 5
   D. 3
   E. 1

4. Block 4 is touched by ___ blocks.
   A. 3
   B. 5
   C. 2
   D. 6
   E. 4

5. Block 5 is touched by ___ blocks.
   A. 4
   B. 3
   C. 5
   D. 6
   E. 2

GROUP 6

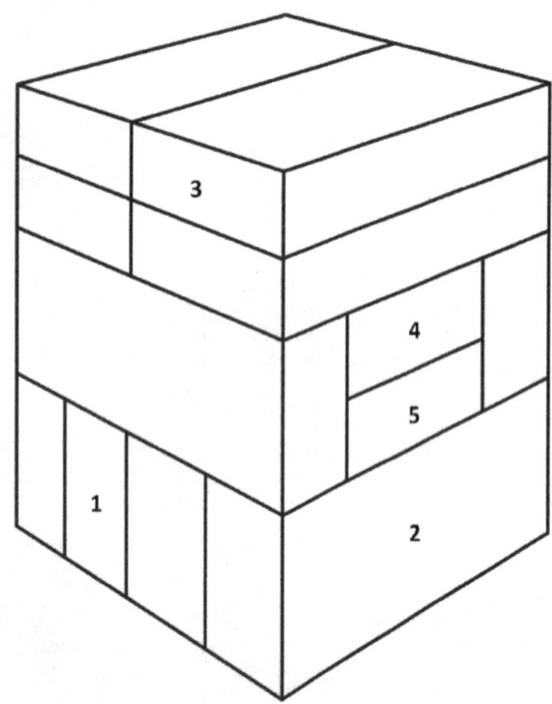

1. Block 1 is touched by ___ blocks.
   A. 4
   B. 3
   C. 2
   D. 6
   E. 5

2. Block 2 is touched by ___ blocks.
   A. 3
   B. 4
   C. 5
   D. 2
   E. 6

3. Block 3 is touched by ___ blocks.
   A. 4
   B. 6
   C. 5
   D. 2
   E. 1

4. Block 4 is touched by ___ blocks.
   A. 5
   B. 4
   C. 3
   D. 1
   E. 6

5. Block 5 is touched by ___ blocks.
   A. 6
   B. 4
   C. 3
   D. 2
   E. 7

Arithmetic Reasoning

1 — Emma borrowed a total of $1,200 with simple interest. She took the loan for as many years as the rate of interest. If she paid $432 in interest at the end of the loan period, what was the rate of simple interest on the loan?

A. 5
B. 15
C. 9
D. 6

2 — In mathematics class, you have taken five tests and your average test grade is 91%. On the next test, your grade is 78%. What is your new test average?

A. 84.5
B. 90.5
C. 87.5
D. 88.8

3 — Jorge and his younger sister Alicia have ages that combine to a total of 42. If their ages are separated by eight years, how old is Alicia?

A. 25
B. 32
C. 17
D. 11

4 — You are making a budget for your money very carefully. Buying a smoothie each day costs $3.59 during the week and $3.99 on weekends. How much does your weekly budget allow, if you have a smoothie each work day and one day on the weekend?

A. $22.74
B. $23.54
C. $23.94
D. $21.94

5 — Four out of twenty-eight students in your class must go to summer school. What is the ratio of the classmates who do not go to summer school in lowest terms?

A. 6/7
B. 1/7
C. 4/7
D. 3/7

6 — Gourmet cookies are regularly priced at 89 cents each. Approximately how much is each cookie if one and a half dozen sell for $12.89?

A. 65 cents
B. 82 cents
C. 72 cents
D. 80 cents

7 — Which of the following is not an integer?

A. 0
B. 1
C. -45
D. All of the answer choices are integers

8 — Subtracting a negative number is the same as adding a __________ number.

A. Positive
B. Negative
C. Zero
D. Irregular

9 — What are the factors of 128?

A. 2
B. 2, 64
C. 2, 4, 8, 16
D. 1, 2, 4, 8, 16, 32, 64, 128

10 — What are the two even prime numbers?
A. 0, 2
B. -2, 2
C. Cannot answer with the information given
D. There is only one even prime number

11 — What are the prime factors of 128?
A. 2
B. 2, 3
C. 2, 4, 8, 16, 32, 64
D. Cannot answer with the information given

12 — What is the proper "name" for the following: [(52 + 25) + 3] / 58x
A. An equation
B. An expression
C. A polynomial
D. An exponent

13 — What is the Greatest Common Factor (GCF) of 16 and 38?
A. 2
B. 16
C. 19
D. Cannot determine with the information given

14 — What is the Least Common Multiple (LCM) of 5 and 8?
A. 13
B. 40
C. 80
D. Cannot determine with the information given

15 — What is the value of 7! ?
A. 127
B. 3,490
C. 5,040
D. 12,340

16 — Which of the following is an irrational number?
A. $\sqrt{4}$
B. $\sqrt{9}$
C. $\sqrt{17}$
D. All of the above

17 — A "20% off" sale is on at the men's store. The new shirt that you want is priced at $27.95. Your final cost will include a 6% sales tax. How much will you pay for the shirt?
A. $22.36
B. $20.68
C. $23.70
D. $24.03

18 — Henrietta and her younger brother Henry have ages that combine to a total of 96. If their ages are separated by twelve years, how old is Henry?

A. 38
B. 40
C. 42
D. 44

19 — Subtracting a negative number results in what type of operation?

A. Adding a positive number
B. Adding a negative number
C. An irrational number
D. A prime number

20 — A coffee shop sells an average of 16 coffees per hour. The shop opens at 6:00 in the morning and closes at 5:30 in the afternoon. If each coffee costs $3.05, how much does the shop make in one day?

A. $581.95
B. $561.20
C. $545.29
D. $672.00

21 — At Wilson Elementary School, the sixth grade class includes 38 students in a class. Sixteen of the students are male. What percent of the class is female?

A. 42%
B. 58%
C. 56%
D. 62%

22 — What is the value of $x^{1/2}$?

A. -x
B. $\sqrt{x}$
C. x^2
D. 2x

23 — What is the Greatest Common Factor (GCF) of 15 and 36?

A. 2
B. 3
C. 4
D. 5

24 — What the relationship between 240 and 2?

A. =
B. >
C. <
D. None of the above

25 — What is the value of f ? $f = (2^{-2} * 8) / (0.5 * 4)$

A. √2
B. 1
C. 4
D. Cannot determine with the information given

26 — The Ice Cream Shoppe sells an average of 70 ice cream cones per hour. The shop opens at 10:30 in the morning and closes at 11:30 in the evening. If half of the ice cream cones sold cost $3.00 and half of the ice cream cones sold cost $4.50, how much does The Ice Cream Shoppe make in one day?

A. $840.00
B. $1,255.50
C. $2,420.75
D. $3,412.50

27 — Which of the following is an integer?

A. 9.75
B. 5 1/2
C. √2
D. 21

28 — What are the prime factors of 14?

A. 1, 14
B. 1, 2, 7, 14
C. 1, 2, 3, 5, 7, 11, 14
D. None of the above

29 — At Walla Wall High School, there are a total of 857 students. Twenty four of the students are in the TAG program. Half of the students in the TAG program are male. Eighty per cent of the seniors in the TAG program have been accepted at Ivy League universities. What percent of the student body is NOT in the TAG program?

A. 88%
B. 92.3%
C. 97.2%
D. 99.3%

30 — You are now "on your own", and have decided to create a basic budget to track your income and expenses. Buying a coffee at Starbucks each day during weekdays costs your $3.89. On the weekends, you indulge yourself with a $6.20 super smoothie at a health store both days. How much will your weekly "drink allowance" cost you per year?

A. $834.50
B. $852.20
C. $1,656.20
D. $4,190.00

31 — Write the √63 in simplest form.
A. 3√7
B. √9 * √7
C. 7√9
D. 7√3

32 — Write the √(45 / 7) in simplest form.
A. 3√7
B. √9 * √7
C. 3/7 √35
D. 7√3

33 — The decimal value for √78 lies between which integer pair?
A. 6 and 7
B. 7 and 8
C. 8 and 9
D. 9 and 10

34 — Write the $\sqrt{(72s^3b^7)}$ in simplest form.
A. $6bs\sqrt{2sb^6}$
B. $6bs\sqrt{2s^2b^3}$
C. $6b^2s\sqrt{2sb^3}$
D. $6b^3s\sqrt{(2sb)}$

35 — The decimal value of 7/11 is ________________?
A. 1.57
B. 0.70
C. 0.6363…
D. 0.77

36 — The decimal value of 5/8 is ________________?
A. 0.625
B. 0.650
C. 0.635
D. 0.580

37 — The fractional value of 0.5625 is ________________?
A. 7/15
B. 11/23
C. 5/8
D. 9/16

38 — The fractional value of 0.3125 is ________________?
A. 5/16
B. 4/24
C. 6/19
D. 9/25

39 — Express 17/10,000 in scientific notation.
A. $17 * 10^{-3}$
B. $17 * 10^{-4}$
C. $1.7 * 10^{-3}$
D. $1.7 * 10^{-4}$

40 — Express 736.589 in scientific notation.
A. 7.36589 * 10-3
B. 7.36589 * 10-2
C. 7.36589 * 103
D. 7.36589 * 102

Mathematics Knowledge

1 — If x = 15, find the value of f in the following equation: $f = (x^2 /3) - 8$
A. 67
B. 667
C. 57
D. 83

2 — What does 638,000 signify in scientific notation?
A. 6.38 * 1000
B. $6.38 * 10^5$
C. $6.38 * 10^{-5}$
D. 638 * 1000

3 — Solve the following ratio: 11! / 8! [note: this ratio could also be expressed like this: 11! : 8!]
A. (11/8)!
B. 1.375
C. 990
D. 12.5

4 — What is the value of 8^3 ?
A. 64
B. 48
C. 24
D. 512

5 — Solve for the unknown variable P: P = (Q + 7) (Q + 3)
A. 2Q+10
B. $Q^2 + 10Q + 21$
C. $Q^2 + 4Q + 21$
D. $Q^2 + 4Q + 10$

6 — Place the following fractions in order from largest to smallest: 3/5, 1/4, 3/8, 5/9.
A. 1/4, 3/8, 3/5, 5/9
B. 5/9, 3/8, 3/5, 1/4
C. 1/4, 3/5, 3/8, 5/9
D. 3/5, 5/9, 3/8, 1/4

7 — What is the mode of the following sequence of numbers? 2, 3, 3, 5, 5, 5, 7, 7, 8, 10, 10, 12
A. 3
B. 5
C. 10
D. 12

8 — If a kid's toy rocket is designed to shoot half-a-mile into the air, but it only goes up 70% of that height, how many yards in altitude did the toy rocket reach?
A. 422
B. 610
C. 616
D. 921

9 — If y = 4, given the following equation, what is the value of x? x = (2y - 5) ÅÄ 2
A. 0.2
B. 1.5
C. 39
D. 40

10 — Solve the following ratio and express it in simplest form: 36:4!
A. 1:1
B. 1.5:1
C. 3.5:1
D. 64:1

11 — What percentage of 20 is 15?
A. 15%
B. 20%
C. 50%
D. 75%

12 — 12 is 15% of some number. What is 20% of that same number?
A. 8
B. 12
C. 16
D. 24

13 — If x = 3, find the value of f in the following equation: $f = (x^2 /3) - 3$
A. -3
B. 0
C. 3
D. 6

14 — What is the mode of the following sequence of numbers?
2, 3, 3, 3, 5, 5, 7, 7, 8, 10, 10, 12, 12, 13, 13, 14, 14, 15, 15

A. 3
B. 5
C. 10
D. 12

15 — What is the value of 13^3 ?

A. 160
B. 170
C. 176
D. 2,197

16 — Assume that X is 60% of Y, and Y is 80% of Z. If Z is 40, what is the value of X?

A. 4.8
B. 19.2
C. 20.4
D. 22.6

17 — Place the following fractions in order from largest to smallest: 2/5, 1/3, 3/7, 5/8.

A. 5/8, 2/5, 3/7, 1/3
B. 1/3, 2/5, 3/7, 5/8
C. 5/8, 3/7, 2/5, 1/3
D. Cannot determine with the information given

18 — A brown bag contains 4 yellow, 3 violet, and 4 black balls. All of the balls are of different sizes. Two balls are chosen from the bag. How many combinations can result in the selection of at least 1 yellow ball?

A. 12
B. 34
C. 48
D. 64

19 — If x and y are natural numbers, what are the possible solutions for x and y for the following equation: $3x + 2y = 11$

A. (1,4)
B. (4,1)
C. (3, 1) and (4,1)
D. (1,4) and (3,1)

20 — What is the average weight of the group of watermelons (listed below) that were delivered to Joe's Corner Store, and how much should Joe pay if he is paying $0.32/pound?
Watermelon weight: 6, 7, 7, 9, 12, 12, 15, 23, 23

A. 11.46 pounds; $32.45
B. 12.67 pounds; $36.48
C. 16.73 pounds; $45.22
D. 26.80 pounds; $45.22

21 — Is the value of Y a prime number, assuming A = 2? $Y = [(A^3 + A) / 2] - 2$
A. Yes
B. No
C. Cannot determine from the information given
D. No, but the value of Y is a polynomial

22 — Solve the following equation for R, assuming that $\beta = 36$ and $\mu = 144$: $R = (\sqrt{\beta} * \sqrt{\mu}) / (\beta - \mu)$
A. -0.67
B. 1.56
C. 1.94
D. Cannot determine with the information provided

23 — What is the average weight of the group of apples shown below that were delivered to Jack's Deli, and how much should Jack pay if he is paying $0.86/pound?
Apple weight: 6, 7, 7, 7.5, 8, 8, 9.5, 11, 11
A. 5.54 pounds; $62.45
B. 8.33 pounds; $64.50
C. 11.3 pounds; $75.25
D. 16.9 pounds; $88.50

24 — Solve the following equation to determine the value of Z: $Z = (R + 5)(R + 30)$
A. $R^2 + 35R + 35$
B. $R + 35R + 150$
C. $R^2 + 35R + 150$
D. $R^4 + 35R^2 + 150$

25 — If NASA produced a rocket booster that is designed to launch three-and-a-half miles into the air before dropping away into the ocean below, but it only went up 92% of that desired height, how many feet in altitude did the rocket booster reach, rounded to the nearest ten feet?
A. 14,224
B. 14,380
C. 17,000
D. 23,560

26 — Evaluate the expression $7x^2 + 9x - 18$ for $x = 7$.
A. 516
B. 424
C. 388
D. 255

27 — Evaluate the expression $x^2 + 7x - 18$ for $x = 5$.
A. 56
B. 42
C. 38
D. 25

28 — Evaluate the expression $7x^2 + 63x$ for $x = 27$.

A. 5603
B. 4278
C. 6804
D. 6525

29 — Simplify the expression $35a^4b^3c^2 + 65a^6b^7c^4$.

A. $5a^4b^3c^2 (7 + 13a^2b^4c^2)$
B. $5 (7a^4b^3c^2 + 13a^6b^7c^4)$
C. $5b^3 (7a^4c^2 + 13a^6b^4c^4)$
D. $5b^3a^4 (7c^2 + 13a^2b^4c^4)$

30 — Multiply the binomials $(x+3) (x-7)$.

A. $x^2 - 4x + 21$
B. $x^2 + 4x + 21$
C. $x^2 + 4x + 21$
D. $x^2 - 4x - 21$

Word Knowledge

1 — Expansive most nearly means:

A. Costly
B. Vast
C. Sensible
D. Competitive

2 — Credible most nearly means:

A. Enthusiastic
B. Dishonest
C. Reliable
D. Professional

3 — Devastation most nearly means:

A. Sadness
B. Restoration
C. Clarity
D. Destruction

4 — Vague most nearly means:

A. Unclear
B. Specific
C. Pessimistic
D. Gloomy

5 — Irreverent most nearly means:
A. Religious
B. Disrespectful
C. Humorous
D. Boring

6 — Aversion most nearly means:
A. Attraction
B. Inclination
C. Optimism
D. Distaste

7 — Laborious most nearly means:
A. Difficult
B. Laid-back
C. Noisy
D. Lonely

8 — Interminable most nearly means:
A. Dull
B. Valuable
C. Endless
D. Rushed

9 — Achromatic most nearly means:
A. Time-related
B. Non-romantic
C. Without color
D. Before history

10 — Cursory most nearly means:
A. Ungodly
B. Rapid
C. Not smooth
D. In a circular motion

11 — Hearsay most nearly means:
A. Bovine
B. Secondhand information that can't be proven
C. Taking place in arid regions
D. Communicative

12 — Magnanimous most nearly means:
A. Latin
B. Large quantities of liquid
C. Forgiving
D. Antipasta

13 — Terrestrial most nearly means:
A. Of the earth
B. Ordinary
C. Something that exists in a "miniature" environment
D. Foreign

14 — Nonchalant most nearly means:
A. Magnanimous
B. Hurried
C. Indifferent
D. Positive

15 — Palpable most nearly means:
A. Tangible
B. Unconcerned
C. Capable of being manipulated
D. Easygoing

16 — Daub most nearly means:
A. Suave
B. Plaster
C. Heinous
D. Muddy

17 — Distend most nearly means:
A. Enforce
B. Soften
C. Swell
D. Indemnify

18 — Gaffe most nearly means:
A. Taciturn
B. Mistake
C. Fishlike
D. Cane

19 — Papal most nearly means:
A. Lightweight
B. Regal
C. Downtrodden
D. Leader of Catholicism

20 — Tarry most nearly means:
A. Delay
B. Black
C. Mossy
D. Cold

21 — Hoopla most nearly means:
- A. Cavernous
- B. Heinous
- C. Commotion
- D. Sweet

22 — Doctrinaire most nearly means:
- A. Negative
- B. Dogmatic
- C. Insipid
- D. Diffident

23 — Plumose most nearly means:
- A. Shy
- B. Sly
- C. Furry
- D. Feathery

24 — Supplant most nearly means:
- A. Amplify
- B. Clarify
- C. Uproot
- D. Stabilize

25 — Vagary most nearly means:
- A. Limitless
- B. Wispy
- C. Capable
- D. Caprice

26 — Calamari most nearly means:
- A. Shamu
- B. Digit
- C. Squid
- D. Matrimony

27 — Lethargic most nearly means:
- A. Apathetic
- B. Cozy
- C. Bouncy
- D. Deadly

28 — Teensy most nearly means:
- A. Adolescent
- B. Immature
- C. Tiny
- D. Feminine

29 — Bland most nearly means:
A. Common
B. Solid
C. Rakish
D. Dull

30 — Fulsome most nearly means:
A. Cruel
B. Copious
C. Graceful
D. Handy

31 — Nomenclature most nearly means:
A. Jealousy
B. Name
C. Steadiness
D. Aggression

32 — Reluctant most nearly means:
A. Casual
B. Timid
C. Intense
D. Unwilling

33 — Shabby most nearly means:
A. Feline
B. Horrid
C. Despicable
D. Miserly

34 — Alms most nearly means:
A. Holiness
B. Burn
C. Charity
D. Beverage

35 — Defer most nearly means:
A. Remove
B. Cancel
C. Quiet
D. Delay

Reading Comprehension

Passage 1:

His obsessions and wealth had brought him to own the most magnificent collection of specimens ever compiled by a single man. He had committed to and invested in the widespread slaughter of some of the most exotic bird species in the world. His greatest passion had destroyed Nature's innocence in a maelstrom of cruel arrogance. He had robbed Nature of its riches, while filling his coffers with its spoils. The ravenous hysteria shown for the rarest of feathers to adorn the hats of the fashionable rich showed no signs of abating. Parisian women were festooned in the feathers and, sometimes the whole skins, of snowy egrets, birds of paradise, ospreys and toucans. Concerning nature, man is rarely content to witness its spectacle without desiring to possess it.

1 — What is the main topic of this paragraph?

A. Fashion
B. Nature
C. Death
D. Wealth

2 — What is the speaker's main point about this topic?

A. It is more important than fashion
B. It can be destroyed by humans
C. It can cause man to be greedy
D. All of the above

3 — The final sentence is:

A. The main topic of the paragraph
B. A sentence that contrasts the main topic to another topic
C. The beginning of a new topic that is not related to the rest of the paragraph
D. None of the above

4 — In line 3 the speaker refers to the destruction of "Nature's innocence". What literary device is the speaker using here?

A. Personification
B. Alliteration
C. Metaphor
D. Simile

5 — The speaker views the destruction of the natural world:

A. As inevitable
B. Sarcastically
C. Cheerfully
D. None of the above

Passage 2:

The working-class gambler is the lowest and vilest player that ever walked amongst God's blessed Earth. Frequenting the "hells" of London by night, the nefarious gamester sustains himself upon a meagre diet of bread and quarter gin measures doled out by the degenerate owners of gambling dens in order to encourage play. The more desperate of these characters bully the weaker to play and prey upon them like hungry parasites when their luck has run its course. The impoverished gamblers, profligates and blackguards at heart, blight our great city with the moral disease of the destitute class. In contrast, the aristocratic gambler begins play at the respectable hour of three and partakes in only the most superior forms of gambling. With morality being on his side, he chooses to squander his inherited wealth with the graceful recklessness expected of his class. The pleasant, well-lit comfort of his surroundings is reflected in his affable and gentlemanly countenance. But there is one common thread of destiny that both the working-class gambler and the aristocratic gambler share alike. The destiny of the gamester will end in only poverty and despair.

6 — What is the main topic of the paragraph?

A. Social class
B. Gambling
C. Morality
D. None of the above

7 — What is the main point of the paragraph?

A. Aristocratic gamblers are immoral
B. There are more working-class gamblers than aristocratic gamblers
C. Gambling is beneficial for society
D. All gamblers will become poor in the end if they continue to gamble

8 — What is the purpose of comparing the "working-class gambler" to the "aristocratic gambler"?

A. To emphasize the differences between the working-class and the aristocracy
B. To show how immoral working-class gamblers are
C. To highlight that class difference is not important if you are a gambler because everyone, whether rich or poor, will end up destitute
D. None of the above

9 — What word best describes the speaker's tone in this paragraph?

A. Ironic
B. Uncertain
C. Resentful
D. None of the above

10 — In line 5, the speaker refers to some of the gamblers as being "like hungry parasites". What literary device is the writer using here?

A. Onomatopoeia
B. Foreshadowing
C. Metaphor
D. Simile

Passage 3:

What had I been waiting for, a sign from above, a notice from the bank, a list of instructions telling me step-by-step how to live life? I had thought for all those years that something or someone would tell me that I had been living. But in that moment, as I was staring fear directly in the face, I realized that something else had gone. I'd gone. Me. I'd simply disappeared. How had I spent forty-five years on this planet and never even realized? I couldn't have been living, because I was already too busy dying. I understood this now with perfect clarity. My death was not an event to be feared, it had already begun. I was already dead.

11 — What is the main topic of the paragraph?
A. Death
B. Fear
C. Love
D. Growing up

12 — What is the speaker's main point about this topic?
A. It is something to be resented
B. It is something to be feared
C. It is something to be laughed at
D. None of the above

13 — Which literary device does the speaker use to present their position?
A. Rhetorical questions
B. Metaphors
C. Pathetic fallacy
D. Similes

14 — The speaker views death as:
A. Inevitable
B. Transient
C. Joyful
D. None of the above

15 — What word best describes the speaker's tone in this paragraph?
A. Didactic
B. Mocking
C. Light-hearted
D. Poignant

Physical Science

1 — What is NOT one of the ways that scientists differentiate between the concentric spherical layers of the earth?
A. The material's state of matter
B. The type of rocks
C. Fossil records
D. Chemical formation

2 — What is the layer of the earth that extends approximately 40-60 miles down from the surface?
A. Mantle/asthenosphere
B. Outer core
C. Onion
D. Lithosphere

3 — What causes the phenomena known as the Aurora Borealis?
A. Weather patterns
B. Charged particles from the sun interacting with the earth's magnetic field
C. High levels of iron and silicon in the "axis" of the earth
D. The igneous rock throughout earth's crust

4 — Which of the following is NOT a type of sedimentary rock?
A. Basalt
B. Shale
C. Coal
D. Sandstone

5 — How much more energetically powerful is a seismic event measuring 6 on the Richter scale compared to an event measuring 2 on the Richter scale?
A. 4 times more energetically powerful
B. 8 times more energetically powerful
C. 1,000 times more energetically powerful
D. 1,000,000 times more energetically powerful

6 — In what atmospheric layer will you be traveling for the majority of the flight distance on a commercial airline flight from London, England to Frankfurt, Germany?
A. Troposphere
B. Stratosphere
C. Mesosphere
D. Exosphere

7 — If you are driving through a thick layer of fog, at or near sea level, you are actually passing through what type of cloud?
A. Cirrus
B. Stratus
C. Cumulonimbus
D. Cumulus

8 — Which of the following statements is true if an atom has an atomic number of 17?
A. Its valence quantity is above the critical level
B. It likely has an atomic mass that is less than 17
C. It has 17 protons
D. The sum of its protons and neutrons is at least 17

9 — Which pair of physical properties is NOT matched with its appropriate SI symbol?
A. Luminous intensity: Candela
B. Electric current: Watt
C. Pressure: Pascal
D. Temperature: Kelvin

10 — Using the common conversion factor between meters and feet, approximately how many miles would an 8K race be?

A. 4 miles
B. 4 1/2 miles
C. 5 miles
D. 6 1/2 miles

11 — What is the composition of Neptune?

A. Metamorphic rock with a thin atmosphere of methane
B. A relatively tiny rock and mineral core with an enormous thick outer layer of gas
C. An iron core covered with a thin layer of ice
D. A solid, frozen methane and frozen water surface, a liquid water middle layer and a rock and mineral core.

12 — The Asteroid Belt is located between which two planets?

A. Venus and Earth
B. Earth and Mars
C. Mars and Jupiter
D. Jupiter and Saturn

13 — What is the correct order of the taxonomy that biologists have established to describe Kingdom Animalia (i.e. animals)?

A. Phylum, order, class, family, genus, species
B. Order, phylum, class, genus, family, species
C. Phylum, class, order, genus, family, species
D. Phylum, class, order, family, genus, species

14 — What characteristic(s) do all organisms in Kingdom Animalia share?
I. Cell walls
II. Ability to actively move on their own from place to place at least at some point in their life cycle
III. A nervous system
IV. A vertebrae

A. I and III
B. II and III
C. III only
D. II only

15 — What organism or category of organism is NOT included in Kingdom Fungi?

A. Yeast
B. Molds
C. Sponges
D. Mushrooms

16 — What does the vertical axis of a taxonomy tree represent?
- A. Phyla
- B. Degree of specialization
- C. Degree of intelligence
- D. Time

17 — What is the main goal of biological evolution?
- A. To change an organism so that it is more likely to produce viable offspring
- B. To create a "better" organism
- C. To make the organism's "society" more complex
- D. To produce new species of organisms

18 — Nature "designs" organisms to improve through the process of natural __________?
- A. Selection
- B. Programming
- C. Randomness
- D. Intention

19 — What type of heavenly body is most likely to have a highly elliptical orbit that "slingshots" itself as it passes around the sun?
- A. Quasars
- B. Comets
- C. Black holes
- D. Asteroids

20 — What are the phases of water?
- A. Evaporation, condensation and sublimation
- B. Solid, liquid and gas/vapor
- C. A solute, a solvent and a solution
- D. None of the above

21 — In which era did "dinosaurs roam the earth"?
- A. Paleozoic
- B. Mesozoic
- C. Cenozoic
- D. Mesoproterozoic

22 — When does geographic speciation occur?
- A. When a population is separated by geographic change
- B. When two species meet in a common place and interbreed
- C. When one population drives another in the same geographic locale to extinction
- D. When biomes lose diversity to human activity

23 — What is the classification of rocks formed by the hardening of molten magma from deep within the earth?

A. Sedimentary
B. Metamorphic
C. Igneous
D. None of the above

24 — How do fungi reproduce?

A. Sexually
B. Asexually
C. Sometimes A, sometimes B, sometimes both A and B
D. None of the above

25 — Which brain lobe receives sensory information from the body?

A. Parietal
B. Temporal
C. Occipital
D. Frontal

26 — What is the formula for determining the weight of an object (with g = gravitational acceleration, v = velocity, m = mass, and a = acceleration)?

A. w = m*v
B. w = m^2 *a
C. w = m*g
D. w = a*g^2

27 — What is the acceleration of a train given the following facts: at time = 0, the train is moving at 43 miles/hour; at time = 3 hours 30 minutes, the train is moving at 64 miles/hour.

A. 3 miles / $hour^2$
B. 6 miles / $hour^2$
C. 21 miles / hour
D. 21 miles / $hour^2$

28 — Three different objects (choices A, B, and C) are dropped from three different heights. Which object has the most potential energy? Assume that the gravitational acceleration is a constant: 32.174 ft/s^2.

A. A 10 pound object dropped from 70 ft
B. A 58 pound object dropped from 4 yards
C. A 0.01 ton object dropped from 300 inches
D. All answer choices are equal

29 — What is the unit for work, according to the International System of Units, the internationally recognized standard metric system?

A. Newton
B. Joule
C. Watt
D. Pascal

30 — What is the "tradeoff" when using an inclined plane?
A. Less "output" force
B. Less distance the object must travel
C. Greater distance the object must travel
D. Both A and C

31 — If you want to lift a very heavy load using a simple lever (in the form of a "teeter-totter") so that the lever arm becomes horizontal, what would be an effective way to accomplish your goal?
A. Increase the applied force
B. Move the fulcrum such that the resistance arm and the effort arm are balanced
C. Increase the height of the fulcrum
D. Move the fulcrum in the direction of the load to be lifted

32 — What is the name of a simple machine that is designed to amplify force by increasing and/or decreasing the amount of torque applied at one of the interacting parts in its "system" of parts?
A. Gear
B. Pump
C. Vacuum
D. None of the above

33 — What is the definition of mechanical advantage?
A. Force : Direction
B. Output Force : Input Force
C. Direction : Magnitude
D. All of the above

34 — If a pulley is an example of a simple machine, which of the following is always true?
A. A pulley changes the magnitude of the applied force
B. A pulley changes the direction of the applied force
C. Both A and B
D. Neither A nor B

35 — How does a wedge create mechanical advantage?
A. Amplifies applied force by transmitting it from a larger surface to a smaller surface
B. Increasing the pressure along the length or the wedge
C. Converting output force to applied force
D. None of the above

36— What is the benefit of having well-greased automobile bearings?
A. Increase mechanical advantage
B. Reduces the coefficient of friction
C. Increases the acceleration of the automobile
D. None of the above

37 — Which object (O) has the least momentum?
- A. O moves at 3 ft/hour and weighs 1 ton
- B. O moves at 5,000 ft/hour and weighs 2 pounds
- C. O moves at 1,000 ft/min and weighs 25 pounds
- D. O moves at 300,000 ft/sec and weighs 0.001 pounds

38 — What "things" can change either the magnitude or the direction of a force?
- A. Inclined plane
- B. Lever
- C. Wedge
- D. All of the above

39 — Why do bicyclists use their low gear when going uphill?
- A. It increases the torque produced
- B. It decreases the number of revolutions of the pedals
- C. It reduces the need to buy lot of bicycle accessories
- D. It both increases the torque and allows you to move your legs slower

40 — Which of the following "simple machines" is NOT an example of a wedge?
- A. Knife
- B. Axe
- C. Door stop
- D. All of the examples listed ARE wedges

41 — A 5 kg mass traveling at 15 m/s needs to be stopped in 3 seconds. How much force is required?
- A. 15 Newtons
- B. 75 Newtons
- C. 25 Newtons
- D. 9 Newtons

42 — Accelerating a 3 kg mass to 12 m/s in 4.5 seconds requires how much force?
- A. 15 Newtons
- B. 0.9 Newtons
- C. 18 Newtons
- D. 8 Newtons

43 — Find your potential energy if you are on a roller coaster at the top of a 25 meter drop and your mass is 95 kg.
- A. 23,275 joules
- B. 37.25 joules
- C. 242 joules
- D. 931 joules

44 — How much kinetic energy is required to launch a 1.3 kg toy rocket to a height of 1500 meters?
- A. 11,307 joules
- B. 14,700 joules
- C. 24,305 joules
- D. 19,110 joules

45 — Find the kinetic energy for your car traveling at 80 km/hr. Assume your car is 1400 kg in mass.
A. 1,097,600 joules
B. 172,840 joules
C. 345,800 joules
D. 7856 joules

46 — What do you call an atom that has a different number of protons and neutrons?
A. Ionized
B. Charged
C. One fundamental unit — 1 amu
D. Neutral

47 — What happens when electricity passes through an inductor in a circuit board?
A. A temperature drop or rise
B. Rectification
C. A magnetic field is generated
D. Two parallel plates with a dielectric (non-conducting) material are "activated"

48 — What is the main difference between alternating current (AC) and direct current (DC)?
A. The presence or absence of a magnetic field
B. Ionization
C. The direction electrons move
D. All of the above

49 — Why is copper the metal most commonly used to make wires that carry electricity?
A. Low resistance, flexible, common
B. High resistance, rigid, common
C. Low resistance, flexible, rare
D. None of the above

50 — How does a resistor change the current and voltage in an electrical circuit?
A. Accumulating charge
B. Operating as a switch for the passage of electrons
C. Generating a magnetic field
D. Reducing the rate that electrons can flow

51 — In a circuit, the greater the resistance, the lower the __________.
A. Voltage
B. Diodes
C. Current
D. Ohm's

52 — What is the "driving force" behind the flow of current?
A. Voltage
B. Amps
C. Resistance
D. None of the above

53 — If you have a 12 volt battery that is powering a circuit with a specified internal resistance of 120 ohms, how many amps is the circuit drawing?

A. 0.064 amps
B. 0.10 amps
C. 0.12 amps
D. 10 amps

54 — What is the measurement of how much electrical current is moving through a circuit?

A. Volt (voltage)
B. Amp (ampere)
C. Bandwidth
D. Alternating current (AC)

55 — What is the measurement of the EMF exerted on electrical charge in a circuit?

A. Volt (voltage)
B. Amp (ampere)
C. Current
D. Direct current (DC)

56 — If Ohm's law says that $V = I * R$, what current results when a 6 volt battery is connected to a circuit with a resistance of 150 ohms?

A. 900 amps
B. 25 amps
C. 40 milliamperes
D. 156 amps

57 — If Ohm's Law says that $V = I * R$, what voltage must be applied to create a 10.5 ampere current in a circuit with a resistance of 50 ohms?

A. 4.8 volts
B. 525 volts
C. 0.21 volts
D. 156 volts

58 — If $V = I * R$, what is the resistance of a circuit with a 7.5 ampere current and a 6 volt power source?

A. 0.80 ohms
B. 45 ohms
C. 800 ohms
D. 1.25 ohms

59 — Current in a wire is a result of __________ mobility.

A. Nuclear
B. Neutron
C. Proton
D. Electron

60 — Electric charge motion is a result of __________________.

A. Resistance
B. Voltage
C. Heat
D. Electron

61 — Increasing the resistance will __________________ electrical current.

A. Increase
B. Decrease
C. Alternate
D. Direct

62 — Increasing the voltage will __________________ electrical current.

A. Increase
B. Decrease
C. Alternate
D. Direct

63 — Mobile charges in a wire flow __________________ a positive battery terminal.

A. Toward
B. From
C. Alternating directions
D. Can't tell from the given information

64 — Capacitors in a circuit will allow electrical current to __________________.

A. Flow with a constant current
B. Flow into the battery
C. Stop after charge is collected on the plates
D. Can't tell from the given information

Instrument Comprehension

1. A
2. D
3. B
4. A
5. C
6. B
7. D
8. C
9. A
10. B
11. D
12. C
13. A
14. D
15. B
16. C
17. A
18. D
19. B
20. C
21. A
22. D
23. B
24. C
25. B

Verbal Analogies

1. B
2. C
3. A
4. B
5. D
6. A
7. A
8. C
9. B
10. A
11. D
12. C
13. C
14. A
15. B
16. D
17. A
18. A
19. B

20. C
21. D
22. C
23. A
24. D
25. B
26. D
27. A
28. B
29. D
30. C
31. A
32. B
33. A
34. C
35. D
36. B
37. A
38. C
39. D
40. A
41. B
42. B
43. C
44. A
45. B
46. C
47. D
48. A
49. D
50. B

Table Reading

1. A
2. D
3. C
4. B
5. A
6. E
7. C
8. E
9. A
10. D
11. B
12. C
13. B
14. E

15. C
16. D
17. A
18. B
19. C
20. E
21. A
22. D
23. E
24. B
25. A
26. B
27. C
28. E
29. E
30. A
31. C
32. B
33. C
34. E
35. B
36. E
37. A
38. D
39. B
40. C

Aviation Information

1. E
2. D
3. A
4. C
5. C
6. B
7. A
8. B
9. E
10. D
11. C
12. A
13. E
14. D
15. D
16. B
17. C
18. A
19. C

20. D

Block Counting

Group 1

1. C
2. A
3. B
4. E
5. B

Group 2

1. D
2. E
3. B
4. A
5. C

Group 3

1. B
2. C
3. A
4. C
5. C

Group 4

1. A
2. C
3. D
4. E
5. E

Group 5

1. C
2. A
3. D
4. E
5. A

Group 6

1. E
2. B
3. D
4. A
5. E

Arithmetic Reasoning

1 — D. 6

The correct answer is D. Rationale: The loan was for $1,200, and the amount paid out was $432. You know that the number of years of the loan and the interest rate of the loan is the same number.

There are the four possible scenarios in the multiple choice answers:

5 — 5 years * 0.05 = 0.25 * 1,200 = $300 paid in interest
15 — 15 years * 0.15 = 2.25 * 1,200 = $2,700 paid in interest
9 — 9 years * 0.09 = 0.81 * 1,200 = $972 paid in interest
6 — 6 years * 0.06 = 0.36 * 1,200 = $432 paid in interest

This method of finding the correct answer is based on eliminating the incorrect ones as much as finding the correct one. Often the time spent trying to find an equation or formula is more than the time needed to just model the possible outcomes.

2 — D. 88.8

The correct answer is D. Rationale: If you have taken 5 tests and your average grade was 91% (0.91), then you have earned a total of 455 points out of a possible 500 points thus far; 5 * 0.91 = 4.55. If you have earned a grade of 78% on the next test, you must have gotten 78 points out of a possible 100 points which can be added to the previous total points for your grade

Therefore, you have earned 455 + 78 = 533 out of a possible 600 points. Since you have taken 6 tests, divide the number of points earned by the number of tests you have taken:

553/600 = 0.8883 or 88.83%.

3 — C. 17

The correct answer is C. Rationale: Rather than try figure out a proper formula, ask yourself, "What if Jorge and Alicia were the same age? If their combined ages are 42, then they would each be 21 years old. Since they are 8 years apart, Jorge has to "get older" by 4 years and Alicia has to "get younger" by 4 years. Therefore, add 4 years to Jorge to get 25 years of age, and subtract 4 years from Alicia to get 17 years of age. It might be good to check your results before basking in the glory of knowing how to do this problem! If Jorge + Alicia should equal 42, then 25 + 17 = 42. Check! Remember, the question is asking about Alicia's age, not Jorge's.

4 — D. $21.94

The correct answer is D. Rationale: In this scenario, you will be buying a smoothie each day during the workweek — five times — and once on the weekend. The weekend smoothie will cost slightly more. Notice that you will NOT be buying a smoothie on one of the two weekend days. The weekly cost of your smoothie consumption (SC) can be determined in the following manner:

SC = (3.59 * 5) + (3.99 * 1)
SC = 17.95 + 3.99
SC = 21.94

5 — A. 6/7
The correct answer is A. Rationale: If 4 out of 28 students ARE going to summer school, then 24 out of the 28 students ARE NOT going to summer school. Therefore, to find out the ratio, you divide 24 by 28, and then simplify your fraction by dividing both the numerator and the denominator by 4, which is the same thing as multiplying the fraction by 1 because 4/4th = 1:

24/28 = (24 / 4)/(28 / 4) = 6/7

6 — C. 72 cents
The correct answer is C. Rationale: Reading the question carefully, you will note that the regular price for the cookies is irrelevant since the question is only about the price for each cookie if you buy one and a half dozen, i.e. 18, cookies. If 18 cookies cost $12.89, then 1 cookie costs 12.89/18 = 0.716, or $0.716, and rounded up they each cost $0.72 or 72 cents.

7 — D. All of the answer choices are integers
The correct answer is D. Rationale: An integer is defined as a number that can be written without a fraction or decimal component. The set of integers includes zero (0), the natural numbers (1, 2, 3...), also called whole numbers or counting numbers. It also includes their additive inverses, the negative integers (-1, -2, -3 . . .).

8 — A. Positive
The correct answer is A. Rationale: Within an equation, subtracting a negative number (-A), will give the same result as adding the corresponding positive number (A). Here's an example:

Z + Y = Z - (-Y)
43 + 6 = 43 - (-6)

9 — D. 1, 2, 4, 8, 16, 32, 64, 128
The correct answer is D. Rationale: Factors are the set of numbers that can be multiplied to form a given number. 128 is created in the following ways:

128 = 2 * 64
128 = 4 * 32
128 = 8 * 16
128 = 1 * 128

Therefore, factors of 128 are simply the set of these factors: 1, 2, 4, 8, 16, 32, 64, 128

10 — D. There is only one even prime number
The correct answer is D. Rationale: By definition, there is only one even prime number; 2. Memorize it. Prime numbers are natural numbers greater than 1 that have no positive divisors other than 1 and itself. A composite number is a natural number greater than 1 that is not a prime number. For example, 7 is prime because no integer (natural number), other than 1 and itself, can be divided into it without remainder. The even number 10, for example, is a composite number because both 2 and 5 can be divided into it without remainder.

11 — A. 2
The correct answer is A. Rationale: The prime factorization of 128 is found in the following way:

128 = 2 * 64 = 2 * 2 * 32 = 2 * 2 * 2 * 16 = 2 * 2 * 2 * 2 * 8 = 2 * 2 * 2 * 2 * 2 * 4

The prime factorization of 128 is the last form in the above list. The question asked what the prime factors of 128 are. In the final form two is the only number in the prime factorization of 128.

12 — B. An expression
The correct answer is B. Rationale: By definition, an equation is a statement that two mathematical expressions are equal. Notice that an equation has, by definition, an equal sign. A polynomial is an expression of more than two algebraic terms, especially terms that contain different powers of the same variables. Notice that a polynomial is a specific type of expression. An exponent is a quantity representing the power to which a given number or expression is to be raised. The exponent is the superscript symbol beside the number or expression. There is no exponent in the given quantity.

Since none of these mathematic terms can be used to describe the given information, it must be an expression. An expression is a collection of symbols that jointly express a quantity.

13 — A. 2
The correct answer is A. Rationale: The Greatest Common Factor (GCF) is found by identifying all of the factors of the two or more numbers in your set, and then finding the largest number that they share.

Factors of 16 are 1, 2, 4, 8, 16
Factors of 38 are 1, 2, 19, 38

The greatest (largest) common factor these two numbers share is 2.

14 — B. 40
The correct answer is B. Rationale: The Least Common Multiple (LCM) is found by listing numbers that are integer multiples of the original number. Multiplying a given number by all of the integers (1, 2, 3, 4, 5, 6 etc.):

For the number 5 — 5, 10, 15, 20, 25, 30, 35, 40, 45, 50, etc.
For the number 8 — 8, 16, 24, 32, 40, 48, 56, 64, etc.

The LCM is the smallest number that appears in both sets of multiples; in this case the number 40.

15 — C. 5,040
The correct answer is C. Rationale: The use of the exclamation sign with a number simply means that the number is multiplied by all of the integers smaller than that number. In this example:

7! = 1 * 2 * 3 * 4 * 5 * 6 * 7 = 5,040

16 — C. $\sqrt{17}$
The correct answer is C. Rationale: If a square root is not expressed as an integer, it is an irrational number. Since $\sqrt{4} = 2$ and $\sqrt{9} = 3$, they are not irrational numbers. However, $\sqrt{17}$ cannot be expressed as an integer because it is irrational. The most notable irrational number is probably "pi", which is very useful in geometry; it is equal to approximately 3.14159. It is important to note that this is an approximate value.

17 — C. \$23.70
The correct answer is C. Rationale: To pay for the shirt, you will pay 20% less because of the sale and 6% more because of the tax; however, it is important to note that you will only pay 6% on the sale price. Therefore, first calculate the sale price:

\$27.95 * 0.80 = \$22.36

Now, calculate the price of the sales tax:

\$22.36 * 0.06 = \$1.34

Finally, add the sale price and the sales tax:

\$22.36 + \$1.34 = \$23.70

18 — C. 42
The correct answer is C. Rationale: If Henry and his sister were the same age (for example, if they were twins), and their combined age was 96, they would both be 48 (96 divided by 2). However, if their ages are 12 years apart, Henrietta's age needs to be increased by 6 years, and Henry's needs to be decreased by 6 years. Since the question is asking only about Henry's age, simply subtract 6 years from the average age of 48 to find that the correct answer is 42 years old.

As a check, Henrietta's age should be 48 + 6 or 54 years old. Their combined ages, therefore, would be 42 + 54 = 96 years, the given part of the problem.

19 — A. Adding a positive number
The correct answer is A. Rationale: Subtracting a negative number, is the same as adding a positive number. Another way to think of it is to think, in simple terms, that "two negatives make a positive."

20 — B. \$561.20
The correct answer is B. Rationale: If the shop opens at 6:00am and closes at 5:30pm, it is open a total of 11.5 hours. Selling 16 coffees/hour, they sell (11.5 * 16) or 184 coffees/day. Each coffee costs \$3.05, so in one day they will take in (184 * 3.05) or \$561.20.

21 — B. 58%
The correct answer is B. Rationale: First, ignore that it is the 6th grade class — that number is perhaps included to distract you. If there are 16 males, there must be 22 female students. If you are looking for the percentage of female students, you divide the number of female students by the total number of students (22 / 38) or 0.5789 or 57.89%. Rounding up to 58% is correct, since all the answer choices are whole numbers.

22 — B. $\sqrt{x}$
The correct answer is B. Rationale: A fractional exponent is equivalent to the root of the number. If the exponent is 1/2, it is equivalent to the square root. If the exponent is 1/3, it is equivalent to the cube root. The word "square" is used because squaring the square root returns the number inside the root; the word "cube" is used because cubing the cube root returns the number inside the root.

23 — B. 3
The correct answer is B. Rationale: The Greatest Common Factor (GCF) is found by identifying all of the factors of the two or more numbers in your set, and then finding the largest number that they share.

Factors of 15 = 1, 3, 5, 15
Factors of 36 = 1, 2, 3, 4, 9, 12, 18, 36

The greatest (largest) common factor these two numbers share is 3.

24 — C. <
The correct answer is C. Rationale: Any integer with zero as its exponent equals one. So, the question is asking, "Is one equal to, greater than, or less than two", or "none of the above." This should be an easy choice. It may help if you remember that the arrow points to the smaller number.

So $1 < 2$.

25 — B. 1
The correct answer is B. Rationale: The formula is: $f = (2^{-2} * 8) / (0.5 * 4)$

A number with a negative exponent is the "fraction" or reciprocal of its value. So, if $2^2 = 4$:

$2^{-2} = 1/4 = 0.25$ and
$f = (0.25 * 8) / (0.5 * 4)$
$f = 2 / 2$
$f = 1$

26 — D. $3,412.50
The correct answer is D. Rationale: First, notice that if half the ice cream cones cost $3.00 and half of them cost $4.50, then the average of all of the ice cream cones sold will be $3.75. Next, notice that the store is open for 13 hours each day. If The Ice Cream Shoppe sells, on average, 70 cones per hour, than you need to calculate how many cones they sell in one day:

13 * 70 = 910 ice cream cones sold in one day

Now you can calculate how much money the store takes in during an average day:

910 * $3.75 = $3,412.50

27 — D. 21
The correct answer is D. Rationale: An integer is a number that can be written as a whole number (without a fractional or decimal component). The set of integers consists of zero, the whole/counting/natural numbers (1, 2, 3, …), and the additive inverses of those numbers (-1, -2, -3, …).

28 — D. None of the above
The correct answer is D. Rationale: Prime factors of a positive integer are the prime numbers that divide into that integer exactly. Since 1 and the integer given do not "divide" the number, they are not

included in the list of prime factors for a given number. Therefore, the prime factors of 14 are 2 and 7; a choice not listed as one of the answers.

29 — C. 97.2%
The correct answer is C. Rationale: After reading the question and specifically what the question is asking — the "percent of the student body that is NOT in the TAG program" — you should first notice that there is extraneous information. The fact that 50% of the students in the TAG program are male, and the fact that 80% of the seniors in the TAG program have been accepted at Ivy League universities, are both irrelevant and are intended to distract you. If you read the question carefully, you will realize that it is fairly simple. In this example, one of the important numbers is in word form:

24/857 = 0.028 = 2.8%

So, 2.8% of the students ARE in the TAG program. Notice, however, that they are asking you what percentage are NOT in the TAG program:

100% - 2.8% = 97.2%

30 — C. $1,656.20
The correct answer is C. Rationale: To calculate your weekly drink expenses (WDE), knowing there are 5 weekdays (Monday-Friday) and 2 weekend days (Saturday and Sunday):

WDE = (3.89 * 5) + (6.20 * 2)
WDE = 19.45 + 12.40
WDE = 31.82

However, the question asks you for your yearly drink expenses, and there are 52 weeks in a year:
$31.82/week * 52 weeks/year = $1,656.20

Wow! When you look at it this way, that's a lot of money for a drink each day! If you could manage not to have that habit, but instead put that money under your mattress for 30 years, you'd have almost $50,000 saved!

31 — A. 3√7
The correct answer is A. Rationale – √63 can be rewritten as the product of two radicals, √9 * √7. The part of that product that can be expressed as an integer is √9, which is 3. In simplified form, the square root can be written as 3√7.

32 — C. 3/7 √35
The correct answer is C. Rationale – √(45 / 7) can be rewritten as the ratio of two radicals, √45 / √7, but mathematical conventions do not allow a radical in the denominator. To "rationalize" that ratio, both the numerator and denominator must be multiplied by √7. In a simplified form, the ratio can be written as (√45 * √7) / 7. This can still be simplified because √45 can be written as the product of √9 * √5. The part of that product that can be expressed as an integer is √9, which is equal to 3.

Therefore, since √5 * √7 equals √35, in final simplified form, the ratio becomes 3/7 √35.

33 — C. 8 and 9

The correct answer is C. Rationale – The perfect squares are as follows:

$6^2 = 36$
$7^2 = 49$
$8^2 = 64$
$9^2 = 81$
$10^2 = 100$

Since 78 is between 64 and 81, the $\sqrt{78}$ lies between 8 and 9.

34 — D. $6b^3s\sqrt{(2sb)}$

The correct answer is D. Rationale – $\sqrt{(72s^3b^7)}$ can be rewritten as the product of three radicals: $\sqrt{72} * \sqrt{s^3} * \sqrt{b^7}$. This method allows the solution to focus on one factor at a time. The numerical part of that square root product, which can be expressed as a product of two square roots, is $\sqrt{72} = \sqrt{36} * \sqrt{2}$. Since the $\sqrt{36}$ equals 6, the numerical part of the solution is $6\sqrt{2}$. The factor $\sqrt{s^3}$ can be written as $\sqrt{s^2} * \sqrt{s^1}$, which simplifies to $s\sqrt{s}$. Finally, $\sqrt{b^7}$ can be written as $\sqrt{b^6} * \sqrt{b^1}$, which simplifies to $b^3\sqrt{b}$. In simplified form, the square root $\sqrt{(72s^3b^7)}$ can be written as the product of all three parts, i.e. $6b^3s\sqrt{(2sb)}$.

35 — C. 0.6363…

The correct answer is C. Rationale – The ratio 7/11 implies division, so the decimal value can be determined by the long division problem of 7 divided by 11. The long division results in the repeating decimal 0.6363… However, there is another method that may be simpler. The ratio 7/11 is the product of 7 times 1/11. The ratio 1/11 is the repeating decimal 0.0909…, so multiplying that decimal by 7 is 0.6363..., which is the same answer. If this method seems easier or faster, remember that every fraction with 11 in the denominator can be determined in the same way.

36 — A. 0.625

The correct answer is A. Rationale – The ratio implies division, so 5/8 can be determined by the long division problem of 5 divided by 8. The long division results in the decimal 0.625. However, there is a method to find this decimal that may be simpler. The ratio 5/8 is the product of 5 times 1/8. The ratio 1/8 is the decimal 0.125, so multiplying that decimal by 5 is 0.625, which is the same answer. If this method seems easier or faster, remember that every fraction with 8 in the denominator can be determined in the same way.

37 — D. 9/16

The correct answer is D. Rationale – The numerator in the correct ratio will be equal to the given decimal times the correct denominator. It is simply a result of cross-multiplying. But first, these problems can be greatly simplified if you eliminate incorrect answers.

For example, answers A and B can both be eliminated because they are both less than 0.5 or 1/2. If you can't see that, then multiply 0.5 times 15 and 0.5 times 23. In answer A, 0.5 times 15 is 7.5, so 7/15 is less than the fractional value of 0.5625. In answer B, 0.5 times 23 is 11.5, so 11/23 is less than the fractional value of 0.5625.

Now, evaluating fractional answers this way, you may look at answer C and realize that 0.6 times 8 equals 4.8. Since 4.8 is less than the numerator and 0.6 is larger than the given decimal value, C can be eliminated. The correct answer is D.

38 — A. 5/16
The correct answer is A. Rationale – The numerator in the correct ratio will be equal to the given decimal times the correct denominator. It is simply a result of cross-multiplying. But first, these problems can be greatly simplified if you eliminate incorrect answers.

For example, answer B can be eliminated because it can be simplified to 1/6, which is much less than 0.3125. If you can't see that, then divide 1 by 6, which equals 0.167.

For answer D, the ratio 9/25 is a simplified form of 36/100 or 0.36. This value is greater than the given decimal of 0.3125, so answer D can be eliminated.

Now, evaluating fractional answers this way, you may eliminate answer C for a very simple reason. 19 times 0.3125 will always leave a value of 5 in the ten-thousandths place because 19 times 5 equals 95. That means the product can never be the whole number 6, so answer C can be eliminated.

The correct answer is A because you have logically eliminated all the other possible choices.

39 — C. $1.7 * 10^{-3}$
The correct answer is C. Rationale – The ratio 17/10,000 implies division, which is 0.0017. These ratio conversions are simpler if the correct description is used for 17/10,000. In other words, the ratio is "seventeen ten thousandths" or 0.0017. The scientific notation must begin with 1.7, and since the decimal place will be moved three places to the right, the correct value is $1.7 * 10^{-3}$.

40 — D. $7.36589 * 10^{2}$
The correct answer is D. Rationale – The number 736.589 conversion to scientific notation starts with the decimal expression 7.36589. Since the decimal place was moved two places to the left, the correct value is $7.36589 * 10^{2}$.

Mathematics Knowledge

1 — A. 67
The correct answer is A. Rationale: Substituting 15 for x in the equation, it becomes: f = (152/3) - 8

Since 152 = 225
f = 225/3 - 8
f = 75 - 8
f = 67

2 — B. $6.38 * 10^{5}$
The correct answer is B. Rationale: Scientific notation is a way to simplify large numbers by writing the number into a number that is one or more but not up to ten, followed by ten to the nth power. Here's an example that helps illustrate this concept:

$123{,}456 = 1.23456 * 10^{5}$

If the decimal place in 1.23456 is then moved over 5 places, you will get the original number — 123,456.

In the same way, 638,000 can be simplified into scientific notation by shifting the decimal place over 5 places:

$638{,}000 = 6.38 * 10^5$

Answer choices A and D cannot be correct because they do not include an exponent to indicate the "power of 10". Answer choice C would lead to a very small number instead of a large one since any number with a negative exponent becomes one divided by the number with a positive exponent.

3 — C. 990
The correct answer is C. Rationale: A number followed by an exclamation mark has a value found by multiplying all of the counting numbers beginning with one and ending with that specific number. In this example, you would find the following values for the two given numbers:

11! = 1 * 2 * 3 * 4 * 5 * 6 * 7 * 8 * 9 * 10 * 11
8! = 1 * 2 * 3 * 4 * 5 * 6 * 7 * 8

You could find the value of each of these numbers:

11! = 39,916,800
8! = 40,320

The ratio would be found simply by dividing these two numbers: 39,916,800/40,320 = 990. Therefore, the ratio would be 990:1.

There is a less "laborious" way to find this result. If you are dividing these two numbers, they share all the terms between 1 and 8; therefore, those terms can be factored out, leaving only the following:

9 * 10 * 11 = 990

4 — D. 512
The correct answer is D. Rationale: You can answer correctly easily when you observe that 83 = 8 * 8 * 8 = 64 * 8 = 512. Remember that another way to write this is the following: 83 = 82 * 81 = 64 * 8.

5 — B. $Q^2 + 10Q + 21$
The correct answer is B. Rationale: This is an example of polynomial multiplication. When you recognize a formula in this form, you need to do the following:

1. Multiply the first term in each set of parentheses: $Q * Q = Q^2$
2. Add the product of the first and last terms in each set of parentheses: 7Q + 3Q = 10Q
3. Multiply the second terms in each set of parentheses: 7 * 3 = 21

If you now put these three results in the same expression, you get the following:

$P = Q^2 + 10Q + 21$

Here's an example with the assumption that Q = 3:

$P = (Q + 7)(Q + 3)$
$P = (3 + 7)(3 + 3)$
$P = 10 * 6$
$P = 60$

Now, you want to substitute Q = 3 into the formula developed:

$P = Q^2 + 10Q + 21$
$P = 3^2 + (10)(3) + 21$
$P = 9 + 30 + 21$
$P = 60$

The numerical example of the equation checks out correctly!

6 — D. 3/5, 5/9, 3/8, 1/4.
The correct answer is D. Rationale: This question can be answered converting each fraction into its decimal equivalent:

3/5 = 0.6
1/4 = 0.25
3/8 = 0.375
5/9 = 0.555

The decimal equivalents, from largest to smallest, would be 0.6, 0.555, 0.375, 0.25.

Therefore, the fractions, from largest to smallest, would be 3/5, 5/9, 3/8, 1/4.

7 — B. 5
The correct answer is B. Rationale: The "mode" in a set of data is simply the one item that occurs most often; in this question, the number 5 repeats itself 3 times, more than any other number.

8 — C. 616
The correct answer is C. Rationale: Two conversion factors will be required: one mile = 5,280 feet and one yard = 3 feet.

The rocket is designed to go to a height of 5,280 feet / 2 or 2,640 feet. Because it only reaches 70% of its designed altitude, the rocket achieved an altitude of 2,640 feet * 0.7 or 1,848 feet. To convert this into yards, divide by 3: 1,848 feet / 3 feet/yard or 616 yards.

9 — B. 1.5
The correct answer is B. Rationale: Substitute the value of y into the given equation:

$x = (2y - 5) / 2$
$x = [(2 * 4) - 5] / 2$

x = (8 - 5) / 2
x = 3 / 2
x = 1.5

10 — B. 1.5:1
The correct answer is B. Rationale: The key here is to find the value of 4! The value of a number ending with an exclamation is that number multiplied by all the other whole numbers less than that number; for example:

4! = 4 * 3 * 2 * 1
4! = 24

Now substitute this number into the given ratio and simplify it:

36:24 or 1.5:1

11 — D. 75%
The correct answer is D. Rationale: A percentage problem is a simple ratio. The expression "what percentage of 20" can be designated as the unknown variable x. "Percentage" means a value divided by 100. The expression "of," implies multiplication. The expression "is 15" just means = 15. So, to find the percentage of 20 that is 15:

x = 15 / 20 = 0.75
x = 0.75 * 100 = 75%

To change a decimal into a percentage, simply multiply by 100.

12 — C. 16
The correct answer is C. Rationale: The first step is to write an equation to solve for "some number":

"12 is 15% of some number" translates to x = 12 / 0.15 = 80

However, the question is asking for 20% of that number, 80. To find 20% of 80, multiply by the decimal equivalent of 20%, or 0.2; this then translates to y = 80 * 0.2 = 16.

13 — B. 0
The correct answer is B. Rationale: If you substitute 3 for x in the equation, you get the following:

f = (32/3) - 3

Since 32 = 9

f = 9/3 - 3
f = 3 - 3
f = 0

14 — A. 3
The correct answer is A. Rationale: The "mode" in a set of data is simply the one that occurs most often; in this question, the number 3 repeats itself 3 times, more than any other number.

15 — D. 2,197
The correct answer is D. Rationale: You can easily answer this correctly when you observe that 133 = 13 * 13 * 13 = 169 * 13 = 2,197. Remember that another way to write this is the following: 133 = 132 * 131 = 169 * 13

The values for answer choices A, B. and C are all close to 169 or 132, and the value of 132 still has to be multiplied by another 13!

16 — B. 19.2
The correct answer is B. Rationale: To solve this problem, first write out what you know:

X = 60% of Y
Y = 80% of Z
Z = 40

You can substitute the value of Z into the second equation, remembering that you can always convert a percentage into a decimal by dividing by 100:

Y = 80% * 40 = 0.8 * 40 = 32

Now, in a similar operation, substitute the value of Y into the first equation:

X = 60% * 32 = 0.6 * 32 = 19.2

17 — C. 5/8, 3/7, 2/5, 1/3
The correct answer is C. Rationale: This question can be answered in several ways, but perhaps the easiest is to convert each fraction into its decimal equivalent:

2/5 = 0.4
1/3 = 0.33
3/7 = 0.429
5/8 = 0.625

The order of the decimal equivalents, from largest to smallest, would be the following:

0.625, 0.429, 0.4, 0.33

Therefore, the order of the fractions, from largest to smallest, would be the following:

5/8, 3/7, 2/5, 1/3

It should have been easy to put 5/8 first on the list because it was the only one greater than 1/2.

18 — B. 34
The correct answer is B. Rationale: First, consider the scenario with one yellow ball and one non-yellow ball being selected. Since there are 4 yellow balls, there is a 4:11 chance that one yellow ball will be chosen. Since there are 7 balls that are either violet or black, there is a 7:11 chance that a ball of another color will be chosen. Therefore, there will be 28 (4 * 11) combinations that allow both a yellow ball and a ball of another color to be chosen. There are 110 (11 * 10) total combinations.

Next, consider the possibility that both of the balls chosen are yellow. If these 4 balls are labeled as Y1, Y2, Y3, and Y4, next determine how many combinations there can be.

If Y1 is chosen, its "partner" can be Y2, Y3, or Y4 (3 possible choices)
If Y2 is chosen, its "partner can be Y3 or Y4 (2 possible choices)
If Y3 is chosen, its "partner" can be Y4 (1 possible choice)

To summarize:

Y1 + Y2
Y1 + Y3
Y1 + Y4
Y2 + Y3
Y2+ Y4
Y3 + Y4

Since there are 28 combinations involving one yellow ball and 6 combinations involving two yellow balls, there are 34 combinations that allow at least one yellow ball to be chosen.

19 — D. (1,4) and (3,1)
The correct answer is D. Rationale: The natural numbers are the whole positive numbers beginning with 1. Also, notice from the answer choices that the only possible answers include the numbers 1, 3, and 4, and any equations that have 2 as either x or y should not be considered.

If $x = 1$
$3x + 2y = 11$
$(3 * 1) + 2y = 11$
$3 + 2y = 11$
$2y = 8$
$y = 4$

Therefore, one possible pair of natural numbers are $x = 1$ and $y = 4$.
Remember, $x = 2$ should not be considered. If $x = 2$ then $y = 5/2$. It must be an integer

If $x = 3$
$3x + 2y = 11$
$(3 * 3) + 2y = 11$
$9 + 2y = 11$
$2y = 2$
$y = 1$

Therefore, another possible pair of natural numbers are $x = 3$ and $y = 1$.

If $x = 4$
$3x + 2y = 11$
$(3 * 4) + 2y = 11$
$12 + 2y = 11$
$2y = -1$
$y = -1/2$

Because -1/2 is not a natural number, this pair of numbers should not be considered.

20 — B. 12.67 pounds; $36.48
The correct answer is B. Rationale: You calculate the average weight by adding the weights of all the watermelons delivered and dividing that total by the number of watermelons delivered.

watermelon-weightavg = (6 + 7 + 7 + 9 + 12 + 12 + 15 + 23 + 23) / 9
watermelon-weightavg = 114 / 9
watermelon-weightavg = 12.67 pounds

If Joe is paying $0.32/pound for 114 pounds of watermelons, he will have to pay the following amount:

114 pounds * $0.32/pound = $36.48

21 — A. Yes
The correct answer is A. Rationale: Substitute the value of A into the given equation:

$Y = [(A^3 + A) / 2] - 2$
$Y = [(2^3 + 2) / 2] - 2$
$Y = [(8 + 2) / 2] - 2$
$Y = (10 / 2) - 2$
$Y = 5 - 2$
$Y = 3$ (a prime number)

22 — A. -0.67
The correct answer is A. Rationale: Substitute the values you know:

If . = 36, then $\sqrt{36} = 6$
If $\mu = 144$, then $\sqrt{144} = 12$

Now you can insert those values into the given equation:

$R = (\sqrt{\beta} * \sqrt{\mu}) / (\beta - \mu)$
$R = (6 * 12) / (36 - 144)$
$R = 72 / -108$
$R = -0.67$

Sometimes these problems might look difficult because the Greek letters represent the variables. The Greek letters are no different than the x's and y's that we normally use.

23 — B. 8.33 pounds; $64.50
The correct answer is B. Rationale: You calculate the average weight by adding the weights of all the apples delivered and dividing that total by the number of apples delivered.

apple-weightavg = (6 + 7 + 7 + 7.5 + 8 + 8 + 9.5 + 11 + 11) / 9
apple-weightavg = 75 / 9
apple-weightavg = 8.33 pounds

If Jack is paying $0.86/pound for 75 pounds of apples, he will pay $64.50.

24 — C. $R^2 + 35R + 150$
The correct answer is C. Rationale: This is an example of polynomial multiplication. When you recognize a formula in this form, remember that this type of formula can always be solved in this manner:

$(P + 3) (P + 7) = P^2 + (3+7)P + (3 * 7)$

To check to see if this formulation works, assume P = 4

$(P + 3) (P + 7) = P^2 + 10P + 21$
$(4 + 3) (4 + 7) = 42 + [(10)(4)] + 21$
$7 * 11 = 16 + 40 + 21$
$77 = 16 + 40 + 21$
$77 = 77$

Okay, the equivalence works! Now, apply the method to this question:

To check your answer, assume that R = 2:

$(R + 5)(R + 30) = R^2 + 35R + 150$
$(2 + 5)(2 + 30) = 2^2 + [(35 * 2)] + 150$
$7 * 32 = 4 + 70 + 150$
$224 = 224$

25 — C. 17,000
The correct answer is C. Rationale: To solve this problem, we will use the following conversion of units:

one mile = 5,280 feet

This is because the given units are in miles but the answer units are in feet. The rocket booster is designed to go up three and a half miles:

5,280 feet * 3.5 = 18,480 feet

Because it only reaches 92% of its designed altitude, the maximum becomes:

18,480 feet * 0.92 = 17,001 feet.

Rounded to the nearest ten feet, the correct answer is:

17,000 feet

26 — C. 388
The correct answer is C. Rationale – The value can be expanded as 7 * 49 added to 9 * 7, with 18 subtracted from the total. That becomes 343 + 63 -18, with the answer equal to 388.

27 — B. 42
The correct answer is B. Rationale – The value can be expanded as 25 added to 5 * 7, with 18 subtracted from the total. That becomes 25 + 35 -18, with the answer equal to 42. There is another simple way to evaluate this expression. The expression can be rewritten as the product of two expressions (x+9)(x-2). If you substitute 5 for x, then this product becomes 14 * 3, which is also 42.

28 — C. 6804
The correct answer is C. Rationale – The simplest way to evaluate this expression is to rewrite it as the product of two expressions. Factoring common factors out, the given expression becomes 7x(x+9). "7x" becomes 189 and x+9 becomes 36. The product of 189 and 36 becomes 6804. In the interest of eliminating incorrect answers, the product of the values in the "ones" column is 6 * 9, which is 54. The correct answer must end in 4, so the correct answer must be C.

29 — A. $5a^4b^3c^2$ $(7 + 13a^2b^4c^2)$
The correct answer is A. Rationale – The best way to simplify an expression such as this is to identify term by term the greatest common factors (GCF). In the integer coefficients, the GCF of 35 and 65 is 5. The numerical coefficients inside the parentheses become 7 and 13. Similarly, the GCF of a^4 and a^6 is a^4. The other two GCF factors are b^3 and c^2. Factoring common factors outside of the parentheses leaves the expression $7 + 13a^2\ b^4\ c^2$ inside the parentheses.

30 — D. $x^2 - 4x - 21$
The correct answer is D. Rationale – Multiplying the two binomials together with FOIL means that the first term is the product of the two x's, or x^2. However, the last term is the product of 3 and -7, which means that answer D is the only correct answer. The middle term is the sum of 3x and -7x, which is -4x. Again, answer D is the only correct answer. If you choose to use the box method to solve these products, you will see the same results and the same factors.

Word Knowledge

1 — B. Vast
Expansive means covering a wide area regarding space or scope; extensive; wide-ranging.

2 — C. Reliable
Credible means able to be believed; convincing; plausible; tenable.

3 — D. Destruction
Devastation means great destruction or damage; ruin, havoc, wreckage.

4 — A. Unclear
Vague means of uncertain, indefinite, or unclear character or meaning; indistinct; ill-defined.

5 — B. Disrespectful
Irreverent means showing a lack of respect for people or things that are generally taken seriously; disdainful; scornful; derisive; contemptuous.

6 — D. Distaste
Aversion means a strong dislike or disinclination; abhorrence; antipathy.

7 — A. Difficult
Laborious means a task, process, or journey requiring considerable effort or time; arduous; strenuous.

8 — C. Endless
Interminable means unending; monotonously or annoyingly protracted or continued; unceasing; incessant.

9 — C. Without color
Achromatic means free from color.

10 — B. Rapid
Cursory means hasty and therefore not thorough or detailed; perfunctory; desultory; casual; superficial.

11 — B. Secondhand information that can't be proven
Hearsay means information received from other people that one cannot adequately substantiate; rumor; gossip.

12 — C. Forgiving
Magnanimous means very generous or forgiving, especially toward a rival or someone less powerful than oneself; generous; charitable; benevolent.

13 — A. Of the earth
Terrestrial means of, on, or relating to the earth.

14 — C. Indifferent
Nonchalant means having an air of indifference or easy concern.

15 — A. Tangible
Palpable means capable of being touched or felt; tangible.

16 — B. Plaster
Daub means plaster; to cover or coat with soft adhesive matter; to apply crudely.

17 — C. Swell
Distend means to enlarge from internal pressure; to swell; to become expanded.

18 — B. Mistake
Gaffe means a social or diplomatic blunder; mistake; faux pas.

19 — D. Leader of Catholicism
Papal means of or relating to a pope or the Roman Catholic Church.

20 — A. Delay
Tarry means to delay or be tardy in acting or doing; to linger in expectation; wait.

21 — C. Commotion
Hoopla means a noisy commotion; boisterous merrymaking.

22 — B. Dogmatic
Doctrinaire means very strict in applying beliefs and principles; dogmatic; dictatorial.

23 — D. Feathery
Plumose means having feathers or plumes; feathered.

24 — C. Uproot
Supplant means to supersede another, especially by force or treachery; uproot; to eradicate and supply a substitute for; to take the place of and serve as a substitute, especially because of superior excellence or power; replace.

25 — D. Caprice
Vagary means an erratic, unpredictable, or extravagant manifestation, action, or notice; caprice.

26 — C. Squid
Calamari means squid used as food; the inky substance the squid secretes.

27 — A. Apathetic
Lethargic means indifferent; apathetic; sluggish.

28 — C. Tiny
Teensy means tiny.

29 — D. Dull
Bland means smooth and soothing in manner or quality; exhibiting no personal concern or embarrassment; unperturbed; not irritating, stimulating, or invigorating; soothing; dull; insipid; stories with little plot or action.

30 — B. Copious
Fulsome means characterized by abundance; copious.

31 — B. Name
Nomenclature means name, designation; a system of terms used in a particular science, discipline, or art.

32 — D. Unwilling
Reluctant means holding back; averse; unwilling; disinclined.

33 — C. Despicable
Despicable means mean; despicable; contemptible; clothed with worn or seedy garments; threadbare and faded with wear; ill-kept; dilapidated.

34 — C. Charity
Alms means something (as money or food) given freely to relieve the poor; charity.

35 — D. Delay
Defer means to put off; delay; postpone; suspend.

Reading Comprehension

1 — B. Nature
The subtopics of fashion, the destruction of nature and the inherently greedy nature of man are all introduced through the lens of nature. Several text features elucidate the importance of the main topic with, for example, the personification of Nature. The final sentence ties together the relevance of the preceding information to make a conclusive observation on the main topic of nature.

2 — D. All of the above
Fashion is presented as extravagant and frivolous in comparison to nature through the use of hyperbole, the "ravenous hysteria" of the fashionable women implies their inferiority in regard to the contrasting theme that they are pitted against; nature. The destructive nature of humans is directly expressed through the violent language used, the "widespread slaughter" that occurs, and with the mere fact that a man's "cruel arrogance" has succeeded in destroying "Nature's innocence". Man is shown to be greedy in regard to nature by the way the subject is presented as a thief, robbing "Nature of it's riches". It is not only of pecuniary greed that man is guilty of in relation to nature, but of the desirous need to "possess" and therefore, own nature's beauty.

3 — A. The main topic of the paragraph
The last sentence links the strands of the subtopics together by making a judgement on the relationship of man to nature. The reason why man seeks to destroy nature is because it is inherent in man's nature to own and "possess" it.

4 — A. Personification
The speaker personifies nature by capitalizing the word. This makes it appear as one living entity, emphasized by the fact that it is imbued with human qualities, such as "innocence".

5 — A. As inevitable
The destruction of the natural world is painted as wholly inevitable by the final sentence, which states that man is "rarely" concerned with only viewing nature, but must "possess" it. For man to possess nature they must in some way interfere with the natural order of the world; it can no longer conceivably remain in an untouched state.

6 — B. Gambling
While social class and questions of morality do feature heavily throughout the extract, gambling is the overarching theme that is ubiquitous throughout the extract. This is emphasized with the final sentence, which suggests that morality and class are irrelevant as the fate of a "gamester" will remain the one overriding factor.

7 — D. All gamblers will become poor in the end if they continue to gamble
The revelatory nature of the final sentence elucidates the main point that the speaker is trying to make. He contrasts different types of gambler in order to reveal that these differences are wholly irrelevant as all gamblers share the same "destiny" which is "poverty and despair".

8 — C. To highlight that class difference is not important if you are a gambler because everyone, whether rich or poor, will end up destitute
The comparison between the working-class gambler and the aristocratic gambler is purposely set up to contrast their different modus operandi in terms of how they gamble and the lives that they lead. However, this is set up in order to prove, with the final sentence, that no matter which social class a gambler is from, they will all end up destitute in the end as that is a gambler's "destiny".

9 — D. None of the above
Initially, the speaker's tone appears to be accusatory. The speaker launches biting critiques of the moral degeneracy of the working-class gambler, who is, amongst other things, a "bully" of the "lowest and vilest" order, and they appear to take the side of the aristocratic gambler. However, the revelation in the final sentence that regardless of wealth both gamblers share the same fate. This considerably changes the tone of the extract, as what initially appears as a biting critique of the working class becomes a biting critique of gambling itself.

10 — D. Simile
The speaker compares the working-class people who frequent gambling dens to "hungry parasites". The simile works as hyperbole to convince the reader of the predatory nature of this subsection of society.

11 — A. Death
The speaker's realization revolves around the unfulfilled life they have lived. While they are still physically living, the speaker comes to the realization that something had always been missing to the point where they are figuratively "already dead".

12 — D. None of the above
The speaker shows little of their feeling towards the subject of their death as the extract revolves around the epiphanic moment where they realize that they are dead, but by the mere fact that death "was not an event to be feared" it implies that this realization had put them beyond feeling because they had already faced the worst fear imaginable.

13 — A. Rhetorical questions
The writer uses several rhetorical questions to emphasize the speaker's mental state. The absurdity of the idea that the speaker didn't before realize what they know now is an indication of the gravity of the epiphany they have experienced.

14 — A. Inevitable
The speaker not only views figurative death as inevitable, but so much so that is has already happened without them realizing, they are "already dead".

15 — D. Poignant
The speaker expresses disbelief of the fact that they hadn't realized that they weren't living. Regret and sadness is implied through this belief as she has lead a life unfulfilled.

Physical Science

1 — C. Fossil records

Rationale: The earth is composed of four distinct concentric spherical layers of material. At the center of the earth is the inner core, composed of a solid metallic sphere of nickel and iron. The next layer is the outer core which surrounds the inner core and is composed of molten liquid nickel and iron. The third concentric layer is the mantle. The mantle surrounds the outer core. The mantle is composed primarily of rocky silicate mineral compounds. At the deepest regions of the mantle, this material is extremely hot and behaves like a molten liquid. The mantle material cools as it approaches the surface of the earth, becoming more like a solid substance with the consistency of putty. Although this region is technically a rocky solid, it can flow or ooze when subjected to pressure. The outermost layer is the earth's crust, a thin layer of solid rocky mineral compounds that literally floats on top of the upper mantle layer. At the crust layer, the surface material interacts with the surface environment of the earth to produce a wide variety of solid rocky mineral compounds that are not found in the deeper mantle. Although fossils are found only on or within the earth's crust, scientists do not use this fact to distinguish the crust from the other layers of the earth. If the earth sustained no life, it would have no fossils, but it would still have a crust layer.

2 — D. Lithosphere

Rationale: The lithosphere is the solid outer layer of the earth. It includes the earth's crust and the upper layer of the underlying mantle.

3 — B. Charged particles from the sun interacting with the earth's magnetic field

Rationale: The sun continuously emits vast amounts of charged particles into space. This is known as the solar wind. When these particles intercept the earth, they are directed and concentrated by the earth's magnetic field to the north and south poles. As this concentration of charged particles collides with air molecules, it emits light of varying colors, resulting in a beautiful dynamic display of curtains of changing colors across the extreme northern and southern latitudes. At the North Pole regions, this phenomenon is called the Aurora Borealis. At the southern pole regions, it is known as the Aurora Australis.

4 — A. Basalt

Rationale: Sedimentary rock is formed by accumulating particulate material that is gradually deposited in layers and compressed, fusing and transforming the material together over very long periods of time. Shale, coal and sandstone are examples of sedimentary rock. Basalt is formed right when it cools from a molten state, such as molten lava from a volcano. Rock formed in this fashion is known as igneous rock.

5 — D. 1,000,000 times more energetically powerful

Rationale: The Richter scale is logarithmic — for every increase of one Richter unit number, the measured intensity of ground motion or earthshaking that results from an earthquake increases by a power of 10. The energy required to increase an earthquake's ground shaking motion by a factor of 10 requires approximately 32 times as much energy compared to an earthquake that is one Richter unit smaller than the larger earthquake. Therefore, since the difference between 6 and 2 is 4, the Richter scale 6 earthquake generates 104 times (10,000 times) more intense ground shaking compared to the Richter scale 2 earthquake. This corresponds to an increased energy of 32 * 32 * 32 *32 = 1,048,576 or approximately 1,000,000 (one million) times more energy required to generate a Richter scale 6 earthquake compared to a Richter scale 2 earthquake.

6 — B. Stratosphere
Rationale: Modern aircraft cruise in the Stratosphere, at about 35,000 feet above the earth.

7 — B. Stratus
Rationale: Depending on the altitude at which you encounter fog, it may be almost any type of cloud, particularly at very high elevations near mountain peaks. Stratus clouds are the only type of cloud that can form at ground level at the lowest elevations, which by definition, are the elevations at or near sea level.
8 — C. It has 17 protons
Rationale: This is the definition of an atomic number. The number of protons found in the nucleus is the same as the charge number of the nucleus since protons are positively charged. The atomic number uniquely identifies a chemical element. In an uncharged atom, the atomic number is equal to the number of electrons, since each electron has a negative charge.

9 — B. Electric current: Watt
Rationale: Current is measured in amperes (amps) — memorize it!

10 — C. 5 miles
Rationale: A meter is approximately 3.28 feet. An 8K race refers to a race covering a total distance of 8,000 meters. This converts to a distance in feet of 8,000 times 3.28, which is 26,240 feet. A mile is 5,280 feet. 26,240 divided by 5,280 is equal to about 4.97. Therefore, an 8K race would be 4.97 miles, or about 5 miles.

11 — B. A relatively tiny rock and mineral core with an enormous thick outer layer of gas
Rationale: Neptune and the other "gas giants" — Jupiter, Saturn and Uranus — are planets with rocks on the inside and enormous volumes of gas on the outside. The inner four planets — Mercury, Venus, Earth and Mars — have negligible "atmospheres" over their solid surfaces. Answer D describes the composition of several moons of the gas giants (and possibly many other objects, including large comets and asteroids, within our solar system).

12 — C. Mars and Jupiter
Rationale: The Asteroid Belt is located between Mars and Jupiter. It consists of numerous irregularly shaped bodies called asteroids. Astronomers believe the Asteroid Belt represents material that would have formed a planet between Mars and Jupiter if the gravitational forces of Jupiter did not have such a disruptive effect on the planet-forming processes. The total mass of the Asteroid Belt is about 4% that of Earth's moon. The largest four asteroids are named Ceres, Vesta, Pallas and Hygiene.

13 — D. Phylum, class, order, family, genus, species
Rationale: The biological classifications, in descending order, are:

1. Life
2. Domain
3. Kingdom
4. Phylum
5. Class
6. Order
7. Family
8. Genus
9. Species

14 — D. II only
Rationale: All animals have the ability to move actively on their own at some stage of their life cycle. Cell walls are distinctive biological envelopes of cells found outside of the inner cell membrane. They are features of bacterial, plant and fungal cells, but are not characteristic of animal cells. Although almost all members of the animal kingdom have a nervous system, sponges (which are members of the phylum Porifera of the animal kingdom) do not have nervous systems. All vertebrates are animals, but not all animals are vertebrates. There are more species of animals without vertebrae than with vertebrae.

15 — C. Sponges
Rationale: Sponges are not fungi. Sponges are animals of the phylum Porifera, or "pore bearers". They are multicellular organisms that have bodies full of pores and channels, allowing water to circulate through them. Sponges do not have nervous, digestive or circulatory systems; instead, they rely on maintaining a constant water flow through their bodies to obtain food and oxygen and to remove waste. Yeast is a broad common term for two classes of organisms within the fungi kingdom – the class Ascomycetes and the class Basidiomycetes. Most molds are also members of the fungi kingdom (the exception is slime molds, which are members of the protista kingdom). All species of mushrooms are members of the fungi kingdom.

16 — D. Time
Rationale: Taxonomy trees represent changes over time. Generally, the past is represented at the bottom of the tree, and the present is represented
at the top of the tree.

17 — A. To change an organism so that it is more likely to produce viable offspring
Rationale: Biological evolution is the process where mutations in an organism's genetic code result in an increased probability that the code will be passed to future generations of the organism. This process allows organisms to adapt to changes in the environment and to compete more successfully for survival.

18 — A. Selection
Rationale: This two-word term is a key concept in understanding evolution. The word design is in quotation marks because that word implies intention, and evolution is, by definition, a neutral process that does not require any outside intelligence to occur.

19 — B. Comets
Rationale: Asteroids orbit the sun in approximately the same way planets do. Comets, however, have elongated elliptical orbits that bring them in the vicinity of the sun only occasionally. This is why Halley's Comet is visible only every 75 years. The best way to visualize the difference is to think of comets moving quickly toward the sun and then being thrown way back into deep space in a slingshot-like motion.

20 — B. Solid, liquid and gas/vapor
Rationale: Matter can exist in one of four phases: solid, liquid, gas and plasma. In the solid phase, water molecules are locked into a fixed position and cannot move relative to surrounding water molecules – this is the solid form of water (ice). As the temperature of the water molecules increases to the melting point of water, the water molecules become energetic enough to begin to move freely with respect to other water molecules, but are still attracted to each other, so they remain in physical

contact – this is the liquid phase of water. The gas phase of water occurs when the water temperature reaches the boiling point. The water molecules are so energetic that they cannot be constrained by their attraction to each other. They become freely moving individual molecules that expand away from other water molecules and fill the entire volume of any container or, if uncontained, mix with the other gas molecules in the atmosphere. The plasma phase does not exist for water molecules. In the plasma phase, the temperatures are so high that the water molecules are broken down into individual hydrogen and oxygen atoms. The electrons of the individual atoms have so much thermal energy that they break free from their atomic nuclei. This results in a phase of matter consisting of a mixture of very hot atomic nuclei and free electrons.

Evaporation is the term for a phase change of a substance from a liquid to a gas. This is also known as boiling. Condensation is the term for a phase change of a substance from a gas to a liquid. Sublimation is the name for a phase change of a substance from a solid directly to a gas. This process can be observed in the laboratory as a sample of frozen carbon dioxide (or "dry ice") turns directly to vapor at room temperature.

In chemistry, the terms solute, solvent and solution refer to volumes of liquids that have other chemicals dissolved in the liquids. The liquid is the solvent. The dissolved chemicals are the solutes. The combination of the liquid and the dissolved chemicals are called the solution.

21 — B. Mesozoic
Rationale: Dinosaurs roamed the earth during the Mesozoic era, which consists of the Triassic, Jurassic and Cretaceous periods.

22 — A. When a population is separated by geographic change
Rationale: Geographic speciation occurs when a subpopulation of a species is geographically separated from the other members of the species. This subpopulation is no longer able to interbreed with the other species members. Over time, this subpopulation will evolve independently from the original species and can eventually evolve into an entirely new species.

23 — C. Igneous
Rationale: The answer choices are the three main rock types. Igneous rock is formed through the cooling and solidification of magma or lava. Memorize it! It may be interesting (or not) for you to know that igneous rocks are classified according to mode of occurrence, texture, mineralogy, chemical composition and geometry.

24 — C. Sometimes A, sometimes B, sometimes both A and B
Rationale: Fungi can reproduce sexually or asexually because they can produce both haploid and diploid cells. This allows them to adjust their reproduction to conditions in their environment. When conditions are generally stable, they reproduce quickly asexually. Fungi can increase their genetic variation through sexual reproduction when conditions are changing, which might help them survive.

Almost all fungi reproduce asexually by producing spores, which are haploid cells produced by mitosis, and so they are genetically identical to their parent cells. Fungi spores can develop into new haploid cells without being fertilized. Sexual reproduction involves the mating of two haploids. During mating, two haploid parent cells fuse, forming a diploid spore that is genetically different from its parents. As it germinates, it can undergo meiosis, forming haploid cells.

25 — A. Parietal
Rationale: The parietal lobe is one of the four major lobes of the cerebral cortex in the brain. It integrates sensory information from all parts of the body. This region of the cerebral cortex is called the primary somatosensory cortex.

26 — C. w = m*g
Rationale: It's important to remember that mass is defined as the amount of matter that exists in an object. Matter possesses inertia, so it is a measure of an object's resistance to movement. On the other hand, weight is defined as the product of the object's mass and the gravitational acceleration being applied to that object. Therefore, w = m*g.

27 — B. 6 miles / $hour^2$
Rationale: Acceleration is defined as the change in velocity over time:

$A = \Delta V/\Delta T$

In this question, the change in velocity has been from 43 miles/hour to 64 miles/hour for a change of 21 miles/hour. The change in time is 3.5 hours. Therefore, you can calculate the acceleration simply by substituting the numerical values:

$A = \Delta V/\Delta T$ = 21 miles/hour ÅÄ 3.5 hours = 6 miles/$hour^2$

28 — A. A 10 pound object dropped from 70 ft
Rationale: Potential energy (PE) is measured by the following equation:

PE = M*G*H

where M is the mass, G is the gravitational acceleration, and H is the height. Gravitational acceleration is simply the acceleration of an object caused by the force of gravity on the earth; the conventional standard value is 32.174 ft/s^2 (9.8 m/s^2).

To answer this question correctly, it is important that you convert all units so that they correspond. First, convert each of the three scenarios, remembering the following:

1 foot = 12 inches
1 yard = 3 feet
1 ton = 2000 pounds

Now, convert each of the three scenarios given:

10 pounds dropped 70 ft
58 pounds dropped 4 yards = 58 pounds dropped 12 ft
0.01 tons dropped 300 inches = 20 pounds dropped 25 ft
Since the gravitational constant is the same for all objects and all masses, the PE can be compared by multiplying the two terms:

10 * 70 = 700

58 * 12 = 696
20 * 25 = 500

Answer choice A is the largest of the three numbers (700). Now you have to multiply it by the gravitational constant to calculate the potential energy:

PE = M*G*H = 700 * 32.174 ft/s^2 = about 22,520 joules.

In this case, the "winner" involves the lightest object dropped the greatest distance.

29 — B. Joule
Rationale: Work, by definition, only occurs whenever a force has been applied to an object, and that object moves some distance. Remember the product of Newtons (force) and meters (distance), determines Joules.

30 — C. Greater distance the object must travel
Rationale: A 500 pound steel ball must be placed onto its pedestal three feet above the ground. Your maximum applied force is not adequate to lift the ball vertically. But if you arrange an inclined plane with a sloping surface of about 5 degrees, the top of the ramp ends at the top of the pedestal. It will now be possible to roll the steel ball up the ramp to place it on the pedestal. The ramp can then be removed, and your sculpture is complete and ready to be admired. The ball had to be moved 40 feet up the ramp instead of a vertical height of 3 feet, but you were able to move it using the simple machine, which allowed you to achieve the goal of lifting the massive sphere.

31 — D. Move the fulcrum in the direction of the load to be lifted
Rationale: Increasing the force generated by your body at will is not feasible, so answer choice A is not a viable option. Balancing the lever on the fulcrum may not necessarily help, since it depends on where it was originally, so answer choice B may not be helpful for you to achieve your goal. Increasing the height of the fulcrum simply increases the distance that the load must be moved, so answer choice C is unlikely to be helpful. Only answer choice D (moving the location of the fulcrum so that it is closer to the load) will necessarily be helpful. Experience on a teeter-totter tells us that this is true.

32 — A. Gear
Rationale: This is the definition of the mechanical advantage of a gear. For example, in turning a smaller gear, it means you will turn it more times in order to complete one rotation of a larger gear, but it translates into an increase in the torque that will be applied due to the larger radius of the larger gear. In the same way, if you turn a larger gear, you will have to apply more torque, but it will result in a faster rotation of the smaller gear, and that might be the desirable result of using the gear system.

33 — B. Output Force : Input Force
Rationale: Mechanical advantage is simply the ratio of the output force to the applied input force. Again, a simple machine increases either the amount or the direction of an applied force. Inevitably, the simple machine increases the output force; therefore, the mechanical advantage must be greater than "one." For example, a simple inclined plane allowed the Egyptians to raise very heavy blocks of stone high enough to place them on top of the previous level of stone blocks. The Egyptians did not have electrical or chemical power to move enormous stones of the pyramids. Only by using huge earthen inclined planes could the Egyptians increase the magnitude of the applied force generated by

humans and animals to move those stones and construct the magnificent pyramids over 3,000 years ago.

34 — D. Neither A nor B
Rationale: A system of pulleys can change the magnitude of the applied force when used in the form of a "block-and-tackle." However, the simplest form of a pulley (with a single fixed rotating disk) simply changes the direction of the applied force without increasing the output force. It is possible to have a pulley system that moves the load in the same direction as the direction of the applied force; for example, you could have a block-and-tackle on a sailing ship that lowers the sails by pulling down on the rope. Therefore, neither answer choices A nor B are necessarily always true.

35 — D. None of the above
Rationale: A wedge is a simple machine that is designed to amplify the applied force. The mechanical advantage is defined as the ratio of the length of the slope divided by the height of the wedge. The more gradual the slope, the longer the incline. The longer incline will increase the mechanical advantage. Similarly, the smaller the height of the wedge, the greater the mechanical advantage since the ratio is dividing by a smaller number

$Force_{output} = Force_{applied}$ * length of the incline/height of the incline

If we apply a force of 10 Newtons, to the face of the wedge with an incline length of 10 cm, and an incline height of 1 cm, what is the corresponding output force of the wedge, The use of the wedge amplifies the input force by 10 times! The output force would be 100 Newtons.

36 — B. Reduces the coefficient of friction
Rationale: The reason cars have wheels is to reduce the friction coefficient between the ground and the wheel; i.e., to reduce the friction force experienced when performing work. This makes the wheel one of the greatest inventions/discoveries in the history of humankind. The wheel replaces the ground friction coefficient with a friction coefficient at the axle of the wheel. If the axle is well-greased and/or has good bearings, then the friction coefficient is significantly reduced, meaning that the force required to pull or push an object becomes greatly reduced.

37 — A. O moves at 3 ft/hour and weighs 1 ton
Rationale: The momentum of an object is equal to its mass multiplied by its velocity; in other words, momentum is an object's tendency to keep moving. To answer this question correctly, it is important that you do two things: (1) convert all units so that they correspond, and (2) notice that the question is asking which scenario has the least momentum, not the most.

First, "convert" each of the four scenarios using the following conversion factors:

1 hour = 60 minutes
1 hour = 3,600 seconds
1 minute = 60 seconds
1 ton = 2,000 pounds

Now "convert" each of the four scenarios given:

3 ft/hour that weighs 1 ton has momentum as follows:

3 ft/3,600 sec * 2,000 pounds or
0.00083 ft/sec * 2,000 pounds or
1.76 pounds-ft./sec.

5,000 ft/hour that weighs 2 pounds has momentum as follows:
5,000 ft/3,600 sec * 2 pounds or
1.39 ft/sec * 2 pounds or
2.8 pounds-ft./sec.

1,000 ft/min that weighs 25 pounds has momentum as follows:
1,000 ft/60 sec * 25 pounds or
16.67 ft/sec * 25 pounds or
417 pounds-ft./sec.

300,000 ft/sec that weighs 0.001 pounds has momentum as follows:
300,000 ft/sec * 0.001 pounds or
300 ft-pounds/sec.

Since all answers are in pounds-ft. /sec, the scenario with the least momentum is 1.76 pounds-ft./sec. In this case, the smallest momentum is a very heavy object that is moving very slowly.

38 — D. All of the above
Rationale: Inclined planes, levers, and wedges are all examples of simple machines. A simple machine does not "create" force; instead, it enables applied force to be used in a useful way.

39 — A. It increases the torque produced
Rationale: When you are in a lower gear on a bicycle, your legs move rapidly in order to maintain an adequate speed. However, it's also easier to climb hills in a lower gear, because you're able to apply more torque to the bicycle wheels. Remember that when going uphill, you must exert more force against gravity. As you know intuitively, climbing a hill in a higher gear may not be possible, because you can't move the pedals enough to apply the required torque to the wheels.

40 — D. All of the examples listed ARE wedges
Rationale: The basic shape of the three objects listed are the same. The axe is probably the most "dramatic" example of how powerful a wedge can be in amplifying applied power. Using only the power that a human body can generate, a person can cut through the trunk of a tree. This is done by applying muscle power to a very thin edge, and the reduction in surface area increases the effectiveness of the applied force.

41 — C. 25 Newtons
Rationale – Since force is the product of mass times acceleration, the acceleration is the change in velocity divided by the time. For this problem, acceleration is 15/3. The force is 5 * 15/3, or 25 Newtons of force.

42 — D. 8 Newtons
Rationale: Since force is the product of mass times acceleration, the acceleration is the change in velocity divided by the time. For this problem, acceleration is 12/4.5. The force is 3 * 12/4.5, or 8 Newtons of force.

43 — A. 23,275 joules
Rationale – Since the potential energy in Earth's gravity is the product of mass times gravitational acceleration times the height, you need the gravitational acceleration value, which is 9.8 m/s^2. The product becomes 25 * 95 * 9.8, which is 23,275 joules of potential energy.

44 — D. 19,110 joules
Rationale – Since the potential energy in Earth's gravity is the product of mass times gravitational acceleration times the height, you need the gravitational acceleration value, which is 9.8 m/s^2. The kinetic energy that you apply must be enough to equal the potential energy at the peak of the trajectory. The product becomes 1.3 * 1500 * 9.8, which is 19,110 joules of energy.

45 — C. 345,800 joules
Rationale – The kinetic energy formula is one half the product of the mass times the square of the velocity. The conversion of 80 km/hr to meters per second means multiplying by one thousand and dividing by 3600 (the number of seconds per hour). That value is 22.22, which must be squared and divided by two, or ~247 $(m/s)^2$. Multiplying by 1400, the answer becomes 345,800 joules.

46 — A. Ionized
Rationale: Elements usually have the same number of electrons as protons. In the case where the opposite is true (if an atom has different number of protons and electrons), it is described as being "ionized." When an atom is ionized, it acquires a negative or positive charge by gaining or losing electrons.

47 — C. A magnetic field is generated
Rationale: An inductor is a component in an electric circuit that is able to store voltage as a magnetic field. As electrons pass through an inductor (or coil), a magnetic field is generated.

48 — C. The direction electrons move
Rationale: Alternating current (AC) and direct current (DC) are both forms of electricity in that they both are based on the movement of electrons through a circuit; however, the electrons move through the circuit differently. With DC, the flow of electrons is constant and unidirectional. The best example of a direct current source is a battery. With AC, the flow of electrons moves back and forth in an alternating "wave."

49 — A. Low resistance, flexible, common
Rationale: Electrical resistance in a wire is a direct function of the wire's material and its thickness — the more conductive the wire's material, and the larger the diameter of the wire, the lower the resistance. Copper has very low resistance, and is most often used as a material for wire/cable. Other materials have low resistance and flexibility properties, but are not so commonly used, because they are rare and/or more expensive. Copper is relatively common and affordable.

50 — D. Reducing the rate that electrons can flow
Rationale: Resistors are simply components that are made to reduce the rate at which electrons can flow; therefore, resistors change the voltage and current within a circuit.

51 — C. Current
Rationale: If electrons move through a wire made of conductive material, the concept can be modeled as similar to water moving through a hose. A longer hose limits flow like a longer wire, and a larger diameter hose allows flow similar to a larger diameter wire. When the "hose" is a wire, that means it has resistance. Friction opposes and limits the motion/flow. Resistance is "friction" at an atomic level, and the energy lost from electrons and atoms "rubbing against each other" is converted to heat. The term for measuring resistance is ohms. Note: The terminology is incorrect to describe the "flow of current," since that is the "flow of the flow of charges." Current is more correctly thought of as the "quantity of charge motion."

52 — A. Voltage
Rationale: The amount of current (amperes) moving through a circuit is determined by the resistance in the circuit and the voltage that is applied. The voltage is measured in volts, and it is a measure of how much each electron's kinetic energy increases. Higher voltage means each electrical charge experiences a greater attraction in the circuit. Voltage propels current through resistance, so the higher the voltage, the more current will pass through a given resistance.

Voltage is sometimes referred to as electromotive force or EMF. It is unrelated to how much electricity there is, just as the pressure in a hose doesn't tell you how much water is present. EMF propels current through the circuit. Without EMF, electrical charge still exists in each conductor, but it will have no motion.

53 — B. 0.10 amps
Rationale: This is simply a problem that requires knowledge of Ohm's Law. If you want to find the number of amperes (amps), or current (I) flowing through a circuit, use this formula:

I = V/R
I = 12/120
I = 0.1 amps

54 — B. Amp (ampere)
Rationale: This is the definition of an ampere, and it is critically important to know.

55 — A. Volt (voltage)
Rationale: The amount of current moving through a circuit is determined by the applied voltage or EMF. When there is water (electrons/current) in the hose (circuit), it is always full, but it may come out with a pressure that squirts it 5 feet, or it might come out with a pressure that squirts it 50 feet—depending on the pressure. Volts are a measure of the force moving the current through a circuit. Without applied voltage, electrical charge is in the circuit, but it is not mobile; therefore, there is no charge motion (current) in the circuit.

56 — C. 40 milliamperes
Rationale: Ohm's Law tells you that current (I) is the ratio of V/R. Since V = 6 volts and R = 150 ohms, the current is 6/150 amperes. That ratio is 0.040 amperes, or 40 milliamperes.

57 — B. 525 volts
Rationale: Ohm's Law tells you that voltage (V) is the product of I * R. Since I = 10.5 amperes and R = 50 ohms, the current is 10.5 * 50 volts. That product is 525 volts.

58 — A. 0.80 ohms
Rationale: Ohm's Law tells you that resistance (R) is the ratio of V/I. Since V = 6 volts and I = 7.5 amperes, the resistance must be 6 / 7.5 ohms. That ratio is 0.80 ohms.

59 — D. Electron
Rationale: Neutrons and protons are part of the nuclear structure and are fixed in the structure of the conductor. Electrons are the mobile charges that are in the orbitals of the conductor molecules. Voltage applied to a conductor creates a force that moves those charges through the conductor.

60 — B. Voltage
Rationale – Electromotive force (EMF) is a term that is the same as voltage. When EMF is applied, the electrons are the mobile charges that are attracted to a positive potential and repelled by a negative potential. Voltage applied to a conductor moves those charges through the conductor.

61 — B. Decrease
Rationale – If V = I * R, a larger resistance will reduce the current for an applied voltage.

62 — A. Increase
Rationale – If V = I * R, a larger voltage will increase the current for a given resistance.

63 — A. Toward
Rationale – When a positive voltage is applied, the mobile negative charges (electrons) will always be attracted to the positive voltage.

64 — C. Stop after charge is collected on the plates
Rationale – If a voltage is applied, the mobile negative charges (electrons) will flow through the conductor until the charge on the capacitor plates have a charge equal to the potential of the battery. Unless there is a significant resistance in the circuit, this stoppage will happen almost immediately.

CPSIA information can be obtained
at www.ICGtesting.com
Printed in the USA
BVHW061506250319
543610BV00025B/1391/P